In the Shadow of the Patriarch

MERCER
UNIVERSITY PRESS

Endowed by
TOM WATSON BROWN
and
THE WATSON-BROWN FOUNDATION, INC.

In the Shadow of the Patriarch

The John J. Crittenden Family in War and Peace

Damon R. Eubank

MERCER UNIVERSITY PRESS
MACON, GEORGIA

MUP/H786

First Edition.

Books published by Mercer University Press are printed on acid free paper that meets
the requirements of American National Standard for Information Sciences—
Permanence of Paper for Printed Library Materials.

Mercer University Press is a member of Green Press initiative
(greenpressinitiative.org), a nonprofit organization working to help publishers and
printers increase their use of recycled paper and decrease their use of fiber derived from
endangered forests. This book is printed on recycled paper.

Library of Congress Cataloging-in-Publication DataEubank, Damon.
In the shadow of the patriarch : the John J. Crittenden family in war and peace /
Damon R. Eubank. -- 1st ed.
p. cm.
Includes bibliographical references and index.
ISBN-13: 978-0-88146-151-0 (hardback : alk. paper)
ISBN-10: 0-88146-151-2 (hardback : alk. paper)
1. Crittenden, John J. (John Jordan), 1787-1863—Family. 2. Crittenden, George
Bibb, 1812-1880. 3. Crittenden, Thomas Leonidas, 1819-1893. 4. Coleman,
Chapman, Mrs., 1813-1891. 5. Kentucky—History—19th century—Biography.
6. Kentucky—History—Civil War, 1861-1865. 7. Crittenden family. 8. Kentucky—
Biography. I. Title.
E340.C9E94 2009
976.9'03--dc22

2009011287

For

Lorin and Micah

Contents

Acknowledgments

No one can undertake any research project without accumulating numerous professional and personal debts. This author is no exception to the rule.

First, I want to thank the library staff at Campbellsville University, in particular Karen Lynema for her diligent aid in locating hard-to-find research materials through interlibrary loan.

In a similar way, the staff at the Filson Club, the Kentucky Historical Society, the University of Kentucky Special Collections, the Kentucky Library at Western Kentucky University, and Duke University Special Collections all gave me wonderful advice. They provided everything required to complete the project.

I also desire to express appreciation to my employer, Campbellsville University, for sponsoring an American Civil War Institute Symposium in 1997, from which this project had its birth. Several scholars at that symposium, Kent Masterson Brown, Lowell Harrison, and William C. Davis among others, gave me encouragement to complete this project. The university also generously provided me with an opportunity for a sabbatical to finish the project.

My colleagues and students at Campbellsville University have also encouraged me along the long path to publication. I would like to mention two esteemed colleagues in particular, Dwayne and Susan Howell. Susan, a psychology professor, gave me valuable insight into the impact of birth order on child development and allowed me to bounce around several ideas about the Crittenden siblings. Dwayne suggested that I consider Mercer University Press for the manuscript and thankfully I listened to his advice.

My mentor, John F. Marszalek, suggested numerous changes to the project as it developed. He went far beyond the reasonable call of academic duty. Thanks so much for what you did; it has been truly appreciated.

I also have several personal debts. My wife Lori allowed me the personal time to research, write, and rewrite this manuscript. She has patiently listened to so much about the Crittendens that she probably thinks she is an honorary member of the family. My children Lorin and Micah allowed Dad the extensive time he needed to complete this project, and it is to them that I dedicate this book.

Damon R. Eubank
Campbellsville, Kentucky

Prologue

Senator John J. Crittenden of Kentucky had long been a key figure in American politics, as his biographer Albert D. Kirwan so aptly portrayed in *John J. Crittenden: Struggle for the Union.* The senator's children would also play a significant role in the Civil War era, but Kirwan's work discussed Crittenden family issues only from the perspective of the patriarch. The children's voices have thus remained mute. I hope this work will redress that omission.

Senator John J. Crittenden held most of the public offices that the commonwealth of Kentucky had to offer. Although best remembered today for his last-minute attempt to avert the Civil War during the troubled winter of 1860–1861, the Kentucky senator had a long and illustrious career. He had served in the state legislature, as governor, as a United States representative, as a senator, and as a cabinet member. Crittenden had been a key leader in the Kentucky and national Whig party councils and in 1848 had served as a kingmaker for Zachary Taylor. The Kentuckian had also been mentioned frequently as a possible candidate for even higher office. However, despite these accomplishments, for most of his career he labored in the shadow of Henry Clay. Not until 1962 did Crittenden receive a full-length biography.

The senator was married three times and fathered nine children. Despite the best efforts of the family patriarch, Civil War deeply divided the Crittenden family. The Crittendens present a very public portrait of the deep divisions that Kentucky's leadership class suffered in the Civil War. The children differed in their loyalties and these differences impacted their relationship with their father and with each other.

Just as Henry Clay overshadowed Senator Crittenden for most of his career, so too did the senator overshadow his children during most of their lifetimes. Several of the senator's children deserve study in their own right. Two became significant military commanders during the Civil War, while another was one of the most remarkable women of antebellum Kentucky. The other Crittenden children were also leaders in their respective communities.

The senator's eldest three children, George, Ann Mary, and Cornelia, had pro-Confederate sympathies, and the eldest son George became a Confederate general. He never lived up to his father's high expectations and attempted to escape this disappointment by breaking with his father over secession and turning to alcohol for solace. George had some admirable qualities such as personal bravery and loyalty to friends, but he never overcame his personal weaknesses. If George had not been the son of Kentucky's elder statesman, he could have made only an acceptable regimental or perhaps brigade commander. He definitely was not "general" material.

Most previous military studies have roundly condemned George B. Crittenden for his obvious failures at Mill Springs. Among these works are Thomas L. Connelly's *Army of the Heartland: The Army of Tennessee, 1861–1862,* Raymond E. Myers *The Zollie Tree,* and Stephen E. Woodworth's *Jefferson Davis and His Generals: The Failure of Confederate Command in the West.* Although Charles D. Roland's criticism of Crittenden is less strident in *Albert Sidney Johnston: Soldier of Three Republics,* the book still depicts the Kentuckian as a failure. No amount of revisionist work will make George Crittenden one of the great Confederate captains, but I hope this study will humanize this troubled man. Perhaps it will remove some of the stain of his personal flaws and those coming from his close association with the unpopular Jefferson Davis.

Ann Mary Chapman, the senator's eldest daughter, led a remarkable life. As a teenager, following the premature death of her mother, she served as hostess of the Crittenden household. Widowed in her late thirties, she managed a substantial property on her own and dealt with the difficulties of single parenthood at a time when this was the exception rather than the rule. Ann Mary had a close relationship with her father and knew more about American political happenings than the vast majority of American women. Like her brother George, she broke with her father over the issue of secession, and the two did not reconcile before his death.

Thomas, the second son, wanted to please his father and would not repeat the mistakes of his older brother. As a result, he developed considerable political skills and probably should have entered politics rather than the military. Most historians have condemned Thomas's poor performance as a Union commander. In the postwar era, Henry Cist in

Army of the Cumberland sought to make Thomas a scapegoat for the failures of the Army of the Cumberland. More recent studies, such as Peter Cozzens trilogy of the battles of the Army of Cumberland, and Larry J. Daniels's *Days of Glory: The Army of the Cumberland, 1861–1865*, are more balanced in their treatment of Crittenden. However, the extremely negative press coverage Thomas L. Crittenden received after the second day of the Battle of Chickamauga colors all evaluations of him. Before that fateful day, Crittenden had shown average to sometimes above-average ability as a military commander. Similar to his older brother, on the Confederate side, Thomas received promotion beyond his ability. With experience, he probably would have made a fine division commander.

The work presented here is a family history and a social history. The other siblings remain in the background, only brought into the family story as the documentary evidence allows. My purpose is to discover why a Kentucky leadership-class family divided over the issue of secession and how this influenced their familial relationships. The postwar Crittenden family reconciliation will also be examined.

At the same time, this work is a military study. Both George and Thomas deserve attention for the important positions they held during the war. Ann Mary's life illustrates many of the problems civilians faced on the home front in a border state. Senator Crittenden's importance has resulted in his children's voices being kept historically silent. I hope this book gives these siblings the attention they deserve in their own right.

John J. Crittenden and the Establishment of a Family Heritage

The Crittendens came from an old and distinguished family lineage. According to a genealogy compiled by the senator's eldest daughter, the family descended from, among others, Rollo the Duke of Normandy, William the Conqueror, Edward I of England, and numerous kings of Scotland. The senator's mother was a cousin to Thomas Jefferson. The Crittendens were established English gentry.[1]

During the colonial era, the Crittendens migrated from Essex County, England, to Virginia and established themselves among the Virginia gentry sometime between 1663 and 1674. The senator's father, Major John Crittenden, migrated to Kentucky in 1783 with his wife Judith Harris and settled in what is now Woodford County. It was there in 1786 that the future senator John Jordan was born, the eldest of eight children. His younger brothers Thomas and Henry later served in the Kentucky legislature and his youngest brother Robert was a prominent attorney in Arkansas. Unfortunately, all of these siblings died young, and the senator took a keen interest in the wellbeing of his nephews and nieces.[2]

The Crittendens prospered on the Kentucky frontier. Major Crittenden, a veteran of Daniel Morgan's Riflemen, represented the Bluegrass area in the Virginia legislature in the 1780s. He eventually acquired title to almost 75,000 acres of land. Young John received the best education the frontier offered, at the College of William and Mary. Between 1804 and 1806, however, Major Crittenden died unexpectedly from an accident, and young John had to return home to support his family. John Jordan began to practice law.

---

[1] "Genealogy," John J. Crittenden Papers, Duke University, Durham NC; Albert D. Kirwan, *John J. Crittenden: Struggle for the Union* (Lexington: University of Kentucky Press, 1962) 3–5.

[2] Kirwan, *Crittenden*, 3–5, 98–99.

In many ways, John typified a firstborn child. Firstborns are often serious and achievement oriented. Firstborns, especially ones such as John Jordan, who assumed surrogate father responsibilities, enjoyed the power of their position. They tend to have moralistic, disciplinarian, and perfectionist traits. Firstborns, particularly if they act as surrogate parents, expect a lot from their younger siblings and from their own children as well. John Jordan's trait served him admirably as a firstborn brother but less so as a future parent.[3]

In order to establish himself as an attorney, John moved to Russellville in Logan County in 1807. There he fell in love with Sarah Lee, the granddaughter of Richard Lee and a first cousin of future president Zachary Taylor. The young couple married on 27 May 1811 at Sarah's home in Woodford County. They lived in Russellville in a house on the corner of 9th and Main Streets.[4]

Crittenden's legal career expanded, and so did his family. George Bibb arrived in 1812 and Ann Mary in 1813. Cornelia made her appearance in 1816 and Thomas Leonidas followed in 1819. Because of the increasing demand on John to argue cases in Frankfort, the family moved to the state capital in 1820. There, three more children were born: Sarah Lee (called Maria by the family), Robert, and Eugenia.[5]

In 1824, tragedy struck the growing family when Sarah Lee Crittenden died. She was buried in the Bellevue cemetery on Leestown Road. Crittenden grieved the loss of his wife but remarried within two years. His second wife was Maria Innes Todd, the daughter of respected Kentucky jurist Harry Innes and the widow of John Harris Todd, son of associate justice Thomas Todd.[6]

The second Mrs. Crittenden brought to the union two daughters, Elizabeth and Catherine, and a son, Harry. This second marriage produced two more children, John Jordan and Eugene. One observer noted that Mrs. Crittenden was a "fine looking lady and one whom manners add much to her personal attractions" and that "she is frank and friendly in her

---

[3] Ibid., 6–14. Lucille Forer and Henry Still, *The Birth Order Factor: How Your Personality Is Influenced by Your Place in the Family* (New York: Pocket Books, 1976) 193.

[4] Kirwan, *Crittenden*, 14, 16, 17.

[5] Ibid., 30, 35, 43.

[6] Kirwan, *Crittenden*, 45, 64–65.

remarks." The same observer took notice of the admiration and affection the senator showed his wife. This was, like his first marriage, a happy union.[7]

The surviving correspondence between parents and children and between the Crittenden children themselves does not seem to suggest that relations were strained or that the remarriage caused any significant rift between father and children. Likewise, contemporaries did not note any particular family tension in the public setting.

Sadly, Maria Todd Crittenden died on 8 September 1851. One of her stepsons, Thomas, said that he had "lost the best of mothers" and that life had "lost one of its chief charms." Thomas described the loss of his stepmother as a "terrible misfortune" and a "great calamity" and worried about how his father would deal with the loss.[8]

John Crittenden could not remain alone for long. In 1853 he married for the third time, in this case to Elizabeth Ashley, a wealthy Missouri widow. The newlyweds enjoyed the social whirl at Washington and Frankfort. Theirs too was a happy union. As one friend noted, "When till now did any man have three such wives?"[9]

John Crittenden's public life mirrored the satisfaction of his private one. He lived in a large rambling house in Frankfort that bordered Main and Washington Streets in the city's leading neighborhood. The Crittenden children knew important people throughout Frankfort: two associate justices of the Supreme Court, Thomas Todd and John Harlan; a cabinet officer, George Bibb; six diplomats; three admirals; two generals; six congressmen; and seven governors. Ann Mary, the eldest daughter, fondly remembered the frequent times when neighbors would drop by to talk to her father. From an early date, the Crittenden children were exposed to people of influence and cultivated many useful lifelong contacts from

---

[7] Ibid., 64–65, 98; James Simmons to Sarah S. Simmons, 14 August 1841, James Fowler Simmons Papers, Filson Club, Louisville KY.

[8] Thomas L. Crittenden to Harry Innes Todd, 29 October 1851, Todd Family Collection, Kentucky Historical Society, Frankfort.

[9] Kirwan, *Crittenden*, 282–283.

these informal social gatherings. Early on, parental expectations were high for the Crittenden children.[10]

In most respects, the Crittendens indulged their children. When Thomas needed money to finance a trip to Texas that Senator Crittenden disapproved of, the money still came. When Ann Mary's husband needed a substantial loan to keep his business afloat, the senator offered the money. This generosity continued throughout the senator's life. At his death, Thomas, Robert, and Cornelia still owed him money.[11]

The Crittendens attempted to show their concern for their children in a variety of other ways as well. One method was by simple words of encouragement and advice. For instance, when Thomas attempted to establish himself in business at New Orleans his father wrote, "I indulge the best, fondest hopes," adding that he had "all confidence" in Thomas's integrity. Years later, Crittenden wrote to his son, "I think you have a capacity for great things—do not allow it to be frustrated by little things— by little inattentions, little negligences, little indulgences."[12]

Thomas and his younger brothers received numerous such admonitions concerning their work ethic. For example, Thomas and Robert received stern warnings about the dangers of idleness. Robert had not applied himself at Miami University; as a result his father removed him from school and warned his daughters not to allow their brother to remain idle while at home. Likewise, Thomas received extensive warnings about idleness while trying to establish himself in business at New Orleans. When he failed and returned to Kentucky, Crittenden wrote to his eldest daughter to "see that Thomas avoid idleness." Crittenden warned that "if he is not *well* employed if it cannot be but [that] he will be *ill*-employed" and he feared that Thomas had "adversely contracted some idle habits."

---

[10] Francis Hudson Oxx, *The Kentucky Crittenden: The History of a Family Including Genealogy of Descendent in Both Male and Female Lives, Biographical Sketches of its Members, and Their Descent from Other Colonial Lives* (n.p., 1940) 81–82.

[11] John J. Crittenden to Ann Mary Coleman, 23 February 1838; John J. Crittenden to Ann Mary Coleman, 19 March 1842; and memorandum, 30 June 1859, John J. Crittenden Papers, Duke University.

[12] John J. Crittenden to Thomas L. Crittenden, 10 December 1836, John J. Crittenden Papers, Library of Congress. John J. Crittenden to Thomas L. Crittenden, 28 November 1862, John J. Crittenden Papers, Duke University.

Thomas's father believed that "employment, constant employment" was the only "security for his future success." Thus, the senator requested that Ann Mary's husband find a place for Thomas in his Louisville firm.[13]

The firstborn patriarch had worked hard as a young man to support his mother and younger siblings. He exerted pressure on his sons to follow his example of hard work. The senator had accepted responsibility for himself and others at a young age, and he naturally assumed that his children would do likewise. His sons did not have their father's work ethic or his sense of responsibility. Hence, tensions arose between parent and child.

Senator Crittenden frequently offered advice to his children about a variety of other topics. Thomas received instruction about business ethics, his shy mannerisms, and his handwriting. His father also did not neglect to give him advice on military affairs. Ann Mary received advice about finances and careers for her children. The senator involved himself in many aspects of his children's lives.[14]

George received a great deal of advice about his intemperate lifestyle, but unfortunately it had little effect. His father pleaded with him to stop drinking "for the sake of honor—of every earthly interest" and not to sacrifice himself "to that only weakness which has given you as well as all of us so much anguish." When Crittenden tried to help George return to the army in 1848, the secretary of war noted that he would base anything he could do "solely upon the grounds that your son has totally changed his most unfortunate habits." George did reenter the army, but he did not stop drinking. The senator later noted that resigning would be better for George than to "expose himself to the inevitable disgrace that must attend his continued intemperance." Crittenden pleaded with Ann Mary to apply her sisterly influence on her wayward brother.[15]

---

[13] John J. Crittenden to Ann Mary Coleman, 4 January 1838; John J. Crittenden to Ann Mary Coleman, 14 January 1838; and John J. Crittenden to Ann Mary Coleman, 1 June 1838, John J. Crittenden Papers, Duke University.

[14] John J. Crittenden to Thomas L. Crittenden, 10 December 1836; and John J. Crittenden to Thomas L. Crittenden, 28 April 1838, John J. Crittenden Papers, Library of Congress. John J. Crittenden to Thomas L. Crittenden, 28 November 1862; and John J. Crittenden to Ann Mary Coleman, 17 September 1851, 20 February 1858, and 2 July 1859, John J. Crittenden Papers, Duke University.

[15] John J. Crittenden to George B. Crittenden, 14 April 1848, John J. Crittenden Papers, Kentucky Historical Society. William Marcy to John J. Crittenden, 5 November

Thomas similarly received a great deal of advice about his intemperate lifestyle. His father warned, "Do not frequent the haunts of the idle and dissipated, be not seen at any gaming or drinking house. Even the suspicion arising from such things will be a stain upon your character, and impair confidence in you." Crittenden advised Thomas to "avoid taverns & the use of liquors or wines." Thomas's "own sense of propriety" must be his guide and his conduct must "be the subject of daily self-examination." Clearly Thomas had to avoid the mistakes of his older brother.[16]

Apparently the entire family enjoyed taking a drink, although only George became an alcoholic. The senator worried a great deal about alcohol fostering a spirit of laziness and irresponsibility in the lives of all his children. If George or any of the other siblings failed, alcohol could bear the blame. George drank too much, as most of his contemporaries readily admit, and it was easier for the senator to blame his failures on drink than on his firstborn son's desire to avoid the parental expectations of hard work, success, and responsibility.[17]

The senator also used his political influence to help his children. When Mexicans captured George in 1843 during an ill-fated expedition, his father became "distressed" to hear of the capture and wrote a letter to Santa Anna begging for clemency for his son. Crittenden also enlisted old political associates Daniel Webster and Waddy Thompson to help secure George's release. Later, when George faced court martial over another drinking incident, his father pleaded for his restoration to the army.[18]

1848; John J. Crittenden to Ann Mary Coleman, 29 January 1852; and John J. Crittenden to Ann Mary Coleman, 17 May 1852, John J. Crittenden Papers, Duke University.

[16] John J. Crittenden to Thomas L. Crittenden, 10 December 1836, John J. Crittenden Papers, Duke University. John J. Crittenden to Thomas L. Crittenden, 28 April 1838, John J. Crittenden Papers, Library of Congress.

[17] John J. Crittenden to Maria Crittenden, 5 February 1843, John J. Crittenden Papers, Library of Congress.

[18] John J. Crittenden to Robert P. Letcher, 24 February 1843; Waddy Thompson to Antonio Santa Anna, 9 March 1843; Antonio Santa Anna to Waddy Thompson, 13 March 1843; and Waddy Thompson to Daniel Webster, 18 March 1843, John J. Crittenden Papers, Library of Congress. John J. Crittenden to Waddy Thompson, 6 February 1843; Daniel Webster to John J. Crittenden, 21 February 1843; and John J. Crittenden to Chapman Coleman, 28 August 1848, John J. Crittenden Papers, Duke University.

Crittenden also attempted to get an army commission for Ann Mary's son Crittenden, but he failed. However, he did successfully secure appointments for George and Eugene at West Point and at Annapolis for Sarah Lee's son. Likewise, Crittenden's influence won Thomas a valuable consulate in Liverpool.[19]

While the Crittenden children benefited from parents who loved them and could provide for them generously, they also dealt with some negative parental qualities. For example, Crittenden sometimes blamed others for his own children's weaknesses. This particularly applied to his eldest son George. When George made poor decisions, such as participating in an ill-fated expedition against Mexico or defying military superiors during the Mexican War, his father rescued him. When George cast his lot with the Confederacy, his father noted that others had deluded his son into the Rebellion. According to his father, George had acted under more "honorable" motives than any others. In a similar vein, after criticism of George's conduct at the Battle of Mill Springs surfaced, his father criticized "the worthless and lawless scoundrels [George] was bravely trying to serve." The senator once ruefully noted to his eldest daughter, "My poor boys—my heart has bled over them. But I will chasten myself.... There is a divinity that shapes our end."[20]

The senator had successfully overcome difficulties in his own life, and he expected the same of his children. The Crittenden children had an important legacy to live up to. Their parents came from distinguished families and many people recognized John Crittenden as a leading legal and political figure in Kentucky and the nation. Such pressure to excel can prove troublesome. George fell victim to several vices as he grew older, and his failure to deal with them only placed more pressure on the younger siblings. Robert and Eugene had difficulty meeting this expectation. Thomas developed a fear of failure that drove him to find acceptance and approval

---

[19] John J. Crittenden to Ann Mary Coleman, 27 April 1858, 9 May 1849; and Ann Mary Coleman to John J. Crittenden, 3 October 1856, John J. Crittenden Papers, Duke University.

[20] John J. Crittenden to George D. Prentice, 8 May 1862, John J. Crittenden Papers, Kentucky Historical Society. John J. Crittenden to Ann Mary Coleman, 23 February 1862; and John J. Crittenden to Ann Mary Coleman, 23 February 1838, John J. Crittenden Papers, Duke University.

from others and made him reluctant to take risks, whether political or military. He never came close to matching his father's accomplishments. All of the Crittenden daughters married well and apparently had influence in their respective communities. Ann Mary showed the most talent and accomplished much in an era that limited women's scope of activity.

For the most part, the siblings seemed to have had a good relationship. Frequent letters passed between them, and a common theme was their concern over the welfare of other family members. Occasional disputes occurred, but these did not permanently divide the family. Thomas, Ann Mary, and Robert shared rent on a summer home in Pee Wee Valley on the eve of the Civil War, and the siblings also frequently traveled together.[21]

Yet, during the secession crisis, despite having the same heritage, an open and positive relationship with each other, and an obviously caring father, the siblings divided on the issue of secession. Other families throughout Kentucky and the Border States made similar difficult decisions in 1861. For the Crittenden siblings this conflict would literally be a brothers' war pitting elder Rebel siblings against younger Union siblings. This was not the heritage the senator hoped to leave his children; rather, he had hoped to bequeath a legacy of excellence in service to state and country.

The Crittenden siblings received their father's heritage of excellence in various ways. Within the large Crittenden family constellation, each child had a unique personality and a unique parental expectation. The birth order of the child played a significant, if not determining, role in how the senator viewed his children and how their personalities developed. Birth order also contributed to how each child perceived the bestowal of the parental heritage of excellence. An examination of the siblings according to their birth order will provide clues as to why the Crittenden family so deeply divided over the secession issue.

---

[21] Ann Mary Coleman to John J. Crittenden, 3 July 1860, John J. Crittenden Papers, Duke University.

2

The Crittenden Siblings and the Receiving of a Family Heritage

Senator Crittenden's three eldest children, George, Ann Mary, and Cornelia, formed a distinct block within the family. As older children, they had better memory of their mother than the younger children, and this may have made them less susceptible to their father's influence. They might also have had more opportunity to harbor resentment against their father for his quick remarriage than the younger siblings, who had only a vague memory of their birth mother. For the younger siblings, the second Mrs. Crittenden was essentially the only mother they ever knew.

The elder trio also tended to defy their father's wishes, either directly or indirectly. Perhaps they resented the senator's domineering influence much more than the younger siblings did. Unlike the younger children, in fact, they refused to give in to their stronger father. Instead, they confronted and often disappointed him. The three elder siblings were pro-Confederates and defied their father's public and privately expressed opinion on the issue. In many ways, they attempted to reject or at least modify the heritage their father had bequeathed to them.

George, the eldest son, had great promise never realized. He graduated from West Point in 1832, ranking twenty-sixth in a class of forty-five. Never marrying, he served in the Black Hawk War and in the Arkansas territory before resigning in 1833 to return to Kentucky to practice law with his father. George found the practice of law boring and returned to military life. In 1836, he commanded a company in the Kentucky state militia; soon thereafter he moved to Texas and entered the Texas army.[1]

---

[1] Mark M. Boatner II, *The Civil War Dictionary* (New York: David McKay Company, 1959) 208; Francis Hudson Oxx, *The Kentucky Crittenden: The History of a Family Including Genealogy of Descendent in Both Male and Female Lives, Biographical Sketches of its Members, and Their Descent from Other Colonial Lives* (n.p., 1940) 73, 93; Kentucky

In 1842, George participated in an expedition against Mexico. He was captured, and when an escape attempt failed he and the other captives had to pick beans (*diezmo* or black beans) in a lottery for their lives. Those who picked a white bean would live, while those who picked a black bean would die. George drew the white bean, but he gave it to a friend and drew a second time. Fortunately for him, he picked a white bean again. In February 1843, the elder Crittenden learned of his son's capture and felt distressed about newspaper accounts of the harsh treatment the prisoners were receiving. He began to make arrangements to secure George's release. He referred to the mission as a "miserable expedition" and felt that friends had induced his son through poor counsel. Fortunately, the Mexican president was amendable to the idea of release, and the elder Crittenden son gained his freedom.[2]

In 1846 George reentered the army, performed admirably in combat, and won a brevet for gallantry at the Battle of Churubusco. However, he was constantly intemperate in his personal conduct. He had been charged with drunkenness several times, resigned his commission, and through the efforts of his father been reinstated in the army. His father had warned him of the dangers when he wrote:

> You have won them [honors] fairly—take care to wear them worthily…. For the sake of honor—of every earthly interest—do not sacrifice yourself to that only weakness which has given you as well as all of us so much anguish. I am honored in my sons—their honor is mine and as dear to me as life. To enjoy them fully, I want to feel secure in them. I have but one cause of apprehension—you can remove them—I ask you to do it—It will be the greatest favor.[3]

Mounted Gunmen Volunteer Regiment, Miscellaneous File, Filson Club, Louisville KY; George B. Crittenden to John J. Crittenden, 21 April 1839, John J. Crittenden Papers, Duke University, Durham NC.

[2] Oxx, *Kentucky Crittendens*, 93. John J. Crittenden to Robert P. Letcher, 5 February 1843; Waddy Thompson to Antonio Santa Ann, 9 March 1843; Antonio Santa Anna to Waddy Thompson, 15 March 1843; and Waddy Thompson to Daniel Webster, 18 March 1843, John J. Crittenden Papers, Library of Congress.

[3] Stephen E. Woodworth, *Jefferson Davis and His Generals: The Failure of Confederate High Command in the West* (Lawrence: University of Kansas Press, 1990) 63. John

In 1848, however, George was again arrested for drunkenness. This time President Polk was not inclined to let him escape court martial. In a letter to his son-in-law, the senator described his concerns about George: "I have this day written to the Secretary earnestly in his behalf and have I think pointed out insurpassable objections to the competence of the court and the validity of the sentence.... I want him to return home immediately and remain with me till I have exhausted every effort for his restoration."

The senator pleaded for the help of others such as Jefferson Davis, an old family friend. Davis sincerely believed that George was innocent of the charges and spearheaded the lobbying for George's reinstatement in the army. Senator Crittenden pleaded with the secretary of war that George's "offense has not been of so unpardonable a character as to preclude him from forgiveness & the opportunity of future advancement by good service." The senator admitted worry about his son's future. The secretary accepted Crittenden's argument, and George was reinstated in the army. The senator expressed pride in his son when he said, "I can hardly express my dear son, the pride I feel these honors won & obtained by you." He could only hope that George had learned his lesson and had truly changed.[5]

Unfortunately, George did not change his bad habits. The senator, in a letter to his eldest daughter, noted George's continuing problems with alcohol:

> George, you say, has not received orders. Poor fellow, unless he changes his habits, it will be well for him never to receive them—I can not even hope but [he] will be disgracefully dismissed from the army as soon as he goes, unless there is a total reformation of

---

Crittenden to George B. Crittenden, 14 April 1848, John J. Crittenden Papers, Kentucky Historical Society, Frankfort.

[5] William C. Davis, *Jefferson Davis: The Man and His* Hour (Baton Rouge: Louisiana State University Press, 1991) 186; John J. Crittenden to William L. Marcy, 20 March 1847, John J. Crittenden Papers, Filson Club. Woodworth, *Jefferson Davis and His General,* 63.

conduct. He had better excuse himself if he can, on the score of his health or any other grounds, from joining the army, than to expose himself to the inevitable disgrace that must follow his continued intemperance...I wish he would resign.

The father had apparently lost confidence in his eldest son's ability to fight the demons within. George's love for alcohol proved far stronger than his sense of personal responsibility. Unlike his father, George had little willpower and relatively little concern for the family's reputation.[6]

George could also have a touchy disposition. Unlike his father, who never fought a duel nor was ever issued a challenge, George had taken offence over some matter during his service in the Mexican War. He requested that Cassius Clay, the Kentucky abolitionist, carry a letter to the party who had insulted him. According to Clay, the matter was resolved peacefully by the actions of some unnamed intermediaries, and the duel never took place. Clay did not mention whether alcohol played a role in the confrontation, but no doubt it did.[7]

Some years later David Meriwether, while serving as territorial governor of New Mexico in 1856, met George at Fort Craig. The Kentucky politician was impressed with George and recorded: "Major Crittenden was a gallant officer and had but one fault, and that was too great a fondness in early life for the fishing bowl. I rejoiced at his reformation,... I never again saw any evidence of his falling from grace." In fact, Meriwether had purchased some liquor to give to George as a present. George claimed to have quit using alcohol and told Merewether, "I have no doubt that you purchased this brandy on my account, after you found that I was your guest, because you have often seen me drinking while you were in Frankfort. But I wish to inform you that I have abandoned the use of spirits entirely, and haven't tasted a drop for a year and half." After this

---

[6] John J. Crittenden to Ann Mary Coleman, 29 January 1852, John J. Crittenden Papers, Duke University.

[7] Cassius Marcellus Clay, *The Life of Cassius Marcellus Clay: Memoirs, Writings, and Speeches Showing His Conduct in the Overthrown of American Slavery, the Salvation of the Union, and the Restoration of the Autonomy of the States* (1896; repr., New York: Negro Universities Press, 1969) 216.

exchange George proposed throwing the bottle into a nearby river, but later he began drinking again.[8]

Short-lived reformation such as this did wonders for George's military career. He often impressed people when they first met him. One visitor at Fort Inge, in the New Mexico territory, noted that George was a superb hunter and fisherman and described him as "the most honorable and truthful gentleman I have ever known." By 1857, George reached the rank of lieutenant colonel and was serving on the Rio Grande in the New Mexico territory. He hoped for a transfer to the more hospitable Carlisle Barracks in the east. Due to his many influential contacts, in 1859 George received a year-long leave of absence for his tour of Europe, but by 1860 he was back in the New Mexico territory.[9]

The prewar years highlighted several aspects of George's character. He was personally brave and loyal to his friends, but he often made poor choices of friends and was easily swayed to make rash, unwise decisions. He should have paid the consequences of his actions, but his father's influence usually saved him. Thus he never learned from his mistakes, and this dependence no doubt created resentment. George must have wanted to prove he could make good decisions and succeed on his own without his father's aid.

The prewar years also highlighted the impact of George's birth order on his developing personality. Though also a firstborn, George did not exhibit many of the characteristics his father possessed. John Jordan had the common firstborn strong sense of duty, and his role of surrogate father to his younger siblings while a young man had only strengthened that tendency. John Jordan felt driven to succeed. On the other hand, George did not have a strong sense of duty. Rather, he had a strong sense of inadequacy. Firstborns often feel a sense of loss when the second child arrives, and they wish to regain their lost position. If the father is also a firstborn, as was the senator, and demands perfection from his own firstborn child, then the feeling of inadequacy only intensifies. This anxiety

---

[8] David Meriwether Memoirs, 1856, Filson Club.

[9] Http://sunsite.unc.edu/pub/academic/histo...litary/civil_war_/D_H_Maury/DHM_ 06,TXT, accessed 9 November 1997. John J. Crittenden to Ann Mary Coleman, 10 February 1857; John J. Crittenden to Ann Mary Coleman, 17 September 1857; and John J. Crittenden to Hamilton Fish, 1 May 1859, John J. Crittenden Papers, Duke University.

over time can create anger and grow into rebellion of either a direct or an indirect nature. No doubt George's alcoholism arose from a firstborn's cry for attention and approval from a perfectionist father. When the approval did not materialize, the destructive behavior continued as a means of lashing out and embarrassing his demanding father.[10]

George's birth order may also explain another prominent characteristic. Throughout George's life, he often seemed to make hasty, unwise decisions based partially on a poor choice of friends. His father criticized this personality trait several times. Some psychologists suggest that the loss of a family member, especially a mother, creates incredible insecurity in the mind of a child. As a result, he or she would frequently enter into new relationships hastily and far less critically than normal. The child fears the loss of a loved one so much that he or she is constantly reaching out for companionship. Thus, in his intense desire for acceptance George often made questionable friends.[11]

The senator's second child, Ann Mary, might have been the most talented of all of the Crittenden children. She had the social graces and astuteness that would have made her a political success had she not been a woman. In many ways she was closer to her father than any of the siblings, and she served as the family matriarch following the death of her mother. The senator would sometimes ask Ann Mary to talk to her brothers about their behavior. The hope was that a little sisterly chide would improve their behavior.[12]

In November 1830 in Frankfort, Ann Mary married Chapman Coleman, a prosperous Louisville merchant. She bore him several children before his untimely death in 1849. The senator thought highly of Coleman and once even offered to lend him $1,000 during a business recession. Mrs. Coleman managed her considerable property for years after

---

[10] Lucille Forer and Henry Still, *The Birth Order Factor: How Your Personality Is Influenced by Your Place in the Family* (New York: Pocket Books, 1976) 10, 41–42, 66, 203.

[11] Walter Toman, *Family Constellation: Its Effects on Personality and Social Behavior*, 4th ed. (New York, Springer, 1993) 38–39, 43.

[12] John J. Crittenden to Ann Mary Coleman, 17 May 1852, John J. Crittenden Papers, Duke University.

the death of her husband, and she even found time to write and to translate German works into English.[13]

On George's recommendation Ann Mary also lived in Europe for a few years, but she worried that her father disapproved of her European stay. The elder children, who prized their independence from their father, were pleased with her travel. The senator reassured her that he still loved her, and Ann Mary's family enjoyed the visit. While in Europe, Ann Mary requested that her father find a consulate post for her son Crittenden. The senator approached Secretary of State Lewis Cass about the possibility but was unsuccessful. Afterward Ann Mary approached her father about getting young Crittenden an army appointment. Her father replied that because of partisanship and budget constraints, the prospects of an army appointment were also slim. He encouraged his oldest daughter to return home. George was in Europe at the time, and the senator hoped he would influence his sister. Ann Mary considered returning herself and allowing her children to remain in Europe, but she eventually decided to return with the children in tow. After her return, she arranged with her brothers Thomas and Robert and a son-in-law to share expenses to rent a summer home in Pee Wee Valley. On the eve of the Civil War, Ann Mary was enjoying life.[14]

The senator often gave his eldest daughter advice on business and legal matters, which she usually followed. Crittenden even often offered advice on personal issues such as childrearing. He once referred to a want of parental authority as cause for the rise of "many dissolute and miserable sons," perhaps thinking of George. Ann Mary rarely followed her father's personal advice, however. She was indulgent with her children. Perhaps she resented the great pressure her father placed on her and her siblings.

---

[13] Albert D. Kirwan, *John J. Crittenden: Struggle for the Union* (Lexington: University of Kentucky Press, 1962) 192; G. Glenn Clift, comp., *Kentucky Marriages, 1797–1865* (1938; repr., Baltimore: Genealogical Publishing Comp., 1966) 62; John J. Crittenden to Ann Mary Coleman, 19 March 1842, John J. Crittenden Papers, Duke University; Kirwan, *Crittenden*, 242; U. S. Grant to Ann Mary Coleman, 3 October 1866, John J. Crittenden Papers, Duke University.

[14] Ann Mary to John J. Crittenden, 8 February 1857, 10 February 1857; John J. Crittenden to Ann Mary Coleman, 17 September 1857, 20 February 1858, 27 April 1858, 2 July 1859; and Ann Mary Coleman to John J. Crittenden, 18 September 1861, 16 December 1859, 3 June 1860, John J. Crittenden Papers, Duke University.

Ann Mary loved her father and had a very close relationship to him, but she also had an independent mind.[15]

Once again, birth order provides some insight into the personality of a Crittenden sibling. The oldest sister of a firstborn brother often tends to move toward their father as a means of coping with a perceived sense of inferiority to the firstborn son. Ann Mary certainly fits the pattern of the oldest daughter drawing close to the father. Other studies have noted that the eldest sister of several younger sisters tends to have more ambition and is frequently more willing than the other children to accept opposition. Ann Mary typified these traits, since she had high ambitions for herself and her family and was willing to oppose her father if she deemed it proper.[16]

A contemporary described Cornelia, the third child, as a "very attractive woman in mind and person" who "left pleasant memories upon all who knew her." On 20 November 1839, Cornelia married John C. Young, a Presbyterian clergyman and president of Centre College in Danville, Kentucky. Cornelia had eight children, and one of her sons later became president of Centre College. The Youngs were well known and highly respected in their Danville community. Among the Crittenden siblings, Cornelia and Dr. Young had reputations as the moral ones. For instance, when one of Ann Mary's sons neglected his studies for the excitement of Danville's social life, Dr. Young expelled him from the college. As the senator approached old age, Cornelia told her father that she was praying for him and begged him "to try and be a Christian." Cornelia did not visit or socialize with her siblings as much as the others, and she is the only one of the Crittenden siblings not buried in the family plot in Frankfort Cemetery. In a genteel, quiet way, she followed her own path just as her sister Ann Mary had.[17]

---

[15] Kirwan, *Crittenden*, 242, 282.

[16] Forer, *Birth Order Factor*, 208; Toman, *Family Constellation*, 18.

[17] Oxx, *Kentucky Crittendens*, 192; Clay, *Life*, 216; Clift, *Kentucky Marriages*, 102; Letter book, 2:179, John C. Young Papers, Centre College, Danville KY; Lowell H. Harrison and James C. Klotter, *A New History of Kentucky* (Lexington: University Press of Kentucky, 1997) 177; John J. Crittenden to Ann Mary Coleman, 17 [MONTH] 1857, 14 February 1852; and John C. Young to John J. Crittenden, 13 November 1862, John J. Crittenden Papers, Duke University.

The younger siblings formed a second distinctive block within the Crittenden family. As a group, they often followed the lead of Thomas, the middle child. The younger children had little memory of their mother, and the last two Crittenden sons were children of Maria Todd Crittenden, the second wife. Maria was apparently a good stepmother. Her children from her first marriage got along very well with the senator's children. For different reasons, the younger children depended on their father more so than the elder children. Sometimes this dependence was financial; sometimes it was psychological or emotional. The younger siblings needed their father's acceptance and approval. Thus, they rarely challenged him.

Thomas was the most successful of the senator's sons. He dabbled in law, business, and a military career with some degree of success. Still he did not rise to the level of influence that his father envisioned for him. Perhaps with less pressure from the senator, Thomas might have had the self-confidence to achieve more.

As a child Thomas studied at the Frankfort Academy. Later, he was sent to Centre College to study under the watchful eye of his sister Cornelia. At Centre, he studied with his boyhood friend John C. Breckinridge. Thomas did not embarrass the family by his performance in school. However, intellectual concerns were not foremost in his mind. He felt the call of adventure.[18]

Thomas's first taste of excitement occurred in 1836. President Andrew Jackson called on Kentucky to provide 1,000 mounted troops to report to Camp Sabine in Louisiana because tensions with Mexico over the Texas War of Independence ran high. Thomas served from 17 August to 18 September 1837 in a company commanded by his brother George. The experience was Thomas's first exposure to military life, and apparently it was one he never forgot. The militia experience planted in Thomas a desire to leave home and try to establish his career.[19]

After release from the militia, Thomas wanted to go to New Orleans and enter business. Despite his youth, he gained his father's permission

---

[18] L. F. Johnson, *The History of Franklin County, KY* (Frankfort: Roberts Printing Company, 1912) 102–103; William C. Davis, *Breckinridge: Statesman, Soldier, Symbol* (Baton Rouge: Louisiana State University Press, 1974) 13–14.

[19] Oxx, *Kentucky Crittendens*, 95.

and made the long journey to the Crescent City. In a letter to his stepbrother Harry I. Todd, the young Crittenden lamented his situation, noting that it was "a devil of a business to be the youngest counting clerk." Thomas had been in New Orleans only three days and was already "mad as a hornet" because he was "waiting here starving while some of these trifling clerks are sitting down in some tavern or coffeehouse smoking their sigars [*sic*] or drinking liquor." The young Crittenden went on and reluctantly stated that "it is a bitter pill, but the doctor says I must take it so here it goes." Thomas had quickly discovered how hard the business world could be. Even with the extra time on his hands, he did not find time to write and the family was beginning to worry about him. Their great fear was that he would follow the poor example of his elder brother and became an idle drinker.[20]

As the months passed, Thomas became lonelier. He was happy that Harry Todd promised to write frequently, but he complained that "Pa or Ma never write to me." Thomas resolved not to write his parents until he received a letter from them. The young Crittenden wished to hear family news such as his sisters' courtships and how his stepbrother was faring in business. Obviously Thomas missed his family and he began contemplating a return to Kentucky.[21]

Thomas also contemplated moving to Texas to find his fortune. The senator insisted that Thomas was "too young" for such an undertaking and that the "adventure itself is unsuited to the character I wish him to sustain." Instead the senator proposed that Thomas return to Kentucky, providing $250 for him to make the journey. He also requested that Ann Mary's husband provide Thomas employment in his Louisville business. He hoped that Thomas would not be depressed by his experience in New Orleans, saying that it was "unworthy of his spirit and resolution."[22]

---

[20] Kirwan, *Crittenden*, 110; Thomas L. Crittenden to Harry I. Todd, 12 December 1836, Todd Collection, Kentucky Historical Society; Ann Mary Coleman to John J. Crittenden, 20 December 1836, John J. Crittenden Papers, Duke University.

[21] Thomas L. Crittenden to Harry I. Todd, 29 April 1837, Todd Collection, Kentucky Historical Society.

[22] John J. Crittenden to Ann Mary Coleman, 14 January 1838, 23 February 1838, John J. Crittenden Papers, Duke University.

The senator worried about his second son. Thomas had great promise, and with George's failure the family hopes fell squarely on him. The senator said of his second son: "He has fine affections and fine principles, but even this may lead him astray in the untried world that is before him…He has I fear, adversely contracted some idle habits…employment constant employment is the only preservative the only security for his future success." The senator went on to express his love for Thomas: "If he only knew how much solicitude I feel for him. If he always remember how much my own pride & happiness is bound up in his destiny & depends on his good conduct & success." Finally, the senator expressed his desire that no child of his would ever do anything dishonorable, since that would destroy their inheritance. In his mind that inheritance included a demonstrated record of hard work, personal and public achievements, and personal responsibility in their private affairs.[23]

While working for his brother-in-law, Thomas faced numerous economic hardships and parental admonitions. He needed to borrow money from his father to make purchases. While in Louisville Thomas apparently gave up the use of tobacco, which pleased his father, and familial pressure was brought to bear on him to give up alcohol as well. Thomas never gave it up, but apparently he also never allowed it to master him or cause him disgrace. The elder Crittenden also complained of Thomas's poor handwriting, noting the need for a fine hand in order to be a more polished gentleman.[24]

Thomas responded to all the parental admonitions by always trying to please his father, but these efforts may have undermined his self-confidence. He rarely trusted his own instincts and seldom acted on them if he thought they might cause conflict. Thomas disliked taking a stand in opposition to anyone because he feared others' displeasure; instead, he sought to please others and gain acceptance. Thomas spent much of 1839 ill, and the family feared he was dyspeptic. He complained of few letters from home and pondered his future, deepening his relationship with his sister, Ann Mary; he stayed with her for approximately a year. By 1840, he

---

[23] Ibid.
[24] John J. Crittenden to Thomas L. Crittenden, 28 April 1838, John J. Crittenden Papers, Library of Congress.

had decided to begin the study of law, following in his father's footsteps. He began study in Louisville and his sister noted his dedication, but she also remarked that he was "not well satisfied" and seemed to be looking for something else. Thomas completed his study of law under his father in Frankfort. Unlike his older brother, Thomas remained deeply influenced by his father and had no desire to challenge him. Instead, he attempted to imitate his father in as many ways as possible.[25]

Along with a new career, Thomas had a new family. He married his step-sister Catherine Lucy Todd, called Kitty by the family. A soldier who saw Kitty during the Civil War described her as "a brunette, but masculine in face," noting that "she has the appearance of a strong minded woman." Thomas and Kitty had three children. Annie was born in 1844 but only lived for four months. John Jordan, named after the senator, was born in 1854 and died with General Custer at Little Bighorn. Maria Innes was born in 1856 and died in 1859. The marriage continued the trend of Thomas's life by binding him even closer to his father. His father, his father-in-law, and his mentor in the practice of law were the same person. In almost every element of Thomas's life, he faced his father's towering shadow.[26]

In 1843, Thomas received an appointment as commonwealth's attorney. His first trial was a murder case in Woodford County, the accused a Dudley Woolfork. According to observers, Thomas performed credibly but Woolfork was still acquitted. Woolfork's defense attorney was John J. Crittenden. Thomas was learning the hard lesson of the futility of opposing his father. Whether in business, family matters, or the courtroom, Thomas realized that he needed to heed his powerful father; opposition would only result in defeat and disgrace.[27]

Still, Thomas's years at Frankfort seemed happy. He was prospering in his law practice and had become involved in civic affairs. For example,

---

[25] Ann Mary Coleman to John J. Crittenden, 8 February 1839; John J. Crittenden to Ann Mary Coleman, 27 January 1840, John J. Crittenden Papers, Duke University; Kirwan, *Crittenden*, 159; Ann Mary Coleman to John J. Crittenden, 11 February 1840, John J. Crittenden Papers, Duke University.

[26] Kirwan, *Crittenden*, 159; George Landrum to sister, 18 July 1862, George W. Landrum Letters, Ohio Historical Society Columbus; Oxx, *Kentucky Crittendens*, 195.

[27] Kirwan, *Crittenden*, 159–60.

he was on a committee that created the Frankfort Cemetery, the sponsors hoping to develop interest in the project by moving the body of Daniel Boone from Missouri back to Kentucky. Missouri agreed to the request but later changed its mind, preferring to build a Boone monument there. Kentucky sponsors appointed a committee consisting of Thomas Crittenden, Phillip Swigert, and Colonel William Boone to bring back the remains.

The committee had to deal with Harvey Griswold, the owner of the property where Boone was buried, and with the numerous Boone relatives in Missouri. Thomas Crittenden apparently presented the case. He argued that he had "satisfactory evidence that the immediate relations of Colonel Boone had been consulted and given their written consent" for the removal of the body. He promised that Griswold would be adequately compensated for the loss of value to his property by the removal of Boone's remains. Crittenden also emphasized that Kentucky would build a substantial memorial to Boone in the new cemetery. Gaining agreement, Crittenden hired three men to exhume the body on 23 July 1845. The remains were not in very good condition, and the Kentuckians eventually brought only bones back to Kentucky. No one, even today, really knows if Crittenden and company actually dug up the right body in Missouri. Unfortunately, Griswold never received compensation for the loss of value to his property and the monument to honor Boone was not completed until 1860.[28]

Still, an aggressive Thomas was showing signs of political skills in debate and in maneuvering against hostile foes. Perhaps he would be the Crittenden politician of the next generation. Throughout the cemetery debate, the Crittenden family supported Thomas's activities by buying burial plots in the new cemetery a short distance from where Boone was buried.

During the 1840s, American relations with Mexico grew tenser. They were not improved by the annexation of Texas in 1845 or the controversy over the boundary between Texas and Mexico. It seemed as if a declaration

---

[28] Nettie Henry Glenn, *Early Frankfort Kentucky, 1786–1861* (Frankfort: Kentucky Historical Society, 1986) 171; Carl E. Krammer, *Capital on the Kentucky: A Two Hundred Year History of Frankfort & Franklin County* (Frankfort: Historic Frankfort, 1986) 131; John Mack Faragher, *Daniel Boone: The Life and Legend of an American Pioneer* (New York: Henry Holt & Comp., 1992) 356–61.

of war was simply a matter of time. In 1846 the war came, and Thomas quickly volunteered to serve on the staff of General Zachary Taylor. Taylor was a Kentuckian, a cousin of Thomas's mother, and he had previously hired the senator as his attorney to represent his Kentucky property. The senator saw in General Taylor a winning presidential candidate and used his son Thomas to gather information about him.[29]

Thomas traveled south and eventually reached Matamoras. From there to Monterrey, another officer named Jefferson Davis accompanied him. The journey was hazardous, and as a result of their adventures Crittenden and Davis became good friends. In many ways, Jefferson Davis looked upon Thomas as a younger brother. After the Battle of Buena Vista, Thomas wrote to Davis's brother Joseph that he had developed "a great personal attachment" for his new friend. Davis would refer to Thomas as "our noble boy" when he wrote Senator Crittenden, and after the wounding of Davis at the Battle of Buena Vista, Thomas tended to his fallen comrade. The Crittenden-Davis connection would have great importance for the family in the years ahead.[30]

At the pivotal battle of Buena Vista, Thomas played a significant role. After the first day's fighting, Taylor sent him to demand the surrender of some retreating Mexican forces. Instead, the Kentuckian was captured and brought before General Santa Anna. The Mexican leader told Crittenden that he had 22,000 troops and had Taylor surrounded, so Taylor should surrender immediately. Crittenden replied that "General Taylor never surrenders," but Santa Anna released him anyway to carry the message to Taylor. Upon hearing of Santa Anna's threats, General Taylor responded, "said he had 22,000 men did he? Ump! He won't have that many tomorrow." Taylor was right—on the second day of the battle, the Mexicans were defeated decisively.[31]

After the victory at Buena Vista, Taylor sent Crittenden and an escort of 250 men under Major Giddings to carry news to President Polk. As the force approached Seralvo, a force of about 1,500 cavalry under General

[29] Kirwan, *Crittenden*, 203; George R. Poage, *Henry Clay and the Whig Party* (Chapel Hill: University of North Carolina Press, 1036) 154.

[30] Oxx, *Kentucky Crittendens*, 96; Davis, *Jefferson Davis*, 159; Woodworth, *Jefferson Davis and His Generals*, 63.

[31] Oxx, *Kentucky Crittendens*, 96.

Urrea attacked them. The American force lost about seventeen men and between forty and fifty wagons. They claimed to have inflicted sixty-five casualties on the Mexicans. The force had to wait about six days for reinforcements to arrive. Still, Crittenden's mission was eventually a success, and he brought the first definite news of Taylor's victory to the American public.[32]

Crittenden's Buena Vista experience sparked a desire to add to his military reputation. As a result, in 1847 Thomas was appointed lieutenant colonel of the newly created 3rd Kentucky regiment. Manilus Thompson, a former lieutenant governor, was colonel of the regiment; Thomas's old childhood friend John C. Breckinridge served as the major. Crittenden's men came primarily from Bluegrass counties with a few Appalachian units thrown in. The 3rd Kentucky saw no combat but served garrison duty in Mexico.[33]

The Mexican War gave Thomas only a brief introduction to military life. While on Taylor's staff he saw how an army was managed. Unfortunately, Taylor was not a good administrator. Service with Winfield Scott's staff would have been more instructive. As lieutenant colonel of the 3rd Kentucky, Crittenden did not see actual combat that could have prepared him for the stress of high command in the Civil War. In short, Crittenden's Mexican war experience was limited.

Much to Senator Crittenden's pleasure, Taylor received the Whig nomination for president and won the election. As a reward, Thomas received a consulate position in Liverpool. The position had great financial possibilities for investors wanting to speculate in American cotton, but the appointment also caused a rift between Ann Mary and Thomas. Ann Mary had hoped that the consulate position would go to her husband instead of Thomas. Thus, she felt that her father favored Thomas over her. The

---

[32] Ibid., 96–97; *Taylor and His Generals A Biography of Major-General Zachary Taylor; and Sketches of the Lives of Generals Worth, Wool, and Twiggs; With a Full Account of the Various Actions of their Divisions in Mexico up to the Present Time; Together with a History of the Bombardment of Vera Cruz and a Sketch of the Life of Major-General Winfield Scott* (Philadelphia: E. H. Butler & Co, 1847) 209; K. Jack Bauer, *The Mexican War, 1846–1848* (New York: Macmillan, 1974) 219.

[33] Damon Eubank, *The Response of Kentucky to the Mexican War, 1846–1848* (Lewiston: Edwin Mellon Press, 2004) 39, 123.

senator had to practice his political conciliatory skills on his children. He told Ann Mary that the position had first been offered to Mr. Coleman but that he had declined it in favor of Thomas, who had not really sought it. Thomas would have stepped aside if he had known how much Ann Mary wanted to go to Europe, as would have Mr. Coleman if he thought Thomas really wanted to go. It was all a big misunderstanding and no cause for disagreement. Apparently, this explanation resolved the issue with no further repercussions.[34]

The voyage to Britain took eleven days, and Thomas's wife Kitty was sick most of the time. After their arrival, Thomas wrote to a friend, "I am in bad spirits about my office, I fear I shall not be able to make any money." He went on to note that office expenses were great and that he and Kitty could only survive with "rigid economy." He concluded with the promise that "if I find after six months trial I can't make money here I shall come home." Thomas suggested that his friends in America use their influence to close consulates in Manchester and Leeds to increase the volume of cotton going through Liverpool.[35]

Eventually, Thomas and Kitty settled into their new surroundings. Thomas reported that "we are getting on tolerably well and making acquaintances gradually, and becoming more and more satisfied with the situation here." Unfortunately, he did not adjust very well to the British climate and was ill much of the time. He wrote home for guidance about places to visit while in Britain, hoping that Ann Mary and Orlando Brown would visit and they could travel together around Europe.[36]

As consul, Thomas had to tend to many mundane chores associated with the position. He obtained autographs of President Zachary Taylor for interested parties. He also gave advice to friends about investments in the

---

[34] Kirwan, *Crittenden,* 251–52; John J. Crittenden to Ann Mary Coleman, 9 May 1849, John J. Crittenden Papers, Duke University.

[35] Thomas L. Crittenden to Orlando Brown, 18 July 1849, Orlando Brown Papers, Kentucky Historical Society.

[36] Thomas L. Crittenden to Orlando Brown, 5 September 1849, Orlando Brown Papers, Kentucky Historical Society; Thomas L. Crittenden to John J. Crittenden, 23 January 1850, John J. Crittenden Papers, Duke University; Thomas L. Crittenden to Orlando Brown, 21 September 1849, Orlando Brown Papers, Filson Club Louisville; John J. Crittenden to Ann Mary Coleman, 23 February 1851, John J. Crittenden Papers, Duke University.

cotton market. He worried about changes in tariff duties and how they would impact his financial investments, and he continued to defend Zachary Taylor from attack. He resented the growing criticism of Taylor during the divisive sectional debates of 1850. He could not "leave a friend," reminding the critics that "if Santa Anna with his 20,000 could not drive him from ground he had chosen, shall a few dollard [*sic*] politicians whose backs and banners are yet dusty from defeat?"[37]

Although Thomas was happy, enjoyed his surroundings, and liked the British people, he and Kitty began to grow homesick for old friends and familiar surroundings. In 1852 Thomas resigned his position and returned to Frankfort, Kentucky. During the 1850s he dabbled in politics and public service. In 1854, when former president Millard Fillmore visited Kentucky, Thomas was one of the introductory speakers joining Charles Morehead, Lazarus Powell, Robert P. Letcher, and Orlando Brown, all very powerful Kentuckians. Clearly Thomas was keeping distinguished company.[38]

As Crittenden's beloved Whig party disintegrated in the 1850s, politicians searched for an alternative party. Thomas flirted with the Know-Nothing movement and in 1855 gave a well-received speech at the group's convention. Perhaps because his father never moved in that direction, Thomas drew back. Instead, he was establishing himself as a public speaker, giving an address, for example, commemorating General Charles Scott. He gave a long speech in the best oratorical traditions of that day.[39]

---

[37] Thomas L. Crittenden to Orlando Brown, 5 September 1849, Orlando Brown Papers, Kentucky Historical Society; Thomas L. Crittenden to A. T. Burnley, 23 October 1850, Bibb-Burnley Papers, Kentucky Historical Society; Thomas L. Crittenden to Orlando Brown, 20 December 1859, 11 May 1850, Orlando Brown Papers, Kentucky Historical Society.

[38] Thomas L. Crittenden to Harry I. Todd, 15 November 1850, Todd Collection, Kentucky Historical Society; Thomas L. Crittenden to Orlando Brown, 18 July 1849, Orlando Brown Papers, Kentucky Historical Society; Thomas L. Crittenden to Orlando Brown, 28 April 1852, Orlando Brown Papers, Filson Club; Thomas L. Crittenden to Orlando Brown, 6 March 1850, Orlando Brown Papers, Filson Club; Johnson, *History of Franklin County*, 137; Kirwan, *Crittenden*, 299.

[39] Thomas L. Crittenden, *Obituary Address Delivered Upon the Occasion of the Re-internment of the Remains of General Charles Scott, Major William T. Barry, and Captain Bland Ballard and Wife in the Cemetery at Frankfort, November, 1854* (A. G. Hodges: State Printer, 1855).

Had Thomas followed his natural inclinations, he could have entered Kentucky politics. He had ambition. He wrote to a friend, "You know I am full of ambition and of high hopes...for I know you must aim high if you would shoot far." Thomas wanted to please and impress his father by succeeding in the political world. Thomas once noted that his father's qualities were "of gold" while his own qualities were only "of brass." Thomas felt he had worthwhile abilities too, but he still felt inferior to his father. It was this sense of inferiority that probably prevented him from entering the political arena in the 1850s. On the eve of the Civil War Thomas told a friend, "I think I could get the nomination to Congress from this district, with a fair chance of being elected." However, as he feared failure and disliked the inevitable comparisons to his father, he never campaigned for the office. If Thomas had held political office during the 1850s, it might have given him more self-confidence and made him less dependent on his father. Thomas's instincts were often sound, but he was unable to act on them aggressively. His Civil War career and postwar life might have been different had these character traits been ingrained in him before the crisis of war exposed their lack.[40]

While in Frankfort, Thomas also took time to be a good friend and son. One of his best friends was Orlando Brown, one-time editor of the Frankfort *Commonwealth* and, like Thomas, a member of one of Kentucky's leading families. The two men wrote and confided in each other frequently. When Orlando was discouraged about his political prospects, it was Thomas who encouraged him to "hold on" because better fortunes "will come after a while." When Orlando was diagnosed with the early stages of consumption, his physician Dr. Hensely asked Crittenden to break the news. Ever the dutiful friends, the two survived the Civil War crisis and were buried close to each other in the Frankfort Cemetery they had helped found. In a similar vein, Thomas tried to be a good son. He worried about his father's health and wished that the elder Crittenden would relax and enjoy life.[41]

---

[40] Thomas L. Crittenden to Orlando Brown, 26 April 1852, 6 March 1850, Orlando Brown Papers, Filson Club; Thomas L. Crittenden to John Coyle, 12 April 1861; Thomas L. Crittenden Letter, Miscellaneous file, Filson Club.

[41] Thomas L. Crittenden to Orlando Brown, 6 March 1850, Orlando Brown Papers, Filson Club; Thomas L. Crittenden to Orlando Brown, 16 March 1858, Orlando Brown

As a member of Kentucky's leadership class, all the Crittendens were wealthy, part of that wealth coming from slave ownership. The senator had made his fortune from the practice of law and lived all of his adult life in an urban setting. Consequently, he never owned more than about a dozen or so slaves, who were household servants rather than field hands. The Crittenden children grew up accepting slavery as an institution that simply existed in the normal course of events. They lent out household servants to each other. Thomas's actions as a slaveholder are recorded in a letter to his stepbrother Harry I. Todd: "Sanders has written to me for permission to get married. Please see him and tell him I have no objections—make him give you an account of what he is doing and tell him if he expects to stay in Frankfort this winter he must send me his wages regularly, or I will be compelled to hire him to some steamboat association. He may have a week's holiday after his marriage." Thus, in attitude and concerns, Crittenden was a typical antebellum Southerner, blind to the immorality of the institution of slavery.[42]

Thomas lived in Frankfort for several years after his return from Britain. His home was only a few blocks from the home in which he had been raised. He practiced law but never lost his early interest in mercantile pursuits. Thus, sometime during the 1850s he moved to Louisville and entered business there. Crittenden & Co. on Wall Street provided brokerage services for Louisvillians. To all appearances, Thomas had settled into a comfortable life as a member of Kentucky's leadership class. Only his lack of self-confidence prevented him from playing an even larger role. Thomas had charisma and charm and some political ability, but he needed an opportunity to develop and display these gifts.[43]

The impact of birth order within the Crittenden family again offers insights into Thomas's personality. Middle children tend to be affable and must learn to get along with others. They often have a more relaxed relationship with their parents because more is expected of the firstborn

---

Papers, Kentucky Historical Society; Thomas L. Crittenden to Orlando Brown, 21 September 1849, Orlando Brown Papers, Filson Club.

[42] John J. Crittenden to A. M. Coleman, 28 January 1855, John J. Crittenden Papers, Duke University; Thomas L. Crittenden to Harry I. Todd, 8 December —, Todd Collection, Kentucky Historical Society.

[43] *Louisville Daily Journal*, (5 September 1860): 4.

than the middle child. Middle children also often feel neglected and thus strive to please the parents and gain favorable attention. Thomas typified these traits since he had an affable personality along with a deep desire to please his father and gain favorable parental attention.[44]

The senator's next child was Sarah Lee, called Maria by the family, the most elusive of the Crittenden children. She was only a small child when her mother died and her father remarried. The second Mrs. Crittenden had a daughter called Elizabeth who was Maria's age, and the two became inseparable. Later they would marry brothers. As teenagers, Maria and Elizabeth attended an academy in Steubenville, Ohio. As an adult, Maria married Dr. Edward Howard Watson of Frankfort, and the couple lived at the Crittenden house in Frankfort. This was not a problem while the senator was in Washington, but it became more stressful for Maria when her father and stepmother returned to Frankfort. Maria wrote few letters that have been preserved, and she was only infrequently mentioned by her siblings in their correspondence. Like her brother Thomas, she did not want to create tension or defy her father.[45]

The senator's youngest son by his first wife was Robert. He entered Miami University in Oxford, Ohio, in 1836 but was such a poor student that the senator removed him from school in 1838. He was sent back to Frankfort to remain under the watchful eye of Crittenden's friend Mason Brown. The senator asked Ann Mary to keep Robert from becoming idle. After a while, young Robert went to study at Centre College under the careful watch of his moral sister Cornelia and her husband Dr. Young. There Robert concentrated on his studies and graduated in 1842. Later, on 17 October 1844, he married Adeline Theobald. The two had several children.[46]

Robert tended to follow the lead of his older brother Thomas. When Thomas was appointed to the consulate at Liverpool, Robert made the journey to England, although his wife wanted him to return to Frankfort because she was sick. She died within a month, with her husband absent.

---

[44] Forer, *Birth Order Factor*, 11, 128.

[45] Oxx, *Kentucky Crittendens*, 192; Kirwan, *Crittenden*, 65, 110, 157.

[46] Kirwan, *Crittenden*, 110, 122, 169; John J. Crittenden to Ann Mary Coleman, 4 January 1838, 1 June 1838, John J. Crittenden Papers, Duke University; Oxx, *Kentucky Crittendens*, 192; Clift, *Kentucky Marriages*, 108.

Since John J. Crittenden was serving as governor of Kentucky at the time, she passed away at the governor's mansion. After Robert's eventual return to Kentucky, he was impressed with the investment possibilities he saw in Europe. He inquired from Thomas's close friend Orlando Brown if there were other consulate positions available at Leeds & Manchester. Although inquires were made, nothing ever come of the idea. After Thomas returned to Frankfort, he and Robert entered into business in their hometown. The two brothers remained close throughout their lives.[47]

Robert never emerged from beneath the shadow of his more talented older siblings. His father placed pressure on him to do well in school and to work hard just as he had with the other siblings. Unfortunately, Robert did not have Ann Mary's ability or George or Thomas's charm. The youngest child of the senator's first marriage never rose to prominence. Robert was a typical youngest child; he always expected someone else, whether his father or one of his siblings, to solve his problems for him. The youngest Crittenden never matured.[48]

The two children born of the senator's second wife Maria Todd, John Jordan Jr. and Eugene, never amounted to much either. John Jordan Jr. died before the start of the Civil War and never had an opportunity to show what promise his life might have held. In many ways Eugene followed the example of his eldest brother George. Like George, Eugene chose a military career. He went to West Point, where he had a mediocre record, and after graduation he began to drink excessively. The senator, worried that the family curse might repeat itself, asked Ann Mary to talk to her little brother. Whatever she said did no good, for Eugene continued his drinking. Eugene also began to spend his money rather freely. He piled up huge debts that his father had to pay. Like George, he never married.[49]

Eugene served on the Western frontier and saw duty during the Mormon War of 1858. Since he was much younger than George, Thomas,

---

[47] Robert H. Crittenden to Orlando Brown, 26 August 1849, Orlando Brown Papers, Filson Club; Glen G. Clift, *Kentucky Obituaries* (1938; repr., Baltimore: Genealogical Publishing, 1979) 152; Kirwan, *Crittenden*, 282; Thomas L. Crittenden to Orlando Brown, 21 September 1849, Orlando Brown Papers, Filson Club.

[48] Forer, *Birth Order Factor*, 11.

[49] John J. Crittenden to Ann Mary Coleman, 17 May 1852, John J. Crittenden Papers, Duke University; Kirwan, *Crittenden*, 476, 282.

and Robert, he had less chance for prominence during the Civil War. Like Thomas, he seemed to have good military and political instincts. He might have done more in the postwar world had he not died prematurely in 1874 while serving in the New Mexico territory.[50]

The younger siblings often followed Thomas's example. While giving their father cause for worry, they tended not to defy his wishes on major matters. They followed their father's example and yielded to his influence. In other words, they were for the most part compliant children.

The Crittenden siblings had a powerful father who put great pressure on them to excel. The family patriarch had achieved great success and wished to pass this heritage on to his children. Some of the siblings could not attain the patriarch's lofty goals and reacted to the pressure in self-destructive and embarrassing ways. At the same time, other siblings reacted to parental pressure by consciously trying to please their father. The Civil War would dramatically show the Crittenden children's different responses to the demands of their powerful father. Instead of a heritage of achievement, the siblings inherited division. The result was a family tragedy.

---

[50] John J. Crittenden to Ann Mary Coleman, 20 February 1858, John J. Crittenden Papers, Duke University.

3

The Civil War and the
Division of a Family Heritage

The American Civil War was the great crisis of the Crittenden siblings' lifetime. Indeed, it was the great crisis of the nation. Kentucky and the Crittenden family would be intimately involved in the crisis. Both state and family would be torn asunder by the war. For the Crittenden siblings, their world would never be the same. They had to publicly take a position, and the glare of public scrutiny would practically destroy several of them.

In the tense presidential election of 1860, the Republican candidate Abraham Lincoln carried most of the Northern states by a narrow vote and thus won a victory in the electoral college. In Kentucky, John Bell of the Constitutional Union party received 66,051 votes; John C. Breckinridge, running on a states rights platform, received 53,143 votes; Stephen Douglas, supporting a popular sovereignty platform, received 25,638 votes; and Abraham Lincoln, running on a platform opposing the expansion of slavery, received only 1,364 votes. Both Bell and Douglas believed in the compromise of sectional issues, and they represented about 63 percent of the 1860 Kentucky vote. Clearly Kentucky agreed with these two men. The election of Abraham Lincoln, unfortunately, led to secession in the lower South.[1]

In such a situation, Kentuckians felt that they had much to lose. As one Kentuckian noted, "The true position of Kentucky in the present crisis is to assume the stand of pacification. She has nothing to gain, but much to lose, by throwing herself into the arms of any new Confederacy, North or South." Kentucky would lose her advantage of a central location and become a hotly contested battle zone. The state's property would be destroyed, its

---

[1] Lowell H. Harrison, *The Civil War in Kentucky* (Lexington: University Press of Kentucky, 1975) 4–5.

citizens killed, and its social institutions devastated by war. Kentucky would suffer the same fate as Virginia. Thus, Kentucky hoped for and worked for peace. Senator Crittenden had intended to retire from the US Senate in 1861, but instead he spent his last months in office trying to save the Union. Unlike his former fellow Kentuckian, the senator could not arrange an acceptable compromise now. The secession movement continued, and the race was on for who would win Kentucky. As President Lincoln once said, "I think to lose Kentucky is nearly the same as to lose the whole game." Kentucky's agricultural production, industrial potential, strategic rivers, and population all made the state desirable.[2]

Kentucky moved slowly in making up its mind about which side to join. Following a visit from Alabama and Mississippi commissioners, on 27 December 1860 Governor Beriah Magoffin called for a special session of the state legislature to convene on 17 January 1861. The special session considered Kentucky's need to call a state convention to vote on secession and to send delegates to a border state conference in Baltimore. Magoffin, a states rights advocate, aroused the fears of Kentucky Unionists.[3]

In response Kentucky Unionists formed a Union state central committee led by George Prentice of the Louisville *Daily Journal*, John H. Harney of the Louisville *Democrat*, and James Speed, a well-known Louisville lawyer. They would proceed with caution, not wanting to upset the very delicate state of affairs. Although the Unionists disagreed with many Northern policies, their desire for the preservation of the Union overrode those fears. As one Unionist wrote to John J. Crittenden, "The great sound conservative heart of the commonwealth who are for the union, the constitution—the whole flag, every strip and every star in its place. This party will struggle for the Union as it was." Kentucky Unionism attracted numerous leading Kentuckians, among them Robert J. Breckinridge, James Guthrie, Garrett Davis, A. G. Hodges, and John J. Crittenden.[4]

---

[2] Fred J. Hood, ed. *Kentucky: Its History and Heritage* (St. Louis: Forum Press, 1978) 137; Thomas D. Clark, *A History of Kentucky* (Lexington: John Bradford Press, 1960) 329, 334; Thomas D. Clark, *Kentucky: Land of Contrast* (New York: Harper & Row, 1968) 125.

[3] Lowell H. Harrison and James C. Klotter, *A New History of Kentucky* (Lexington: University Press of Kentucky, 1997) 187.

[4] Hood, ed. *Kentucky*, 137–139; Thomas Speed, *The Union Cause in Kentucky* (New York: G. P. Putnam & Sons, 1907) 38–39; Clark, *Kentucky: Land of Contrast*, 124–25.

Many Unionists perceived the calling of a state convention as the first step toward secession. As a result the state legislature met and adjourned on 11 February 1861, not to meet again until 20 March. The legislature then remained in session until 4 April. It approved the call for another border state convention in Frankfort on 27 May and supported a proposed 13th amendment that would guarantee slavery where it already existed.[5]

Then the dramatic events at Fort Sumter altered the situation. When the Federal government attempted to resupply the fort, Confederate forces fired upon it. President Lincoln requested militia from the states to put down the rebellion. Governor Magoffin replied to the request of troops from Kentucky with a stinging refusal, declaring, "I say, emphatically, Kentucky will furnish no troops for the wicked purpose of subduing her sister Southern states." It seemed as if Kentucky was on the verge of joining the Confederacy.[6]

At this juncture, the old senator gave a speech in Lexington on 17 April in which he advocated a policy of neutrality for Kentucky in the coming war. He asserted that Kentucky's duty was "to maintain her present independent position, taking sides not with the government and not with the seceding states, but with the Union against them both, declaring her soil to be sacred from the hostile tread of either, and, if necessary, making the declaration good with her strong right arm." Crittenden and many other Unionists realized that neutrality was nothing more than a stall tactic. They reasoned that the longer it took Kentucky to vote on secession, the less likely the state would secede. President Lincoln seemed to agree and tried to let Kentuckian Unionism rise to the surface.[7]

Crittenden and the other Unionists seemed to be right. Emotions cooled after the neutrality proclamation, and as time passed Kentucky Unionism began to rise. During the summer in legislative and congressional elections, Unionists won overwhelming majorities. Instead of retiring, Senator Crittenden found himself a candidate for a US House seat. He won the election and served there until his death in 1863. During the summer, President Lincoln began discreetly sending weapons into

---

[5] Hood, ed., *Kentucky,* 139–40; Harrison, *Civil War in Kentucky.*

[6] Harrison, *Civil War in Kentucky*, 8.

[7] Hood, ed. *Kentucky*, 140–42.

Kentucky so that Unionists such as William "Bull" Nelson could organize Union military units. Kentucky was looking more and more like a Union state.[8]

In the late summer, Federal General John C. Fremont's unauthorized order freeing slaves in Missouri caused a spike in Confederate support in Kentucky. One Unionist referred to the proclamation as "despotism, the most fearful on the globe." Before States Rights Kentuckians could take advantage of this surge in popularity, however, in early September Confederate general Leonidas Polk invaded Kentucky, completely negating any Confederate gains from Fremont's proclamation.[9]

During the Civil War, Kentucky was a divided state. Although figures vary, one historian has estimated that the state provided 76,000 volunteers for the Union and 25,000 for the Confederacy. According to one count, Kentucky provided sixty-seven generals to the Union side and thirty-eight to the Confederate. Just as their home state was divided by war, so too were the Crittendens. The senator and his children were very active in the tense events of 1860 and 1861, and their actions would impact them for the remainder of their lives.[10]

The two oldest sons, George and Thomas, played leading roles in the unfolding drama. Over the course of time, the other siblings fell in line behind one or the other of these brothers. George, the older and ever disappointing son, followed through to once again disappoint his father. Thomas, the ever dutiful son who sought acceptance and approval, faithfully echoed his father's Union position.

As rumors of disunion spread, George was stationed at Fort Craig far away in the New Mexico territory. Secretary of War John Floyd, from Virginia, had stacked the officers at Fort Craig with Southerners. William Loring of North Carolina was the colonel of the unit and would later serve as a Confederate general. George was the lieutenant colonel, and D. H. Maury of Virginia was the adjutant. Some historians have speculated that Secretary Floyd hoped to annex the New Mexico territory to the new

---

[8] Harrison, *Civil War in Kentucky,* 11; Hood, *Kentucky,* 143.

[9] Hood, ed. *Kentucky,* 143–45; Alfred Pirtle Journal, 1 September 1861, Filson Club Louisville; Harrison and Klotter, *New History of Kentucky,* 191–92.

[10] Clark, *Kentucky: Land of Contrast,* 142–43.

Southern republic by staffing it with so many Southern officers. In 1861 George had told friends in Santa Fe, "I am sure that I shall find my father altogether with the South when I get home." Once again George made a rash decision, and this time his father could not alter the consequences.[11]

Unfortunately for George, he had completely misunderstood his father's position. On 30 April 1861 the patriarch wrote his eldest son, expressing his concern about George joining the Confederacy and questioning George's ability to lead: "It is not so much on account of any dangers to which you may be exposed as because of embarrassments and responsibilities that may devolve upon you in new and untried circumstances as serious in which you may be found." The senator went on to express his opinion of George's resignation from the army and of the situation in Kentucky:

> Many officers of the army and navy have resigned for the alleged reason that they belong to some one of the seceded sates, now calling themselves the "Confederate sates" and cannot therefore bear arms against them—This supposes they have *no nation*, no national flag. This is expressing a very questionable position at best. But I hope that you will never have cause for such question or example in your case. Kentucky has not seceded, I believe she never will, she loves the union and will cling to it as long as possible—and so I hope will you. Be true to the government that has trusted in you and stand fast by your nation's flag, the stars and strips. And do not resign under any circumstances without consultation with me. There have been so many instances of distinguished treachery and dishonor in the army that I would be proud to see you distinguished by exemplary loyalty and devotion to your flag and your country—the country that commissioned you…. The spirit of disunion has spread so far and wide, that it may have even reached your distant posts, and infected the minds of some officers. It becomes you to be *vigilant*, very vigilant, and with all your energy and courage, if need be, to resist every attempt at weakening or rebellion against the

---

[11] John P. Dyer, *From Shiloh to San Juan: The Life of Fighting Joe Wheeler* (Baton Rouge: Louisiana State University Press, 1941) 16; http://sunsite.unc.edu/pub/academic/histo...litary/civil_war_/D_H_Maury/DHM_06,TXT.

government…God knows what is to be the end. I do not see how the conflict of arms can be avoided, Kentucky is adverse to this civil war—and it is now, I trust it will continue to be her determination to keep out the strife—and, fighting only in the defense of her own borders when they shall be invaded. To occupy the position of a friendly neutral mediator between the belligerents.

The senator had clearly stated his opinion of the situation and had expressly told George what he expected him to do. Even considering the poor communications with the Western frontier outposts, it is probable that George received this letter before he acted.[12]

On 11 June 1861, the adjutant general office accepted George's resignation from the Federal army. He journeyed back to the Eastern states. Through the old family connection to Jefferson Davis, on 15 August George received an appointment as Confederate brigadier general. Before he could be given an assignment, however, on 9 November he was promoted to major general and placed in command of troops in eastern Kentucky.[13]

In a letter dated 19 July 1861, the senator attempted to dissuade his son. He pointed to the larger population and superior economic resources of the Northern states and argued that the South would be overwhelmed by the North in any war. The senator believed that his son was backing a losing cause. Like many Americans, Senator Crittenden believed that the war would be brief, and news of the Federal defeat at Bull Run stunned him. According to one report, he broke down in tears. The patriarch clearly realized that this would be a long, divisive war that would create deep wounds within his nation and his family.[14]

George rebelled in defiance of his father's expressed wishes. The eldest son now had the opportunity to succeed in something without the aid of his powerful father. No doubt George considered himself one of the

---

[12] John J. Crittenden to George B. Crittenden, 30 April 1861, John J. Crittenden letters, Filson Club.

[13] Francis Hudson Oxx, *The Kentucky Crittenden: The History of a Family Including Genealogy of Descendent in Both Male and Female Lives, Biographical Sketches of its Members, and Their Descent from Other Colonial Lives* (n.p., 1940) 127.

[14] John J. Crittenden to George B. Crittenden, 19 July 1861, John J. Crittenden Papers, Kentucky Historical Society; Anonymous, *Louisville Daily Journal,* (31 July 1861): 1.

coming great generals of the Confederacy. He was a scarce West Point graduate during a time of war, he was a close friend and associate of the Confederate president, and in the prewar years he had established a reputation for personal bravery. Moreover, George could be charming when he chose to be. If he could control his drinking habits and have a little luck on the battlefield, he might become one of the great heroes of the Civil War.

While George was in New Mexico withdrawing from his father's influence, Thomas was in Kentucky growing even closer to his father. Unlike George, Thomas tended to be cautious—perhaps too cautious for his own good, as future events would show. Thomas waited to see where his father stood on the issue of secession and where Kentucky public opinion was headed before he acted. Even so, during this troubled time Thomas seemed to always be on the edge of key events. He was on the verge of greatness if only he could come out from under his father's long shadow.

On 8 January 1861, Thomas had attended a meeting of Kentucky Unionists in Louisville whose purpose was to bring together those who had supported John Bell in the 1860 election and those who had supported Stephen Douglas. This group placed a high value on the Union and viewed the election of Lincoln as insufficient grounds to break it. They denounced the "fanaticism" of the North but still felt that the problems could be worked out peacefully. Thomas spoke at the evening session. The Louisville *Daily Journal* recorded that he "fairly took his audience by surprise with his cogent reasoning, his bold positions, the nervous strength of his language. He inherits the eloquence as well as the patriotism of his father." Even considering that George Prentice, the editor of the *Daily Journal*, was an old family friend, Thomas must have given a very well-received speech to earn such praise. He no doubt enjoyed the favorable comparisons with his father. It seemed as though Thomas had finally found his niche in life. He was a superb public speaker.[15]

In March 1861, Governor Magoffin sent Thomas, Senator Crittenden, Humphrey Marshall, and John W. Russell on a mission to

---

[15] Speed, *Union Cause in Kentucky*, 35–36; Anonymous, *Louisville Daily Journal*, (9 January 1861): 3.

Cincinnati. The Kentucky governor had proposed a league of Kentucky, Indiana, and Ohio to mediate the differences between the North and South. The meeting was proposed for late April, and Magoffin sent the committee to Cincinnati to sound out Governor Morton of Indiana about his interest in the project. Thomas carried a letter that read: "I have been instructed by the Honorable B. Magoffin, Governor of the state of Kentucky, to solicit of yourself and the Honorable William Dennison, Governor of the state of Ohio, in an effort to bring about a truce between the general government and the Seceded states until the meeting of Congress in extraordinary session in the hope that the action of that body may point out the way to a peaceful solution of our national troubles." Governor Morton rejected the idea, claiming that he would only met with Governor Magoffin in person. At the same time that Thomas was being thus rejected, he also wrote to Governor Dennison, asking him to use his influence to arrange a truce. Dennison also rejected the Kentuckians' overtures.[16]

Thomas continued to speak on behalf of the Union throughout 1861, his oratorical skills persistently earning him praise. Patrick Joyes, one of Ann Mary's sons-in-law, reported to her that Thomas had recently given a fine speech for the Union and many people had complimented him for his efforts. If Thomas had concentrated on politics in 1861, he might well have won some elective office and launched a successful political career. However, he could never quite flush the call of the military out of his system.[17]

Within a short period of time, the other siblings followed one or the other of the two elder brothers into one of the warring camps. As events developed, the two eldest sisters would follow George's lead and support the Confederacy, while the younger brothers and sisters would follow Thomas and support the Union. The Crittendens were now truly a family divided.

---

[16] Anonymous, *Louisville Daily Journal*, (21 March 1861): 3; W. H. H. Terrill, *Indiana in the War of the Rebellion: Report of the Adjutant General* (1869; repr., Indianapolis: Indiana Historical Society, 1960) 272; Whitelaw Reid, *Ohio in the War: Her Statesmen, Her Generals, and Soldiers*, 2 vols. (Cincinnati: Moore, Wilstach & Baldwin, 1868) 1:38.

[17] Patrick Joyes to Ann Mary Coleman, 12 June 1861, John J. Crittenden Papers, Duke University, Durham NC.

Such family division was an especially heartbreaking phenomenon throughout the border region, with many Kentucky families facing the same situation as the Crittendens. The Clays, the Breckinridges, and the Prentices all had divided loyalties. Unfortunately, these opposing Kentucky units would face each other in combat several times during the war, and the wounds would take a long while to heal. The Crittenden division was just a microcosm of the region's turmoil.[18]

The oldest sister Ann Mary, despite having always been extremely close to her father, surprised him by supporting the Confederacy. As the war dragged on she actively opposed her father's policies. The eldest Crittenden daughter was the child of a well-known Southern politician and the widow of a prosperous Southern businessman. She felt herself a Southerner, as did most Kentuckians of her generation, and was drawn to support of the Confederacy for several reasons. Ann Mary was much older than the younger siblings. In fact, some of her children were older than the senator's children by Maria Todd Crittenden. Ann Mary probably felt closer to George and Cornelia, who were nearer her age than the younger set of siblings. The younger children looked to Ann Mary almost as a surrogate mother rather than a sister. Another personal factor that played a role in deciding Ann Mary's loyalties was her son Crittenden's Confederate allegiance. When young Coleman entered the Confederate army, his mother felt duty-bound to support him no matter what the senator or the younger siblings thought.[19]

Crittenden Coleman had always been a difficult child. When he entered Centre College, he got into trouble and was expelled by his uncle Dr. Young. When Ann Mary asked her father for parental advice, he told her "to treat him with severity mixed with kindness. He must be made to feel that he has brought disgrace on his family but that he can redeem himself by good conduct in the future." Ann Mary had seen the impact her father's pressure to succeed had made on George and Thomas, and she apparently did not want the same for her young son. She refused to discipline him and instead was an overly indulgent mother. The senator decried this absence of parental authority to no avail. Young Crittenden

---

[18] Speed, *Union Cause in Kentucky*, 162; Clark, *Kentucky: Land of Contrast*, 142.

[19] Historical Sketch, John J. Crittenden Papers, Duke University.

always seemed to be searching for something. He had attempted to enter West Point but failed. He had tried his hand at business but had not done well. There were rumors of duels, and when the war started, Crittenden Coleman enlisted in the Confederacy against his mother's wishes. He died under mysterious circumstances in Pensacola, Florida, in October 1861. The senator had told Ann Mary that he thought it was an "error" for his grandson to enter the Confederate army but that he still loved him. After Crittenden Coleman's death, his mother requested that the senator arrange a pass for her to go to Florida to see the grave. The senator persuaded her that this would not be a wise thing to do. Ann Mary grieved the loss of her son, whom she had essentially set on a pedestal. She hated the thought of her favorite son dying in vain. Thus, she became a diehard Confederate. At one point, she even attempted to smuggle information to Confederate lines.[20]

In 1863, Ann Mary's bitter attitude intensified. Her younger son Chapman wanted to join the Union army. Chapman had apparently visited with his uncle Thomas, now a prominent Union general, and was stirred to join the army. Ann Mary could not stand the thought of her younger son serving in the Union army and fighting against the very cause for which his elder brother had died. Thomas, ever the consummate politician and diplomat, had suggested to his mother that Chapman wait a while before enlisting. Thomas wished to avoid directly confronting and alienating his eldest sister. Ann Mary sadly noted to her father, "It seems to me if I lose one son in the Southern army and the other in the Northern my sons will have been born in vain!" In the end, Ann Mary had her way, and young Chapman did not enter the Union army.[21]

Ann Mary eventually moved to Baltimore in 1863 and quickly became embroiled in sectional politics. The senator, in his last letter to his eldest daughter, admonished her: "I entreat you to be on your guard—have nothing to do with politics. It hardly seems to me to become one to live in

---

[20] Albert D. Kirwan, *John J. Crittenden: Struggle for the Union* (Lexington: University of Kentucky Press, 1962) 282, 447–48; Anonymous, *Louisville Daily Journal,* (25 February 1861): 3; Ann Mary Coleman to John J. Crittenden, 30 October 1861, John J. Crittenden Papers, Duke University; Oxx, *Kentucky Crittendens,* 146.

[21] Ann Mary Coleman to John J. Crittenden, 5 April 1863, 18 May 1863, John J. Crittenden Papers, Duke University.

the Union—to take its protection and at the same time to give...sympathy & voice to the Rebellion." The senator went on to state that he could not understand how a woman as intelligent as his daughter could entertain support for the Confederacy.[22]

In a similar manner, the daughter could no longer understand her father. As time passed, Ann Mary became increasingly angry at Lincoln and his policies. In her last letter to her father, she said did not know how Lincoln could live with himself because of all the pain he had caused. She wanted the war to end, and she believed a Confederate States of America was preferable to continued war. In that last letter to her father she said, "I don't think I love the rebellion but I *accept* it, as the best thing that remains. I want *peace*. I was always opposed to the war...I don't think any result can pay for a civil war in this country...I feel that this country can never be one again, too much has been suffered, too many hearts have been broken!" After a lifetime of close intimacy parent and child were angry, barely writing to one another around the time of the father's death.[23]

The Civil War was a bitter experience for Ann Mary. She lost her favorite son and her close lifelong relationship with her father. Her devotion to the cause that had taken her son caused a strain on her relationship with Thomas and the younger siblings. The rebellious sibling left her beloved Kentucky and did not return until years later.

Cornelia, as usual, took action in a very indirect and soft-spoken way. One of Cornelia's sons entered the Confederate army, and apparently, when many in the Crittenden family and in Kentucky turned their backs on George for his support of the Confederacy, Cornelia remained steadfast. After the war George would live with his sister, and she would take care of him until he died. Unfortunately, correspondence between Cornelia and her family during the Civil War has not been preserved.

The younger siblings followed the example of Thomas and supported the Union. Harry I. Todd, a Crittenden stepbrother, served on the Union committee and latter in the Union army. Robert was a colonel in the Union army and served in Kentucky. Never one to attract attention, Robert failed

---

[22] Kirwan, *Crittenden*, 467–468.
[23] Ann Mary Coleman t John J. Crittenden, 18 May 1863, John J. Crittenden Papers, Duke University.

to distinguish himself in combat. The elusive Sarah Lee (Maria) Watson left no personal record. However, her son John Crittenden Watson, a graduate of the United States Naval Academy, served in the US navy during the war. He was promoted to lieutenant commander and in 1864 served as Admiral Farragut's flag lieutenant at the Battle of Mobile Bay. Watson would later retire as a captain. Finally, young Eugene also served in the Federal army. A West Point graduate, he rose to the rank of colonel of the 12th Kentucky Cavalry and fought in the New Madrid and Perryville campaigns. He also participated in the long Federal pursuit of John Hunt Morgan into Ohio.[24]

Adding to the family's stress during the war years, the senator died on July 26, 1863 with Thomas at his side. The family and the state grieved the lost statesman. Governor Robinson issued a proclamation stating that "when a great man dies, a nation mourns"; he likewise closed all public offices for the funeral and requested that all private business follow suit.[25]

Crittenden left only an $8,000 estate, which was surprisingly small for such a successful lawyer. He gave his surviving wife Elizabeth a portrait of himself, their house, and gold plate for her daughters. Thomas received a bust of the senator; George received a silver plate; Sarah Lee (Maria), Robert, and Eugene each received a portrait of their mother; and Harry Innes Todd received a watch. The assets of the estate were divided equally, with debts owed to the senator by Robert and Thomas deducted from their share. Likewise, as Cornelia had received an advance on her inheritance after the death of her husband, this was deducted from her share. The senator instructed his children not to sell any of the slaves except to other members of the Crittenden family. The will named Thomas and Robert as co-executors. In an impressive state ceremony, the senator was laid to rest in the Frankfort Cemetery that Thomas had sponsored years earlier.[26]

The senator did not leave any personal items for Ann Mary in the will. Sarah Lee (Maria) probably did not even remember her mother, but

---

[24] Anonymous, *Louisville Daily Journal*, (12 December 1860): 2; Anonymous, Indianapolis *Daily Journal*, (31 July 1863): 2; Alfred Pirtle, comp., *The Union Regiments of Kentucky* (Louisville: Courier-Journal Printing Comp., 1897) 99; Oxx, *Kentucky Crittendens*, 137; Kirwan, *Crittenden*, 448.

[25] Kirwan, *Crittenden*, 475; Anonymous, *Louisville Daily Journal*, (29 July 1863): 1.

[26] Crittenden will, John J. Crittenden Papers, Duke University.

the senator gave her, not Ann Mary, their mother's portrait. Personal correspondence does not indicate whether the senator gave his eldest daughters personal items at some earlier period. Ann Mary, even if she arrived for the funeral, did not play a prominent role in the affair.

Some newspapers covering the senator's funeral omitted any mention of George, who did not attend. The patriarch was dead, and the children divided. Some of the children had been bitterly angry at their father before his death, and the opportunity for reconciliation was gone forever. Whatever reconciliation between the siblings was possible would have to wait until the conclusion of the Civil War.[27]

---

[27] Anonymous, Indianapolis *Daily Journal*, (31 July 1863): 2.

4

The Early Days of the War:
Thomas Finds a New Career

Despite the best efforts of Kentuckians such as John J. Crittenden, the Civil War came to Kentucky. Once it arrived it did not leave the state's borders until the war's bitter end, and Kentucky families such as the Crittendens had to choose which side they would support. For Thomas Crittenden the war opened an opportunity in the military he thought would lead him to greater fame and fortune. He entered the conflict through the often ignored or forgotten state guard.

In 1860 Kentucky, sensing the drift toward war, had reorganized its state militia. It created a force of approximately three divisions. Everyone between the ages of eighteen and forty-five who was not exempted by law or already serving in the state militia would constitute a reserve the state could call upon in case of emergency. Power was concentrated in the hands of a newly appointed inspector-general, who could disband units at will. Many Kentuckians viewed this militia act as the first stage toward disunion and thus distrusted the whole idea.[1]

West Point graduate Simon B. Buckner received the appointment as inspector-general and eventually major general of the state guard. Thomas became brigadier general. Among the guard's colonels were future Confederate generals Lloyd Tilghman and Roger Hanson. Within six months of the passage of the militia act, Buckner and Crittenden had raised approximately 61 companies, or about 5,000 men. Soon observers

---

[1] *Kentucky Documents, 1860–1865* (Frankfort: State Printing Office, 1860–1865): 1:142–71; Thomas Van Horne, *The Army of the Cumberland* (1875; repr., New York: Konecky & Konecky, 1966) 8–9.

described the state guard as the best-drilled militia in the country.[2]

The state guard, however, had problems. First, it was short on weapons and ammunition. The sudden spike of enthusiasm could not erase years of fiscal neglect. Governor Magoffin attempted to remedy the situation in January 1861 when he sent Luke P. Blackburn, a Kentucky physician and future Kentucky governor, to New Orleans to purchase arms. At the same time Simon Buckner traveled north on the same mission. Not unexpectedly, neither man was successful as most states in early 1861 were in same condition as Kentucky.[3]

A second problem for the state guard was its suspect loyalty. Unionists in Kentucky feared a strong state guard in the hands of secessionist-leaning Governor Magoffin, so the state legislature stripped the governor of his power to command the guard and instead placed authority in the hands of a Unionist committee. Members of the state guard were also required to take an oath of allegiance to both Kentucky and the national government. The legislature then stripped the guard of its limited funds and financed an alternative home guard that was more pro-Union in its sympathies.[4]

The Unionists had justifiable fears. In February a state guard unit was drilling near the Jefferson County Courthouse, and when it marched by the American flag Buckner did not give the order to salute. Some members of the militia saluted the flag on their own while others walked off in disgust at the thought of such a salute. Shortly thereafter, when the Federal government offered Simon Buckner a commission in the Federal army, he declined. In September 1861, when Federal forces entered Kentucky, Buckner resigned from the state guard and went to the Confederate army. Many of the other members of the Kentucky state guard followed suit.[5]

---

[2] Thomas Speed, *The Union Cause in Kentucky* (New York: G. P. Putnam & Sons, 1907) 116, 125; Arndt M. Stickles, *Simon Bolivar Buckner: Borderland Knight* (Chapel Hill: University of North Carolina Press, 1940) 46.

[3] Van Horne, *Army of the Cumberland*, 9.

[4] Fred J. Hood, ed. *Kentucky: Its History and Heritage* (St. Louis: Forum Press, 1978) 142; Van Horne, *Army of the Cumberland*, 4; Thomas D. Clark, *A History of Kentucky* (Lexington: John Bradford Press, 1960) 337.

[5] Van Horne, *Army of the Cumberland*, 2–3; Lowell H. Harrison, *The Civil War in Kentucky* (Lexington: University Press of Kentucky, 1975) 14.

Thomas Crittenden eventually received command of the state guard despite some doubt about his loyalty. Like his father Thomas was a Unionist, and once his allegiance was discerned beyond doubt, the orders were issued to place him in control. After Buckner's resignation, Thomas urged the loyal members of the state guard to defend Kentucky from Rebel attack. Within a month the loyal remnant of the state guard had entered Federal service, with Crittenden holding command of the Kentucky regiments thus created.[6]

Unionist fears were overstated in the crisis of 1861. In the spring months one member of the state guard had noted, "There are some secessionists I know in the guard, but still, many union men [remain]." The same man later pointed out, "Union men are largely in the majority here now." Although some key leaders supported the Confederacy, the bulk of the organization remained loyal to the Union and would faithfully serve in the Union army for the duration of the war. For these men Thomas Crittenden would always be their leader.[7]

At the time of his appointment the Louisville *Daily Journal* referred to Thomas Crittenden as a "chivalric" leader; other newspapers gushed, "He is among the finest and noblest and best of the martial spirits of the nations. He combines all the qualities of a military leader in an eminent degree. He is cool, prudent, courteous, and wise, and yet, when occasion demands it as daring and impetuous as a cataract." Sadly for Thomas, popularity is fleeting.[8]

Federal authorities set up recruiting centers around the state to enlist Union volunteers: Camp Dick Robinson, Greensburg, Louisville, Owensboro, and Calhoun. Thomas Crittenden served as a key recruiter.[9]

---

[6] US War Department, comp., *The War of the Rebellion: A Compilation of the Official Records of the Union and Confederate Armies*, 128 vols. (Washington, DC: Government Printing Office, 1880–1901) 1st ser., vol. 4:288; Van Horne, *Army of the Cumberland*, 28; Speed, *Union Cause in Kentucky*, 136.

[7] Alfred Pirtle Journal, 15 May 1861 and 4 June 1861, Filson Club, Louisville.

[8] Annymous, *Louisville Daily Journal*, (20 September): 4; Anonymous, *Louisville Daily Journal*, (27 September): 4; and Anonymous, *Louisville Daily Journal*, (3 October 1861): 2.

[9] Alfred Pirtle, comp., *The Union Regiments of Kentucky* (Louisville: Courier-Journal Printing Comp., 1897) 23–24, 27.

The Federal forces that included these Kentucky units took several different names during the war but were most commonly referred to as the Army of the Cumberland. This army was originally commanded by General Robert Anderson of Fort Sumter fame and, later, for a brief period by General William T. Sherman. Sherman was so pessimistic about conditions in the state that Don Carlos Buell replaced him within a month.

Because of the desperate need for Kentucky Unionists to enter the army, the Federal government gave prominent positions to important Kentuckians besides Thomas Crittenden. Regular army officers tended to look down on these political appointees as rank amateurs. Many of the political generals deserved the distain; others did not. A significant number like Thomas Crittenden were a mixture of talent, good raw instincts, and weaknesses such as poor administrative skills and lack of practical experience. Thomas Crittenden got his position because of who he was and where he was from, not for his military excellence. He was not alone in this phenomenon. Thomas was certainly not the greatest political general, but he also was not the worst.[10]

Like the others, Thomas no doubt looked to the postwar era, when he hoped that a prominent war role would pay political dividends. However, as historian Gerald Prokopwicz noted, army life centered on the regiment, and commanders of higher units had a looser claim to the loyalty and devotion of soldiers. Thomas was probably too far removed from the Kentucky soldiers he commanded to reap the political benefits he desired.[11]

When Thomas Crittenden entered the service in September 1861, he had more immediate issues to consider. He worked with General Robert Anderson to counter Confederate moves in Kentucky. Rumors of the establishment of Confederate recruiting centers filtered into the Federal camp, but there was little Anderson or Crittenden could do. They had to concentrate their limited forces in key strategic areas along the northern portion of the state.[12]

---

[10] Gerald J. Prokopowicz, *All for the Regiment: The Army of Ohio, 1861–1862* (Chapel Hill: University of North Carolina: 2001) 45.

[11] Ibid., 101, 114.

[12] Anonymous, *Louisville Daily Journal,* (27 September 1861): 2; *OR*, 1st ser., vol. 4:277.

It was uncertain just who should go and where. At one point, it was suggested that Thomas go to Camp Wildcat near London in eastern Kentucky. T. T. Garrard was raising troops at the camp, but he was having problems training them. Garrard thought Crittenden could train the undisciplined soldiers better than the previous commander had, although Thomas had but little more experience. Thomas's oratorical and political skills might have made a difference; however, this assignment did not materialize.[13]

Within a week, Crittenden received completely opposite orders to Owensboro. As he was boarding the train to go to western Kentucky, William T. Sherman, Anderson's second in command, confronted him. Sherman glared at Crittenden, asking him several questions about his eligibility to serve. Sherman concluded, "He'll do," and let Crittenden proceed on his way. Some days later, Sherman advised Crittenden to make a demonstration against the Confederates since "Kentucky looks for some bold stroke" for the Union cause. Sherman clearly was appealing to Crittenden's desire to impress others and to his dream of entering politics after the war.

Before arriving at Owensboro, Crittenden's command was enlarged to include the neighboring city of Henderson. One estimate held that his brigade consisted of about four regiments with approximately 1,500 men. These units consisted of the 11th Kentucky commanded by Pierce Hawkins at Rochester, the 17th Kentucky commanded by John McHenry at Hartford, the 26th Kentucky commanded by Stephen Burbridge at Owensboro, and 3rd Kentucky Cavalry commanded by James S. Jackson at Owensboro.[14]

Sherman, like many other Federal authorities, doubted the loyalty of Kentuckians. He remarked, "Kentuckians, instead of assisting, call from every quarter for protection against secessionists." Lorenzo Thomas, the Federal adjutant general, noted with alarm Sherman's pessimistic attitude following a visit with secretary of war Simon Cameron. In such an

---

[13] Ibid., 1st ser., vol. 4:286, 290.

[14] *OR*, 1st ser., vol. 4:297, 299, 315; Larry J. Daniel, *Days of Glory: The Army of the Cumberland, 1861–1865* (Baton Rouge: Louisiana State University Press, 2004) 16–17; Van Horne, *Army of the Cumberland*, 56; Richard J. Reid, *The Army that Buell Built* (Fordsville KY: Wendell Sandefur Offset Printing, 1994) 14.

atmosphere of official distrust it is not surprising that Kentucky Unionists grew resentful. Suspicions of Kentuckians' loyalty only grew as the war progressed, and Thomas Crittenden would continually have to deal with such negative attitudes.[15]

As the days of October 1861 slipped by, Crittenden's procrastination did not help his state's cause. General Sherman kept trying to prod Crittenden into demonstrating against Confederate forces in western Kentucky. On 30 October, he suggested a demonstration at Russellville, Thomas's birthplace. The next day Crittenden responded to Sherman by essentially requesting Sherman's advice. The Kentuckian admitted his inexperience as a soldier. Thomas always wanted to please those in authority, and it is regrettable that Sherman or some other professional officer did not take him under his wing at this early point in his career. He certainly needed the help.[16]

Crittenden did, however, order a demonstration against Hopkinsville in late October when he sent a force under colonels John McHenry (400 men) and Stephen Burbridge (250 men) to probe enemy lines. Near the small village of Woodbury, in Butler County, the troops made contact with Confederate forces from the 1st Mississippi Cavalry under Captain Thomas Lewers and defeated it. McHenry, moving from Hartford, likewise encountered and defeated a Confederate force at Morgantown. Unfortunately Crittenden did not know how to follow up these small successes. A more knowledgeable, aggressive, self-confident officer would have continued pressing on and achieved a greater victory. Thomas, however, played it safe. In all fairness, illness also deterred him. Of approximately 6,000 Union troops on the rolls in western Kentucky, over 1,000 were sick, and this surely included some of Thomas's soldiers. The army suffered many illnesses, measles being the major culprit.[17]

Crittenden's probes awakened Confederates to the dangers they faced in western Kentucky. In November, they countered the Union offensive

---

[15] *OR*, 1st ser., vol. 4:300, 313.

[16] *OR*, 1st ser., vol. 4:324; Thomas L. Crittenden to William T. Sherman, 30 October 1861, Thomas L. Crittenden Letters, Miscellaneous file, Filson Club.

[17] Van Horne, *Army of the Cumberland*, 56–57; Anonymous, *Louisville Daily Journal*, (4 November 1861): 2; Daniel, *Days of Glory*, 36; Short Green to brother, 1 December 1861, Green Family Papers, Western Kentucky University, Bowling Green.

with one of their own. Thomas's old playmate John C. Breckinridge advanced from Hopkinsville to Greenville in Muhlenberg County and entered the small village of Rochester. He intended to destroy the Green River locks and cut off Crittenden's lines of communication. Burbridge's regiment detected Breckinridge's movement and slowed it. Having lost the advantage of surprise, Breckinridge did not wish to pursue the matter any further. The whole episode made Crittenden look good. It seemed as though he had turned back a major Confederate probe. Thomas was not one to turn down good publicity, and he did little to cause anyone to doubt that assumption. One newspaper said of the incident: "Gen. Crittenden is fully prepared to receive the private soldier's musket or the brigadier's sword. Indeed, he and his men are all burning with anxiety for active service." In truth, Crittenden preferred the general's stars to service as an enlisted man; he wanted to play a leading role in the war.[18]

Just at this time, the Army of the Cumberland had a change of command and a change of name. William T. Sherman, who had replaced Robert Anderson, was himself replaced as commander by Don Carlos Buell. The Army of the Cumberland became the Army of the Ohio. Don Carlos Buell was fine organizer, but he had few people skills. He was aloof, not one to teach or encourage his subordinates. In December 1861 he reorganized his army. Regimental and brigade units were consolidated into divisions, and Thomas Crittenden received command of the 5th Division at Calhoun near the Green River locks. This division consisted of the 13th Brigade commanded by Charles Cruft and the 14th Brigade commanded by William Sooy Smith. The other division commanders were George H. Thomas of the 1st Division at Lebanon and later Somerset, A. M. McCook of the 2nd Division at Camp Nevin on the Nolin River, O. M. Mitchel of the 3rd Division at Camp John Quincy Adams on Bacon Creek, William "Bull" Nelson of the 4th Division at Camp Wickliffe near New Haven, and Thomas J. Wood of the 6th Division at Bardstown. All of the divisional commanders except for McCook and George Thomas were

---

[18] Van Horne, *Army of the Cumberland*, 57; Anonymous, *Louisville Daily Journal*, (27 November 1861): 3; Anonymous, *Louisville Daily Journal*, (4 December 1861): 2.

Kentuckians, and Crittenden formed a particularly close friendship with Nelson.[19]

Thomas Wood, the son of a state legislator from Hart County and a graduate of West Point, was particularly significant to Crittenden. One historian has suggested that Wood "buttressed" Crittenden as corps commander. One veteran soldier noted that Wood was "a very strict disciplinarian" who exercised his talents in the "development of raw recruits into an army of disciplined soldiers." This soldier also added that the training process was "often very distasteful to the raw material from which the disciplined soldier was being developed." It would have been better for Crittenden had he served under Wood rather than become his commander. Wood could have taught Thomas much about being a soldier.[20]

William Nelson was an early Kentucky Unionist. He was a strict authoritarian and, as one regimental historian surmised, "The troops instinctively felt they had a leader, and although they still feared him to be a harsh disciplinarian, he had already secured their confidence and was rapidly gaining their esteem." Another regimental historian disagreed, insisting that the men did not like Nelson or get along with him. Apparently, Crittenden was one of the few people who seemed to like Nelson.[21]

A. M. McCook was a conservative Democrat who lacked any particular military ability. One reason for his elevation was his close personal ties to the Stanton family. Secretary of War Edwin Stanton promoted McCook far above his ability. One observer said of McCook that he was a "drunken lot" who had "several drunken aides who are perfect court fools" and "merely

---

[19] *OR*, 1st ser., vol. 7:468; Van Horne, *Army of the Cumberland*, 41, 49–57.

[20] Anonymous, *Louisville Daily Journal*, (15 September 1861): 1; Francis F. McKinney, *Education in Violence: The Life of George H. Thomas and the History of the Army of the Cumberland* (Detroit: Wayne State University Press, 1961) 445; John J. Hight, *History of the Fifty-eighth Regiment of Indiana Volunteers Infantry: Its Organization, Campaigns, and Battles from 1861–1865* (Princeton: Press of the Clarion, 1895) 35.

[21] Ebenezer Hannaford, *The Story of a Regiment: A History of the Campaigns, and Associations in the Field, of the Sixth Ohio Volunteer Infantry* (Cincinnati: Ebenezer Hannaford, 1868) 173; Robert L. Kimberly and Ephraim S. Holloway, *The Forty-first Ohio Veteran Volunteer Infantry in the War of the Rebellion, 1861–1865* (Cleveland: W. R. Smellie, 1897) 33.

make fun of their master, laugh at his jokes, mix his liquor for him, and play the flunkey in every conceivable way." Continuing, the observer noted that "if we ever win a battle you take my word for it, that the valor of his men and not the skill or bravery of the Genl. did the work." For better or worse, these key individuals led the Army of the Ohio through most of its battles. Of the original division commanders, only Wood and Thomas were first-rate quality, with Thomas perhaps the most underrated general in the Civil War. Crittenden never developed a close relationship with George Thomas.[22]

During this time of relative calm, Crittenden moved his headquarters to the city of Calhoun, and the local residents had a chance to meet the Union commander and his troops. One visitor noted that Thomas Crittenden was a gentleman and very likeable. The same individual believed that Jackson's 3rd Kentucky Cavalry was the "finest body of men I ever saw and are doing more service than all the others here." The city of Calhoun, he said, was in good order and army discipline was strictly enforced. The sight of Crittenden, with turned-up felt hat, riding his gray warhorse "JJ" become a common sight around the camp. Not everyone had a favorable impression of Thomas or of his Kentucky troops, however. One subordinate,lieutenant colonel James Shanklin of the 42nd Indiana, said of Thomas that "he is a very fine man in his manners, easy and makes you feel at home at once; he possess a great deal of pluk [sic] and courage I have no doubt, but whether he is the man for the place is the question—that is the question." Perhaps the Hoosiers felt the Kentuckians did not behave well in camp.[23]

By late November 1861, the calm began to dissipate. On 25 November, Crittenden heard rumors from a spy that John C. Breckinridge with a force of 4,000 to 6,000 was marching from

---

[22] Whitelaw Reid, *Ohio in the War: Her Statesmen, Her Generals, and Soldiers*, 2 vols. (Cincinnati: Moore, Wilstach & Baldwin, 1868) 1:808; Donn Piatt, *General George H. Thomas: A Critical Biography* (Cincinnati: Robert Clarke, 1893) 174; Sam Starling to daughter, 15 November 1862, Lewis-Starling Collection, Western Kentucky University.

[23] Unsigned to Layfayette Green, 8 October 1861, Green Family Letters, Western Kentucky University; Short Green to brother, 1 December 1861, Green Family Letters, Western Kentucky University; Daniel, *Days of Glory*, 41, 191; *Kentucky Crittendens*, 153; Anonymous, *Louisville Daily Journal*, (18 January 1862): 3.

Hopkinsville toward Rochester with the goal of Lock No. 1 on the Green River. The next day no more such reports surfaced. Crittenden told Buell that he could hold the locks against a Confederate attack unless the Confederates were heavily reinforced by troops from Bowling Green. In fact, no Confederate attack on the Green River locks materialized.[24]

On 26 December another Confederate probe under Nathan Bedford Forrest moved toward Sacramento and came into contact with a detachment of the 3rd Kentucky cavalry led by Major Eli H. Murray. At Sacramento, Forrest first showed the tactical brilliance that would mark the rest of his Civil War career by aggressively and unexpectedly attacking the Federal force.

Crittenden did not want this defeat at Sacramento to mar his rising military reputation, so he quickly sent an explanatory report to Buell's headquarters. He minimized his losses, reporting that he had sent General James Jackson with the remainder of 3rd Kentucky cavalry to push Forrest out of the region. Most telling, Crittenden concluded the report with the comment he had "written this [so] that you may not be deceived by exaggerated reports which will doubtless reach you."[25]

In a fuller account, written a few days later, Crittenden praised the gallantry of Murray and the splendid performance of his men. The Kentuckian noted that "although outnumbered and partially surprised, I think my men had the best of the fight." He complained that if informed of the advance of the Confederates in advance, he could have captured the whole force. Blame for the reversal fell on some unknown soldier who yelled retreat and caused the Federal lines to falter. On the Confederate side, Forrest insisted that he penetrated Murray's lines easily and only called off the pursuit because the horses were getting tired. [26]

After the skirmish, persistent rumors continued of an advance against Crittenden. In most of the rumors, John C. Breckinridge would lead a

---

[24] *OR,* 1st ser., vol. 7:447, 449; Robert H. Ernest to James H. Ernest, 12 December 1861, Robert H. Ernest Papers, Kentucky Historical Society, Frankfort.

[25] *OR,* 1st ser., vol. 7:62.

[26] *OR,* 1st ser., vol. 7:62–63.

force toward Greenville, Kentucky, and attempt to destroy the Green River locks. Fortunately for the Federal forces, these rumors proved false.[27]

After the skirmish at Sacramento, Crittenden moved his headquarters from Calhoun to South Carrollton, one soldier referring to the march during the winter as a trip through the "mud and slush of that malarious region" and "the fiery ordeal of acclimation to camp life." When Crittenden arrived at South Carrollton, he immediately constructed breastworks. He established headquarters in a hotel known locally as the Lovelace Tavern. Secessionists protested the Federal army's use of this building, but to no avail.[28]

Some Confederate guerillas operating in the region approached a local farmer and forged Crittenden's signature on a paper saying that the Federal government would compensate the farmer for horses they took. The farmer let the horses go but discovered his deception when he went to Crittenden to be paid. Crittenden, despite his many political skills, could not resolve the issue.[29]

In other ways Crittenden showed signs of great promise. Unionists named a Zouvare company in his honor. Newspapers lauded his talents. The Louisville *Daily Journal* said of him, "of our Crittenden tis only necessary to say, the bravest among the brave he inspired confidence wherever he went and managed his corps with marked ability." One subordinate, John Beatty, described Crittenden as a "spare man, medium height, lank, common sort of face, well whiskered." Beatty believed that Crittenden swore although he never heard him do so. He also described a good drinker and one who knew how to blow his horn very well. Another subordinate, William B. Hazen, considered Crittenden "kind, just and brave to a fault." He remarked that Crittenden gave an "admirable, almost electrical speech" and "if it had been in my power I would have made him

---

[27] *OR*, 1st ser., vol. 7:66; Albert Fall to sister, 27 January 1862, Fall Family Papers, Kentucky Historical Society.

[28] John A. Rerrick, *The Forty-Fourth Indiana Volunteer: History of its Service in the War in the War of the Rebellion and a Personal Record of its Members* (La Grange IN: John A. Rerrick, 1880) 27–28, 219; Otto H. Rothert, *A History of Muhlenberg County* (Louisville: John P. Morton, Comp., 1913) 258, 262.

[29] Adam R. Johnson, *The Partisan Rangers of the Confederate States* (Louisville: Geo. G. Fetter Company, 1904) 45.

commander in chief of the army." Hazen also noted that Crittenden's men loved him. One of the regimental historians admiringly remembered him as

> a true Kentucky gentleman, every inch a soldier—plain, straightforward, and unpretending, his only thought being to do his whole duty to his country. He esteemed every brave man as a friend and comrade. I have known of his telling his chief of staff that he deserved to be shot, for marching his troops an unnecessary long distance on a blistering day, the hot southern sun heating our rifles so as to be almost unbearable to the touch. His sympathies were with the men, to whose care and comfort he devoted himself without stint. Himself and family were looked upon with the warmest feelings of regard by all the soldiers. They moved amongst us like patriarchs of old, their presence giving a home and kindred feeling to all. In battle he was a Saladin, —with his only child—a boy of some seven years—on his horse behind him, he would have cut his way with his good sword through a host.

Apparently, Crittenden could make quite an impression on his contemporaries.[30]

Unfortunately, Thomas Crittenden did not make the same impression on his father, who had always worried about him. The senator feared his second son would repeat many of his eldest son's errors. Although Thomas drank freely, he did not become a slave to the demon rum. The senator had also worried about Thomas's work habits. As a Civil War general, Thomas Crittenden often proved lax when it came to administrative details. Like other officers, he frequently forgot to sign appropriate paperwork or check into small military details. Crittenden needed a meticulous staff officer to keep him on top of the administrative detail of his position.[31]

---

[30] "My Early Soldiering Days,", Alfred Pirtle Papers, Filson Club; Anonymous, *Louisville Daily Journal*, (12 January 1863): 4; John Beatty, *The Citizen-Soldier; or Memoirs of a Volunteer* (Cincinnati: Wilstach, Baldwin & Co., 1879) 235–236; William B. Hazen, *A Narrative of Military Service* (Boston: Ticknor & Comp., 1885) 152–53; Rerrick, *History of the Forty-fourth Indiana Volunteer*, 263.

[31] Thomas L. Crittenden to John Coyle, 12 April 1861, Thomas L Crittenden Letters, Miscellaneous file, Filson Club; *OR*, 1st ser., vol. 16, pt. 2:115, 162, 249.

Before the senator's death in 1863, he wrote Thomas a long letter admonishing him never to drink and to be diligent in his command. The father wrote, "Be all eyes—all ears and surprise those who would surprise you." The patriarch encouraged his son with an affirmation: "I think you have a capacity for great things"; however, he then proceeded to admonish his son regarding work habits, telling him not to allow his military career "to be frustrated by little things—by little inattentions, little negligences, little indulgences." The senator warned Thomas that he needed to "meditate" and "study" his new position. Looking toward his son's political future, he told Thomas to "make your soldiers love and admire you" and "be among them and talk with them." The veteran politician pointed to the "great advantage" that would accrue to Thomas in times to come. The senator still pressured Thomas even though his son was rising in the military and showing signs of a bright political future.[32]

This letter negated whatever confidence Thomas may have gained during the secession crisis and his rapid military promotions. Thomas would always be the little boy trying to live up to the expectations of a powerful father he very much admired. Sometimes fear of failure motivates individuals toward success, while at other times it saps initiative and energy. Thomas Crittenden was more afraid of failing and disappointing his father than of taking a chance and succeeding, and many challenges awaited him in the future.

---

[32] John J. Crittenden to Thomas L. Crittenden, 28 November 1862, John J. Crittenden Papers, Duke University.

5

A Fallen Star:
George's Civil War Career

In the early days of the Civil War, George Crittenden's career prospects seemed as bright, if not brighter, than those of his younger Unionist brother, Thomas. George had several advantages over his younger brother. He was a graduate of West Point and had served in the army for a number of years. Logically, George should have more military expertise than his more politically oriented brother. Crittenden also had close family connections with the Confederate president. The only cloud on the horizon was George's lack of self-control. Could George control his drinking and his tendency to make rash decisions or would he self-destruct as he had so many times in the past? If George ran into problems, his father could not rescue him this time. For George, this would be an exciting time and a chance to prove himself to his father, to his family, and to himself.

Confederate troops under Albert Sidney Johnston moved into Kentucky in fall 1861 and occupied roughly the southern quarter of the state. Johnston, a native Kentuckian, did not have enough troops to man his position. Therefore he concentrated his troops at key strategic locations throughout the state. The Confederate commander's concern about the eastern portion of his line created the opening George Crittenden needed to enter the war.

The commander of Johnston's eastern flank around Cumberland Gap was Felix Zollicoffer, a Tennessee newspaper editor who had little military experience. Zollicoffer was personally brave and greatly loved by his men but sadly lacking in military knowledge. His men were poorly armed, many with old flintlocks, but they had already fought Union forces at Barbourville and at Wildcat Mountain. Both Johnston and President Davis worried about the situation, and in late fall Johnston requested someone with more military experience be placed over Zollicoffer. That person turned out to be George Crittenden.[1]

The Confederate president called his old friend to Richmond in November and discussed the new assignment. He told George that he was his first choice for the new post. Davis planned for Crittenden to assume Zollicoffer's old command on the eastern flank and press forward into central Kentucky. The president probably reasoned that the Crittenden name would draw Kentuckians to the Confederate side. Unfortunately, George did not have the political skills of his father nor even of his younger brother.[2]

When Crittenden arrived at Zollicoffer's camp, the troops did not greet him with much enthusiasm. The soldiers loved their old commander and looked upon Crittenden as little more than an interloper. Likewise, not all Confederate generals were pleased with the appointment. Humphrey Marshall of Kentucky, for example, was especially irate at the appointment. Marshall prized his independence and disliked the thought of anyone closely supervising him. In a stinging letter to his political associate, vice president Alexander Stephens, Marshall bitterly declared, "What figure will I cut when the men of the state come to serve under me and find myself commanded by the son of John Crittenden who has been the arch-manager in fixing the evils around us all?"

Marshall apparently did not think that George had the political influence to raise troops, nor did he trust a fellow general who such strong Unionist connections. As Marshall knew, George had received his appointment in part because of who he was and where he was from. As events developed, Marshal proved correct about George's political skills. When George issued a proclamation to the citizens of Kentucky, few

---

[1] Steven E. Woodworth, *Jefferson Davis and His Generals: The Failure of Confederate Command in the West* (Lawrence: University of Kansas Press, 1990) 63; Kent Masterson Brown, *The Civil War in Kentucky: The Battle for the Bluegrass State* (Mason City IA: Savas Publishing Comp., 2000) 48–52.

[2] Ibid., 64; William C. Davis, *Jefferson Davis: The Man and His* Hour (Baton Rouge: Louisiana State University Press, 1991) 380.

responded and others ridiculed him for the attempt. George, it seemed, never understood politics.[3]

The Confederate high command's immediate concern was that Zollicoffer, without authorization, had moved his troops north of the Cumberland River and had built a camp at Beech Grove, Kentucky. A small Union force under Albin F. Schoepf moving from London to Somerset had failed to keep the aggressive Zollicoffer south of the Cumberland River. Zollicoffer's move dismayed Johnston, but Zollicoffer pleaded that the flooded river prevented him from retreating, while Johnston correctly perceived that the move also served to cut off an easy line of retreat in case of emergency. After receiving the appointment to his new position, Crittenden was not explicitly ordered to retreat back across the Cumberland River. Johnston's style of leadership left a great deal of discretion in the hands of subordinate commanders. This is a fine leadership style if one has capable subordinates. Johnston probably believed that Crittenden would have the common sense to move his headquarters from Beech Grove to a more defensible position at the first opportunity. Crittenden did order Zollicoffer to recross the river, but he did not take any steps to enforce the order. When George finally arrived at the encampment, it was far too late for him to move the forces.[4]

Crittenden received ten regiments and was authorized to move into Kentucky immediately. The attack force consisted of two brigades, one commanded by Zollicoffer and the other by William H. Carroll. Departmental lines were not very clear, and George chose to establish his headquarters at Knoxville rather than moving immediately into Kentucky. The decision cost George valuable time in the coming campaign. This slowness also pulled him into the quagmire of East Tennessee politics.[5]

The staunchly pro-Union East Tennesseans deeply resented the establishment of the Confederacy. Many looked to William G. Brownlow

---

[3] Raymond E. Myers, *The Zollie Tree* (Louisville: Filson Club Press, 1964) 74, 78; Humphrey Marshall to Alexander Stephens, 30 December 1861, Humphrey Marshall Letters, Filson Club, Louisville.

[4] Woodworth, *Jefferson Davis*, 66; Charles P. Roland, *Albert Sidney Johnston: Soldier of Three Republics* (Austin: University of Texas, 1964) 280–81; Brown, *Civil War in Kentucky*, 53–54.

[5] Woodworth, *Jefferson Davis*, 64.

of Knoxville as their leader. Brownlow, editor of the Knoxville *Whig*, vehemently denounced the Confederacy, and Confederate authorities suspected him of being involved in acts of sabotage against them. When George arrived in East Tennessee, therefore, he was caught up in the controversy.

Crittenden finally reached Knoxville on 20 November 1861, believing that the Confederate authorities were encouraging him to issue a pass to Brownlow to go to Union lines. These officials just wanted to get rid of Brownlow. On 4 December, an arrangement was made that if Brownlow would come in by the assigned time, Crittenden would issue him a pass to cross into Union lines. The argumentative Brownlow did not show up on time, and on 6 December, Confederate civil authorities arrested him. George made no effort to intervene. At the same time he was taken by surprise at the Brownlow arrest. After his arrest, Brownlow bitterly charged Crittenden with acting in bad faith. George felt sensitive about the charge of betrayal and by this point just wanted to get rid of the troublesome editor. Brownlow spent time in prison, however, and the whole incident seemed to be a bad omen for George's future with the Confederacy.[6]

Because of George's problems in Knoxville, in mid-December Jefferson Davis called him back to Richmond. Davis wanted to impress upon his new general the Confederate objectives in the region. George was to move into Kentucky and occupy as much of the state as possible. He was to stay out of Tennessee politics and concentrate on military matters. Unfortunately, George's recall to Richmond cost the Kentuckian even more valuable time. Had he moved his headquarters to Kentucky in mid-December, he might have had time to shift Zollicoffer's troops from their exposed position and prepare to repel an attack.[7]

George did not leave Knoxville until Christmas day and did not arrive at Mill Springs until 3 January 1862. He immediately realized the precariousness of the Confederate position. The swollen Cumberland River blocked their line of retreat. Johnston should have explicitly ordered

---

[6] E. Merton Coulter, *William G. Brownlow: The Fighting Parson of the Southern Highlands* (Chapel Hill: University of North Carolina Press, 1937) 186–87, 191, 199, 200.
[7] Ibid., 66–67.

Crittenden to recross the Cumberland River as quickly as possible in mid-December, and he should have pushed his subordinate to comply. Instead, Albert Sidney Johnston gave his subordinate considerable freedom of action in carrying out his orders. Thus, Crittenden decided to stay put for the moment and wait for events to develop. Crittenden's slowness did not work well with Johnston's causal command style.[8]

While waiting for the river to subside, Crittenden ordered the strengthening of the fortifications protecting the camp. While the Confederates entrenched, George H. Thomas moved a Federal force from Lebanon via Columbia toward Somerset. Likewise, another Federal force under Albin F. Schoepf camped near Somerset awaiting Thomas's arrival. The combined force planned to march toward the exposed Confederate position and engage the enemy. For George Crittenden, the turning point of his life was near.[9]

This Union move, in mid-winter, caught the Confederates off guard. One Confederate soldier, Jefferson Dean, wrote home just days before the battle, noting that the Confederates had built nice cabins to live in and expected to be there until March. He also told his family that rumors of a Federal attack had declined and he did not foresee anything happening in the near future. Dean, like other Confederates, was sadly mistaken.[10]

Upon his arrival at the Confederate camp near Beech Grove, George was surprised to discover than his earlier order to move south of the Cumberland River had not been obeyed. As the superior officer, it was Crittenden's responsibility to make sure that his orders were followed. He needed an efficient staff officer to help him overcome his natural slowness. The Cumberland River was swollen by the winter rains, so George had little choice but to remain where he was.[11]

The arrival of Union troops under George H. Thomas on 17 January and of Albin Schoepf on 18 January at Logan's Crossroads, just 9 miles from the Confederate encampment, made the situation precarious. In this desperate situation, Crittenden took desperate measures. He planned to

---

[8] Myers, *Zollie Tree*, 74; Roland, *Albert Sidney Johnston*, 280–81.

[9] Brown, *Civil War in Kentucky*, 56.

[10] Jefferson Dean to wife, 6 January 1862, Jefferson Dean Letters, Western Kentucky University, Bowling Green.

[11] Myers, *Zollie Tree*, 78.

march from the Beech Grove encampment during the night of 18 January and attack George Thomas's forces at Logan's Crossroads, not realizing that Schoepf had also arrived at Logan's Crossroads. Crittenden's plan was to defeat Thomas before Scheopf's forces could arrive from Somerset. Crittenden also requested that Johnston order a demonstration somewhere else to divert Union attention. Johnston ordered a probe by General Thomas Hindman against Columbia, but this demonstration had little impact on Crittenden's advance.[12]

Crittenden claimed that the decision to attack was unanimously approved by all the Confederate generals in a council of war. Some Confederate officers later disagreed, saying that Zollicoffer had opposed the move as being hopeless, and noted that Crittenden had been drunk during the council. Most of the Confederate generals adored Zollicoffer and probably wanted to safeguard his reputation from being associated with the tragic defeat; this may have slanted their recollection of the council of war. No one wants to be remembered for supporting an ill-advised move. Another factor to consider was that Zollicoffer was a very aggressive commander and it is unlikely that he would have ever suggested retreat rather than attack. In agreement or disagreement, the Confederates marched the night of 18 January in preparation for battle.[13]

The Confederates attacked at dawn. Zollicoffer utilized a ravine as cover to advance against the Union lines early in the battle. In a moment of confusion, dressed in a white overcoat, he rode into Union lines to order troops to stop firing on their own men. Union officer Speed Fry of Kentucky belatedly realized that this officer was a Confederate. At about the same moment Zollicoffer realized that he was on the wrong side of the battlefield. Shot before he could escape, his death created confusion within Confederate lines. [14]

After hearing of the death of Zollicoffer, Crittenden ordered forward his other brigade commanded by William H. Carroll. Unfortunately for Crittenden, George Thomas began to pour Union reinforcements into the

---

[12] Woodworth, *Jefferson Davis*, 67; US War Department, comp., *The War of the Rebellion: A Compilation of the Official Records of the Union and Confederate Armies*, 128 vols. (Washington, DC: Government Printing Office, 1880–1901) 1st ser., vol. 7:103.

[13] Myers, *Zollie Tree*, 112–13.

[14] Ibid., 119–29.

battle. Many of the Confederates had only old flintlocks rendered almost useless by the rain. Union percussion weapons were much more reliable. The Union forces broke the Confederate left. Almost simultaneously, the Confederate right crumbled. The Confederate force became disorganized and the defeat turned into a rout. Crittenden tried in vain to rally his men, but he could do little to stop the mass retreat.[15]

By 3 o'clock, Crittenden's men were back at their camp. George manned the fortifications, expecting to repel a Union attack, but the Federals did not pursue. That night at a council of war, the Confederates decided the cross the Cumberland River under cover of darkness. All night long, the steamboat *Nobel Ellis* ferried Confederates to the southern shore of the river. All supplies were abandoned and the boat burned to prevent its capture by Union forces.[16]

The engagement has received different names, including Mill Springs, Logan's Crossroads, Fishing Creek, and Somerset, although Mill Springs is probably the most common. No matter what name the battle goes by, it was a poorly conceived campaign. One historian has noted two major missed opportunities for the Confederates. First, the Confederates would have been better off to have attacked Union forces almost immediately after crossing the Cumberland River in December. The Confederates could have engaged the Federals before the Federals developed a superiority in numbers and material. Even if the Confederates had not attacked in December, they would still have had a better chance in January by making the Federals attack their entrenchments near Beech Grove. In either scenario, the Confederates could have substantially improved the odds in their favor. They chose not to do so. As another historian has noted, Crittenden acted from desperation more than forethought.[17]

Thus, George had lost his first battle. The total Confederate loses were 559 out of 4,000 engaged. Federal losses totaled 262 men out of over 6,000 engaged. Because of the hasty Confederate retreat, the men also lost 12 cannons, 150 wagons, 1,000 horses, numerous small arms, and a large

---

[15] Myers, *Zollie Tree*, 97–101, 109; Brown, *Civil War in Kentucky*, 66.

[16] Brown, *Civil War in Kentucky*, 69.

[17] Thomas L. Connelly, *The Army of the Heartland: The Army of Tennessee, 1861–1862* (Baton Rouge: Louisiana State University Press, 1967) 96–97; Thomas B. Buell, *The Warrior Generals: Combat Leadership in the Civil War* (New York: Crown, 1997) 156.

quantity of commissary stores. The Confederate retreat was disorganized, and the men were demoralized. One officer, Colonel Woods of the 16th Alabama, referred to the retreat as "a great funeral procession." Many soldiers deserted during the withdrawal. On 26 January the remnants of the force staggered into Gainesboro, Tennessee. From there they moved to Camp Fogg in Smith County on 9 February, to Murfreesboro on 17 February, and finally to Corinth, Mississippi, where Albert Sidney Johnston was concentrating all available troops. [18]

As news of the defeat spread throughout the South, there was an outcry for someone to blame. Mill Springs was the first major Confederate defeat of the war and Zollicoffer was one of the first generals killed in combat. The brave, popular Zollicoffer, now deceased, received no blame for the disastrous defeat. Thus, Crittenden became the target of Confederate blame and Union ridicule.

George Crittenden made a wonderful target for his critics. He was accused of being a closet Unionist and attempting to turn over the Confederate forces to the Union. He was accused of being drunk during the battle and the subsequent retreat. He was a "bespotted inebriate" according to one editor and Colonel Woods of the 16th Alabama declared him unfit for command. As one historian phrased it, his rallying of the troops was "uninspiring" to say the least. George's reputation for drinking, irresponsibility, and slothfulness had preceded him and was now coming back to haunt him. [19]

Even the Northern press decided to get in on the attack. The Louisville *Daily Journal* commented of Crittenden's behavior that he "got drunk at Monticello and was barely able to ride off and make his escape," that "he urged the affrighted rebels to fly for lives," and that "few men are more disgraced than George Crittenden." The paper also denounced George's proclamation to the people of Kentucky as a joke and speculated about his going back to Texas after the disaster in eastern Kentucky. George had fouled his life again. This time, though, almost everyone in the

---

[18] Ibid., 168–69, 107, 110; James Edmonds Saunders, *Early Settler of* Alabama (New Orleans: L. Graham & Sons, 1899) 192

[19] Horn, Stanley F. *The Army of Tennessee.* (Indianapolis: Bobbs-Merrill Comp., 1941): 70; Myers, *Zollie Tree*, 113; Woodworth, *Jefferson Davis*, 68.

country knew about it, and his powerful father was completely helpless to mute or soften the consequences.[20]

Senator Crittenden grieved over George's public disgrace. He poured his heart out to his daughter Ann Mary shortly after the battle, saying that George's decision brought "shame and sorrow" to the family. Yet he professed his continued love for his erring son. The senator believed that the erroneous thinking of those around him "deluded" George. He blamed others for his son's problems. Parental love continued to blind the senator to George's glaring character flaws.[21]

Only rarely did George find defenders in the press. On one of those few occasions, the Louisville *Daily Journal* wrote, "We deem it due to a Kentuckian, even though a rebel, to contradict those false and injurious imputations." The paper concluded that "he was not drinking at all," that he "bore himself most gallantly," and that he was "prudent and discreet, his opinion as to the expediency and even the necessity of risking a battle under the circumstances being confirmed by the opinions his brother officers." Very few Southern newspapers were as kind to Crittenden.[22]

George Prentice of the Louisville *Daily Journal* took a more negative tack in the spring and intensified his criticism of George Crittenden, saying, "George seems hard to satisfy." The editor pointed out that Crittenden was "the recipient of numerous favors from the government against which he rebelled" and that he had "received position, education, and honor from it, and yet, while he was its sworn officer, pledged to its support and by every principle of honor and gratitude, he joined its malignant enemies and became one of the most malignant of those enemies." Prentice went on to note Confederate authorities' suspicions

---

[20] Anonymous, *Louisville Daily Journal*, (29 January 1862): 2; Anonymous, *Louisville Daily Journal*, (10 February 1862): 2; Anonymous, *Louisville Daily Journal*, (10 June 1862): 3.

[21] John J. Crittenden to Ann Mary Coleman, 23 February 1862, John J. Crittenden Papers, Duke University, Durham NC; Francis Hudson Oxx, *The Kentucky Crittenden: The History of a Family Including Genealogy of Descendent in Both Male and Female Lives, Biographical Sketches of its Members, and Their Descent from Other Colonial Lives* (n.p., 1940) 122.

[22] Anonymous, *Louisville Daily Journal*, (23 February 1862): 2.

about Crittenden's loyalty and cuttingly added that he had brought dishonor to his family name.[23]

The senator felt that he had to respond to this scathing attack on George, so he wrote a private letter to George Prentice pleading with the editor to moderate his attacks. The senator confessed, "My son is a rebel—I defend him not—but what public good can such damnations, as that article contains do?" The statesman continued arguing that the article's "exaggerations and misstatements make it ungenerous and unjust as to my guilty son," concluding that "it was useless for any purpose of public good and could inflict wounds upon friends only." The patriarch affirmed that George was "beloved by all his family as one of the *best* & noblest of their race." The senator believed George had acted from "honorable" motives and had been "deluded" into rebellion. The attacks hurt the family, and political friends such as George Prentice should refrain from disparaging the Crittenden family in their hour of pain. The senator's pleas worked, and the Kentucky editor's fiery attacks on George softened. Prentice would himself soon feel the sting of being a Unionist father with a Rebel son, and this might have made him more understanding of the Crittenden family tragedy.[24]

Albert Sidney Johnston and Jefferson Davis both received intense criticism for allowing an allegedly incompetent commander like Crittenden to hold such an important command. Johnston, ever the gentleman, did not lay the blame for the defeat directly on George's shoulders. As the departmental commander, he felt that he bore the brunt of criticism for the collapse. The president authorized Johnston to begin a military investigation, giving the commander the authority to remove Crittenden from command if he deemed it proper.[25]

Before a court of inquiry could investigate the matter, several other events occurred. Johnston began concentrating all available Confederate forces at Corinth, Mississippi, for a counterattack against the advancing Union forces of Ulysses S. Grant and Don Carlos Buell. As a part of his

---

[23] Anonymous, *Louisville Daily Journal*, (5 May 1862): 2.

[24] Ann Mary Coleman, *The Life of John J. Crittenden*, 2 vols. (Philadelphia: J. B. Lippincott & Co., 1871) 2:347.

[25] Davis, *Jefferson Davis*, 388; Roland, *Albert Sidney Johnston*, 282; Woodworth, *Jefferson Davis*, 69–70.

concentration, Johnston gave George Crittenden command of the reserve corps. The Confederate Congress confirmed Crittenden's appointment to the rank of major general by only a one-vote margin. If one Tennessee senator had not gone home, the appointment probably would have been rejected. If George performed well in the coming battle, he could redeem himself. Unfortunately, George once again buckled under the stress. Shortly before the coming battle, a superior officer found him and one of his subordinates, William H. Carroll, drunk. George was immediately relieved of command and placed under arrest. This second incident only seemed to confirm the rumors about his conduct at Mill Springs.[26]

George Crittenden resigned his commission, but it was rejected pending the findings of the court of inquiry. He could still clear his name. A former lawyer, George pleaded that the order authorizing the court of inquiry had a technical error, and thus the court was invalid and his resignation should be accepted immediately. The adjutant general accepted this rationale and Jefferson Davis reluctantly allowed George's resignation. During the whole incident George had not tried very hard to defend himself. Except for Jefferson Davis, most people believed that George was guilty of the charge of drunkenness.[27]

George now volunteered to serve as an aide to General John S. Williams in West Virginia. A Kentuckian, Williams had served as a regimental commander during the Mexican War and would serve as a US senator from Kentucky after the Civil War. In this backwater region of the war, George loyally served without the glare of publicity. One observer said of Crittenden during these years that he was a "very unostentatious ugly gentleman." Apparently George was also "very clever & agreeable & most intelligent." Crittenden was rumored to be in delicate health. He would not return to a major command for the rest of the war.[28]

In 1864, while George served in southwestern Virginia, an unexpected opportunity developed. In the chaos of the titanic struggle in

---

[26] Anonymous, *Louisville Daily Journal*, (13 March 1862): 3; *OR* 1st ser., vol. 10, pt. 2:379.

[27] Woodworth, *Jefferson Davis*, 69.

[28] William C. Davis and Meredith L. Swentor, eds., *Bluegrass Confederate: The Headquarters Diary of Edward O. Guerrant* (Baton Rouge: Louisiana State University Press, 1999).

eastern Virginia between Grant and Lee, a vacancy opened for command of the department in southwestern Virginia. Into that void George Crittenden marched. On 31 May, Confederate authorities made him the temporary commander. Somewhat surprised at his good fortune, the new commander requested clarification about his departmental boundaries. By 4 June, Crittenden requested that Richmond send someone to relieve him of command. Not desiring the close public scrutiny of leadership after the nightmare of Mill Springs, he sought escape from the ordeal. President Davis, however, liked the prospect of his old friend in command once again, and the Kentuckian remained as temporary commander.[29]

Crittenden's major task as departmental commander was to coordinate his forces with those of John C. Breckinridge in the Shenandoah Valley. Breckinridge, an old family friend, wanted Crittenden to transfer John Hunt Morgan's cavalry from their Kentucky raids to the Shenandoah to help defend it against Union attack. Crittenden promised to send Morgan to Breckinridge as soon as possible but the independent Morgan never made it to Virginia. Instead, Morgan planned another raid into Kentucky from East Tennessee. During the planning, however, Union troops killed Morgan. One of Crittenden's sad responsibilities as departmental commander was to arrange for the funeral of his fallen comrade. He organized the largest procession ever seen in southwestern Virginia, and the honorable funeral service pleased the Morgan family.[30]

George maintained his innocence of the charges levied against him at Mill Springs until his death. It was always a sensitive subject for him. In a letter to his old friend Jefferson Davis, written long after war's end, George wrote, "I attribute the loss of the battle, in a great degree to the inferiority of our arms and the untimely fall of General Zollicoffer." He testily noted that "the Battle of Fishing Creek was a necessity, as to how I managed it, I have nothing more to say." To the end, Davis accepted Crittenden's innocence, but few agreed with him.[31]

---

[29] *OR* 1st ser., vol. 39, pt. 2:616, 635; James A. Ramage, *Rebel Raid: The Life of John Hunt Morgan* (Lexington: University Press of Kentucky, 1986) 224

[30] Ramage, *Rebel Raider*, 224, 246.

[31] Jefferson Davis, *The Rise and Fall of the Confederate Government*, 2 vols. (New York: D. Appleton, 1881) 2:21.

George Crittenden was a fallen star. His credentials and connections predicted great success during his early service in the Confederacy, but instead he had disgraced himself and failed once again. His father blamed those around George for his failings, and the question remains whether this was justifiable reasoning or parental love's blinding effect.

In sum, the Confederates fought from an untenable position at Mill Springs. Zollicoffer should not have crossed the Cumberland River without authorization from superiors. Johnston and Crittenden, as superior officers, should have given direct orders about the matter and taken immediate steps to enforce those orders. Officers have been court-martialed for lesser offenses.

Crittenden is not without blame, however; his slowness cost him dearly. He could have moved from Richmond to Kentucky much more quickly than he did. The detour to Knoxville and Tennessee politics with the recall to Richmond cost Crittenden even more time. Even so, had he moved quickly from Knoxville to Zollicoffer's camp, he might have arrived before the flooding of the Cumberland River. More precise orders from Richmond would have speeded the process but Crittenden has final responsibility for his slow movement.

Considering Crittenden's past record of intemperance, it is highly unlikely that he had not taken at least a few drinks before the battle. It is unclear whether he was totally incapacitated during the battle; however, sober or drunk, he performed poorly. During the retreat the Kentuckian probably sensed that his career was over and, in a spirit of self-destruction, he clearly was drunk. Even with these great lapses of judgment, however, he still could have redeemed himself with a credible performance at the upcoming Battle of Shiloh. Crittenden, however, could not stay sober. He was irresponsible, lazy, and alcoholic. He did not have the character to lead. If he could not live up to his father's high expectations, why should he even bother to try? Instead, George chose the route of self-destruction. He effectively destroyed his career and his body.[32]

From his Texas expedition, his Mexican War record, and his service in West Virginia, it seems that George Crittenden was a brave soldier when he performed away from the glare of the public eye and familial

---

[32] Woodworth, *Jefferson Davis*, 68.

expectations. He probably would have made a good colonel and might have risen to higher command through hard work and a little luck. However, cursed by his heritage and high expectations, George never had good fortune. Placed in a higher position than he could handle, his heritage destroyed him.

6

A Rising Star:
Thomas's Combat Experience

In early 1862, as George Crittenden's career reached its nadir, his younger brother Thomas advanced professionally. Thomas served as the commander of the 5th Division and saw his first combat at Shiloh. Throughout the later campaigns, Thomas served admirably and received another promotion shortly before the Battle of Perryville. At this point in the war, many considered Crittenden one of the better political generals. His military and political prospects looked bright.

But first Thomas Crittenden would experience a bizarre episode. Kentucky Confederate officer William Preston wrote to President Davis suggesting that Crittenden, General William Ward, and L. H. Rousseau were growing discontented with the Federal government's mistrust of Kentuckians. Perhaps these Kentuckians would quit the Union war effort and join the Confederacy. This was a pipedream. The Kentuckians would remain loyal to the Union.[1]

On 10 January 1862, Crittenden was ordered to move his forces from Calhoun to South Carrollton and establish a strong position north of the Green River, but instead he occupied the southern bank. Crittenden, ever wanting to please those in authority, quickly wrote a report explaining his reasons for ignoring Buell's order. He argued that the southern bank was a stronger position and added that a move to the northern bank would have cost him precious time. The amateur general also added that one of

---

[1] US War Department, comp., *The War of the Rebellion: A Compilation of the Official Records of the Union and Confederate Armies*, 128 vols. (Washington, DC: Government Printing Office, 1880–1901) 1st ser., vol. 7:802.

his engineers, Captain Edwards, agreed with the move.[2]

Crittenden stayed at his location south of the Green River and continued to send messages to Buell's headquarters justifying his move. On 24 January, he reported rumors of an advance by the Confederates from Bowling Green toward his position. He said he was preparing "to give them a handsome reception." He was also concerned that Buell had not issued him orders regarding the Confederate move. The Kentuckian worried that he "would be left to do nothing while a battle was being fought at Bowling Green." Crittenden desperately wanted the respect of others. Being left out of the decision-making process galled him and hurt his pride.[3]

Crittenden's nervousness increased with the passing days. On 27 January, he notified Buell that he had received reports that Simon Buckner, with a force of about 15,000 men, was on the attack. Thomas told his superior that he had made his position at South Carrollton as strong as possible, but a few more cannon would make him more secure. The fear of being alone and having to make a decision without clear direction ate at Crittenden's already fragile self-confidence.[4]

Eventually General Buell wrote to Crittenden, ordering him to return to Calhoun. The commander considered Crittenden's position "unsafe" and insisted that the move take place "promptly and without interference." A cautious general, Buell did not want to risk a battle or the loss of territory along the Green River. He was not willing to send a strong Union probe along his western flank to exploit possible Confederate weakness as he had recently done along his eastern flank with General Thomas at Mill Springs. Buell's order only strengthened Crittenden's natural inclination not to take initiative. In terms of military prowess, Crittenden's lack of initiative and his tendency to remain ignorant of the overall plan were major flaws.[5]

To Buell's relief, Crittenden complied with the order as quickly as possible. For Buell it was refreshing to have subordinates who readily

---

    [2] US War Department, comp., *The War of the Rebellion: A Compilation of the Official Records of the Union and Confederate Armies*, 128 vols. (Washington, DC: Government Printing Office, 1880–1901) 1st ser., vol. 7:543–544, 558–559.

    [3] *OR*, 1st ser., vol. 7:564.

    [4] *OR*, 1st ser., vol. 7:569.

    [5] *OR*, 1st ser., vol. 7:569.

obeyed orders rather than dispute them. Later, when Buell was consolidating his divisions into corps, he no doubt remembered the cooperative, pleasant Kentuckian who followed orders. The good impression Thomas had made on those around him no doubt enhanced his promotion prospects.[6]

By early February, Crittenden had grown impatient with the seeming standstill on his front. He wanted to have his forces advance against the enemy. On 6 February, Crittenden got his wish. Buell ordered him to detach the 13th Brigade and send it back to the Ohio River for a potential move down the Cumberland River. A week later, he ordered Crittenden's detached brigade and Nelson's division to move to Smithland to prepare for cooperation with Ulysses S. Grant's forthcoming Fort Donelson campaign.[7]

Buell planned to move Nelson's division and eventually two brigades from Crittenden's division to Fort Donelson. Nelson would command Crittenden's vanguard brigade until the second one arrived, at which time command would revert to Crittenden. Naturally, battlefield conditions might alter this arrangement without warning. Once again Crittenden remained on the fringes during a command decision. Buell regularly chose Nelson over Crittenden, but Crittenden nonetheless maintained a good relationship with his fellow Kentuckian.[8]

The movement of Union troops was not without incident. A small skirmish ensued when a Confederate force of about 500 clashed with troops under Stephen Burbridge and John McHenry at Woodland. The Union troops inflicted about fifty Rebel casualties. Rumors about the Union movement spread, and stories in the Southern press suggested that Crittenden's forces might threaten Paris, Tennessee, or move against Confederate lines in Kentucky. Crittenden was on the move, but the public was unsure of his destination.[9]

---

[6] *OR*, 1st ser., vol. 7:570.

[7] *OR*, 1st ser., vol. 7:584, 588, 610.

[8] *OR*, 1st ser., vol. 7:622.

[9] Henry Cist, *The Army of the Cumberland* (New York: Charles Scribners & Sons, 1882) 25; Anonymous, *Louisville Daily Journal*, (5 February 1862): 1; Anonymous, *Louisville Daily Journal*, (6 February 1862): 4.

On 17 February Buell ordered Crittenden to suspend his movement and await further orders, citing concern about whether boats would be able to use the Green River. The real issue was that Buell and Halleck, as competing department commanders, were not working together very well. Neither general wanted to see the other experience too much glory and neither really wanted to share his troops. On 19 February, Buell countermanded his previous orders to Crittenden, allowing the move toward Donelson to continue. Buell also reluctantly informed Crittenden that, in the future, he would receive his orders from Halleck.[10]

Officers were not happy with the new command structure. Their divisions were broken up to help Grant in the coming campaign, with Crittenden's division particularly hard hit. Part of his division still remained at Calhoun, while another segment was en route to Fort Donelson. This situation hurt unit solidarity and officer morale. As a result of much griping, the order was countermanded and some of the Cumberland units were returned to Buell's command. The 13th Brigade never returned to Crittenden's command, however. Instead, Crittenden received the previously unattached 11th Brigade under Jeremiah T. Boyle. This move did little to improve relations between Buell's Army of the Cumberland and Grant's Army of the Tennessee.[11]

Ulysses S. Grant continued his march toward strategic Fort Donelson and in late February that Confederate location fell. The victory made Grant a national hero, but Halleck, an extremely cautious commander, moved very slowly to follow up Grant's great victory at Fort Donelson. Halleck's sluggishness gave Confederate commander Albert Sidney Johnston time to regroup and reorganize his army at Corinth, Mississippi. Only George's drunkenness prevented him and Thomas from opposing one another on the battlefield at Shiloh.

Buell slowly and methodically moved the Army of the Cumberland into Tennessee, Nashville being the great prize awaiting these troops. If Buell and Grant's armies linked up, they could easily capture the key railroad city of Corinth and gain control of much of the lower South. The

---

[10] *OR*, 1st ser., vol. 7:631, 639.

[11] *OR*, 1st ser., vol. 7:651, 654, 671–672; Larry J. Daniel, *Days of Glory: The Army of the Cumberland, 1861–1865* (Baton Rouge: Louisiana State University Press, 2004): 70.

Federal commanders thought that the Confederate army had been shattered beyond repair, so the advance could take place at the Federals' leisure. Perhaps the Rebels would surrender without an invasion. All of this was, of course, wishful thinking, and it cost the Federals valuable time following the fall of Fort Donelson.

The Confederates decided to attack Grant's army before it established contact with Buell's army. Thus, on 6 April 1862 Johnston launched an attack known as the Battle of Shiloh. Grant's forces were not prepared for the attack and, except for a heroic defense by some troops and Grant's doggedness, the Federal army might have been destroyed.

Buell had ordered his divisions to move to Savannah, Tennessee, to cooperate with Grant. Nelson arrived at Savannah on 5 April, concerned about what he perceived as Grant's exposed position at Pittsburg Landing. However, no one, including Grant, seemed very worried. Buell did order Crittenden and McCook's divisions to Pittsburg landing on 6 April, but they did not arrive until nightfall.[12]

As the battle started on 6 April, soldiers in the Army of the Cumberland could hear the cannons booming. When they arrived on the battlefield, they saw the carnage of war. One soldier said that for "six miles square the earth was covered with carnage" and that men and animal lay together in heaps of decaying flesh. General Crittenden arrived late in the day, and during the night his men were unloaded from the steamers. The Kentuckian reported that when he arrived on a steamboat he found between 6,000 and 10,000 demoralized soldiers on the riverbank. He wished to send a regiment aground to drive them away from the river and keep them from demoralizing his men. He was "disgusted" with the situation.[13]

All of Crittenden's division, except Jackson's 3rd Kentucky Cavalry, crossed the Tennessee River and participated in the second day of battle. During the night Buell issued orders for Nelson and Crittenden to form a

[12] Thomas Van Horne, *The Army of the Cumberland* (1875; repr., New York: Konecky & Konecky, 1966) 79–80, 85–86, Ebenezer Hannaford, *The Story of a Regiment: A History of the Campaigns, and Associations in the Field, of the Sixth Ohio Volunteer Infantry* (Cincinnati: Ebenezer Hannaford, 1868) 237.

[13] Jacob Weaver Davis to George Davis, 11 April 1862, Jacob Weaver Davis Papers, Western Kentucky University, Bowling Green; *OR*, 292–295, 355.

line of battle and prepare to attack in the morning. The divisions of
McCook and Wood would arrive later and form next to Crittenden.[14]

In the morning, Buell ordered Crittenden to form up on Nelson's
right; the Army of the Cumberland had responsibility for the Union left
on the second day at Shiloh. Remnants of Grant's army in the vicinity of
their lines were placed under the command of the Army of the
Cumberland divisional commanders. During the day, Crittenden issued
orders to the 8th and 18th Illinois of McClernand's division and the 7th
Iowa from W. H. L. Wallace's division. Nelson's division opened the
attack and Crittenden's force supported the assault. Crittenden's left
brigade faced an area of dense undergrowth, which slowed his advance and
made it difficult for the two divisions to move in concert.[15]

Nelson's division advanced first through Wicker's field and Sarah
Bell's field and achieved some success from about 9–11 A.M. Perhaps
because of the dense underbrush in front of part of Crittenden's division,
known as the Hornet's Nest, he did not advance as quickly as Nelson. As a
result Nelson had to wait for Crittenden to catch up. A Confederate
counterattack led by Hardee stalled Nelson's advance. As the Confederates
attempted to press their advantage, William Sooy Smith's brigade from
Crittenden's division, with strong artillery support from Mendenhall's
battery, deterred the attack.[16]

After repulsing the Confederates in front of Hazen's brigade in
Nelson's division, Buell ordered A. M. McCook's division into action to
the right of Crittenden's division. There was a gap between the brigades of
L. H. Rousseau in McCook's division and Jeremiah T. Boyle in
Crittenden's division. The arrival of William H. Gibson's brigade, which
pushed the 32nd Indiana into the gap, averted potential disaster.
Confederate commander John C. Breckinridge had seen the gap and was
attempting to exploit it. The day had been saved for the Federals.[17]

---

[14] *OR*, 1st ser., vol. 10, pt. 1:354, 292–295.

[15] Van Horne, *Army of the Cumberland*, 89; *OR*, 1st ser., vol. 10, pt. 1:127, 129, 149, 293–294.

[16] Van Horne, *Army of the Cumberland*, 90, 92; *OR*, 1st ser., vol. 10, pt. 1:294; William B. Hazen, *A Narrative of Military Service* (Boston: Ticknor & Comp., 1885) 32.

[17] Van Horne, *Army of the Cumberland*, 93; James M. McPherson, ed., *The Atlas of the Civil War* (New York: Macmillan, 1994) 53.

When Confederate forces attempted to renew the assault in the early afternoon, Crittenden's artillery battery under John Mendenhall stopped the attack. The Union army counterattacked, with Crittenden delivering a direct assault and Nelson a flank attack on the Confederate forces of Hardee and Breckinridge. The Confederate guns were captured by around 3 P.M., and Confederate forces began to give ground. By the end of the second day at Shiloh, all of the Union ground lost on the first day had been regained and Confederate commander P. G. T. Beauregard had decided to retreat.[18]

By horrible circumstance, the Confederate troops Crittenden's division had fought that day were commanded by John C. Breckinridge, Crittenden's old friend. Breckinridge had only recently replaced George Crittenden as commander. Many of the troops who served under Breckinridge were Kentucky Confederate volunteers; this was the first of several instances during the Civil War in which Kentuckian fought Kentuckian. The results of such confrontations were poignantly heartbreaking. One soldier from Muhlenberg County recorded seeing two men from his hometown in the enemy army at Shiloh. Captain John Lewis of the Confederate 5th Kentucky Cavalry was wounded on the battlefield and requested that Crittenden take him to a hospital. The two had been childhood friends. Sadly, Lewis died before Crittenden could reach him and perform the service.[19]

The Battle of Shiloh was the first of many great bloody battles during the Civil War, and American public opinion was not prepared for what was yet to come. Crittenden's division suffered comparatively light losses, with only 465 casualties out of over 13,000 total Union losses.[20]

After the battle, Crittenden got his first real taste of military glory. Buell's report praised Crittenden's actions during the Battle of Shiloh. Many of Crittenden's subordinates also received praise from both superior officers and contemporary observers. As news of the battle spread to the

---

[18] Van Horne, *Army of the Cumberland*, 93; *OR*, 1st ser., vol. 10, pt. 1:301, 365; McPherson, *Atlas of the Civil War*, 53.

[19] Otto H. Rothert, *A History of Muhlenberg County* (Louisville: John P. Morton, Comp., 1913) 269; Francis Hudson Oxx, *The Kentucky Crittenden: The History of a Family Including Genealogy of Descendent in Both Male and Female Lives, Biographical Sketches of its Members, and Their Descent from Other Colonial Lives* (n.p., 1940) 133.

[20] *OR*, 1st ser., vol. 10, pt. 1:107; Larry J. Daniel, *Shiloh: The Battle that Changed the Civil War* (New York: Simon & Schuster, 1997) 322.

public, the praise added to Crittenden's growing reputation. The Louisville *Daily Journal* reported approvingly that Crittenden was "a truly brave and noble man." The paper continued that the Kentuckian was "cool and self-possessed even when the balls and shells of the enemy were falling all around." Years later, one Union soldier remembered how Crittenden had rallied his men after their initial delay at the Hornet's Nest and had splendidly driven the enemy from his position. One early historian of the Army of the Cumberland agreed that Crittenden deserved great praise for his fine performance at Shiloh. Perhaps Thomas's good work at Shiloh would alleviate some of the shame and disgrace George's poor performance in eastern Kentucky had brought on the family.[21]

Shiloh was Thomas's first experience of combat as a commander. He had shown himself brave under fire and had completed his assignment well. His lack of self-confidence and hesitance to take initiative was not obvious at the divisional level. After Crittenden received promotion to corps command later in the year, his personality weaknesses became far more obvious during the heat of battle.

Years afterwards, when Buell wrote an article about his role at the Battle of Shiloh, he consistently praised the work of Nelson's division but said little about the performance of Crittenden, McCook, or Wood. The flamboyant Nelson overshadowed Crittenden. Only superb battlefield performance would elevate Crittenden's image in the minds of Buell and the public. Crittenden did not have such brilliance; possessing only average ability, he did his best to please his superiors.[22]

After the battle of Shiloh, there was a major Union reorganization. Henry Halleck assumed command of all Union forces in the region. Because of rumors about Grant's lack of preparation and possible drunkenness, Halleck removed him from command of the Army of the Tennessee. George H. Thomas from Buell's army replaced Grant, who became second in command. Halleck planned to merge Grant's force with those of Buell and John Pope when they arrived from the Island No. 10

---

[21] *OR*, 1st ser., vol. 10, pt. 1:295; Jacob Davis to George Davis, 11 April 1862, Jacob Weaver Davis Papers, Western Kentucky University; Anonymous, *Louisville Daily Journal*, (5 May 1862): 3; Oxx, *Kentucky Crittendens*, 132; Van Horne, *Army of the Cumberland*, 98.

[22] Don Carlos Buell to E. Hannaford, 6 July 1868, Don Carlos Buell Papers, Filson Club, Louisville.

campaign. Together the troops would launch an assault against Corinth, Mississippi. Crittenden's division would serve as a part of the center as it approached Corinth. Halleck moved at a snail's pace toward his objective.[23]

On 3 May 1862, Crittenden's division crossed Lick Creek at Greers. By 7 May it had reached Chalmer's Creek with Crittenden's division acting as a reserve force for the center. Two days later, Crittenden's division marched to the left to support the advance of Pope's army. By 17 May, the division was within 2 miles of the enemy fortifications. The next day Crittenden established artillery batteries and began to entrench for what was expected to be a long battle. Confederates were not sure they wanted to fight, and only relatively light skirmishing took place. By 29 May, Nelson realized that the Confederates were retreating and the city was in Union hands.[24]

From 29 April to 3 May, Crittenden was too sick to lead his division. During that time Horatio G. Van Cleve assumed commanded. Crittenden remained physically weak for several weeks, so much so that his family worried about him. To assuage their fears, a family friend sent a copy of an official telegram stating that Thomas was well enough to return to duty. Summer in the Deep South did not agree well with Thomas's health; his condition improved only when the army returned to the milder climate of the Upper South.[25]

After the fall of Corinth, Union forces pursued P. G. T. Beauregard's Confederates at the same snail's pace. On 4 June Crittenden was sent on the Baldwin road to reinforce Pope and Rosecrans. On 7 June his forces built a bridge across the Tuscumbia, then moved beyond Rienzi and encamped on 10 June. They moved toward Iuka, reaching the city on 12 June. Eventually, Crittenden's forces advanced as far south as Booneville, Mississippi.[26]

---

[23] Van Horne, *Army of the Cumberland, 101.*

[24] *OR*, 1st ser., vol. 10, pt. 1:673, 701–703.

[25] *OR*, 1st ser., vol. 10, pt. 1:703; Jack D. Welsh, *The Medical histories of Union Generals* (Kent: Kent State University Press, 1997) 82; E. D. Townsend to John J. Crittenden, 21 May 1862, John J. Crittenden Papers, Duke University, Durham NC.

[26] *OR*, 1st ser., vol. 10, pt. 1:701; Rerrick, John A. *The Forty-fourth Indiana Volunteer Infantry: History of its Services in the War of the Rebellion and a Personal Record of Its Members.* (La Grange IN: John A. Rerrick, 1880): 63.

Throughout the maneuvers, Crittenden proudly noted that his men were "always prompt to obey orders" and boasted that "no position assigned to any portion of my division was ever given up to the enemy." A bright future seemed in store for Crittenden and his men.[27]

During this time the Kentuckian also dealt with several family problems. In his military family, Lyne Starling, a fellow Kentuckian, became Crittenden's adjutant. He loyally served with Crittenden until Chickamauga. Thomas had a cousin also named Thomas in Missouri. Thomas T. Crittenden was serving as a garrison commander in Murfreesboro, Tennessee, when attacked by Nathan Bedford Forrest on 13 July. The young Crittenden surrendered the garrison, a decision for which he took sharp criticism in the Northern press. Some newspaper accounts confused the Crittenden cousins, and the Kentucky Crittendens were concerned that another stinging defeat might add to their family reputation. Thomas L. Crittenden was relieved to see the Kentucky press declare that he would never do such a thing as surrender a garrison.[28]

After the fall of Corinth, Halleck broke up his huge army and restored it to its pre-battle organization. Buell's Army of the Cumberland had the strategic objective of Chattanooga. The city was an important rail center and a gateway for invasion of the Deep South. On 11 June Crittenden's division, called back from Booneville, moved toward Florence, Alabama. Crittenden and McCook's divisions would take the lead.[29]

On 15 June Crittenden's force reached the vicinity of Florence. The Federals planned to use ferryboats to move men across the Tennessee River on 22 June but were delayed three days due to rumors of an attack on Nelson's division. The attack never materialized, and on 25 June the force crossed the Tennessee River. By 29 June it had arrived at Athens, Alabama.[30]

The advancing Federal Army often freely foraged the region's resources regardless of whether their commander approved. Buell hoped to

---

[27] *OR*, 1st ser., vol. 10, pt. 1:700.

[28] *OR*, 1st ser., vol. 10, pt. 1:356; *Louisville Daily Journal*, August 8, 1862.

[29] Van Horne, *Army of the Cumberland*, 116; *OR*, 1st ser., vol. 16, pt. 2:116.

[30] Van Horne, *Army of the Cumberland*, 117–118.

arouse Southern Unionists and break the heart of the Rebel resistance but believed that destroying Southern property was not the way to win over citizens. Crittenden and other commanders received instructions to keep an account of property damages for future compensation. This soft approach to the war was becoming increasingly out of favor in the North. Crittenden and other officers might try to prevent the destruction, but this was usually an exercise in futility.[31]

After their arrival at Athens, Crittenden's force, on Buell's command, halted and awaited further orders. He eventually decided to move the division to Battle Creek in order to protect the Nashville and Chattanooga Railroad. By mid-July Crittenden and McCook's divisions were in place near the railroad. Because of the almost constant sabotage of the tracks, the Federal troops spent a great deal of their time making repairs.[32]

As Crittenden reached Battle Creek in mid-July, his cousin Thomas was surrendering Murfreesboro, a significant supply base for Buell's army. Its loss meant that the Federals had to economize their resources. Buell's forces had few reserves and now had to worry about constant Confederate attacks. The advance on Chattanooga bogged down to almost a standstill.[33]

Crittenden moved from Athens to Huntsville to Stevenson to Battle Creek, arriving in mid-July. Buell ordered him to spread word to other Union units of a possible attack. Crittenden was unsure of Buell's intentions and felt constrained by the commander's words of caution. Crittenden could see Rebel pickets guarding a railroad trestle just across from his front and he wanted to attack them as quickly as possible. The Kentuckian also reported rumors of Confederate troop movement through Chattanooga. Thomas was not sure if Confederates troops were moving into or exiting from the region.[34]

Buell did not seem too concerned with destroying the railroad trestle at that time. Instead he told Crittenden to continue to gather information about the movements of Confederate troops. Buell was particularly

---

[31] *OR*, 1st ser., vol. 16, pt. 2:53; See Mark Grimsley, *The Hard Hand of War: Union Military Policy toward Southern Civilians, 1861–1865* (Cambridge: Cambridge University Press, 1995) 63–66.

[32] *OR*, 1st ser., vol. 16, pt. 2:67–68; Van Horne, *Army of the Cumberland,* 119–120.

[33] *OR*, 1st ser., vol. 16, pt. 2:137.

[34] *OR*, 1st ser., vol. 16, pt. 2:108, 137, 152.

concerned with movements to the north of Crittenden, around the area of McMinnville. At the same time Buell was receiving reports of up to 4,000 troops per day marching through Chattanooga. If the rumors were true and these troops moved north of Crittenden's position at Battle Creek, they could threaten the Union supply base at Nashville or possibly even threaten Kentucky. Everything the Union forces had gained since the beginning of the year would be lost.[35]

Buell had justifiable fears. By 19 July Crittenden received reports from a reliable Union spy that the Confederates had about 21,000 men in the Chattanooga region and about 40 pieces of artillery. What Buell did not yet know was that the new Confederate commander, Braxton Bragg, was beginning a bold gamble to reverse the tide of the war in the west. Bragg and Edmund Kirby Smith from Knoxville would march into Kentucky and reclaim that state for the Confederacy. A strong Confederate force in Kentucky threatening the Ohio River would cause Union troops to pull back from their recently gained territories in the South. To counter this move, Buell had to send his divisions north to intercept Bragg's march. Crittenden and McCook's divisions were ordered north to gain control of the Nashville & Chattanooga Road.[36]

Bragg began his move north in August. Buell thought the objective of Bragg's advance was the capital city of Nashville. One reason for Buell's stubborn insistence on Nashville as the Confederate objective was that on 8 August Union troops found a letter from Bragg describing his intent to move into Tennessee. Crittenden, McCook, and their staff officers discussed the contents of the message before sending it on to Buell. The Union commander believed the letter was authentic. As a result, Buell tried to shield the city from a Confederate attack rather than intercept Bragg's move north. Kentucky, not Nashville, was the Confederate objective. Buell discerned this too late to prevent the Confederate invasion.[37]

Buell wished to prevent Bragg from entering the Sequatchie Valley because the Cumberland Plateau would shield Confederate moves across Tennessee. From the valley, Bragg could cross west through one of the gaps

---

[35] *OR*, 1st ser., vol. 16, pt. 2:144, 153, 162–163.
[36] *OR*, 1st ser., vol. 16, pt. 2:183; Van Horne, *Army of the Cumberland*, 128.
[37] *OR*, 1st ser., vol. 16, pt. 2:377; Daniel, *Days of Glory*, 107.

or proceed up the valley to Knoxville. McCook was tasked with preventing Bragg from entering the Sequatchie but he failed. Once in the valley, Buell's best option was to concentrate at a central location between the Sequatchie and the likely Confederate route to Nashville. Buell chose the site of Altamont. Unfortunately, Bragg did behave predictably and instead veered to the North. As Buell continued to guard avenues to Nashville, Bragg edged further north. By the time Buell realized that the Confederate objective was Kentucky, not Nashville, it was too late.[38]

Buell was now in a race to reach Louisville before the Confederates. Crittenden became impatient. No doubt worries over a Rebel invasion made the general and many of his men concerned about their families back in Kentucky. Confederate raids had also left Buell's men short on supplies,. Crittenden would return to his beloved Kentucky, but not in the manner he had intended.[39]

As the weary soldiers marched north, they dealt with harassing Confederate cavalry attacks. On 13 September, while Crittenden was between Nashville and Bowling Geen, his column stopped to await an anticipated attack from Nathan Bedford Forrest that never came. The troops trudged on and finally arrived in Louisville, beating Bragg to the prize.[40]

From January to August 1862, Crittenden had developed as a commander. While not a military genius or a brilliant administrator, he had performed adequately as a divisional commander. He was personally brave and usually carried out direct and precise orders with reasonable speed. He served as a loyal subordinate who apparently got along well with his colleagues and was highly regarded by his men.

---

[38] Ibid., 108–125.
[39] Daniel, *Days of Glory*, 121.
[40] Ibid., 119.

7

The Kentucky Interlude

In fall 1862, Thomas Crittenden returned to his native Kentucky—not as a conquering hero but to defend his state from Confederate attack. The Kentucky campaign provided Crittenden with an opportunity for military and political growth, but as was the case so often in his life, Crittenden failed to take full advantage of the opportunities afforded him.

In June 1862, Senator Crittenden had suggested to Federal authorities that his middle son transfer to Kentucky if Federal troops began to increase their numbers in the Bluegrass State. The senator may have already sensed that Thomas's talents were more political than military and that if the younger Crittenden was in Kentucky, he could use those political talents more freely than if he served elsewhere. Unfortunately, the transfer did not take place. Instead, William Nelson was the Kentuckian called back home to organize a new Federal force. On 30 August Nelson suffered a devastating defeat at Richmond. Crittenden, with his limited military ability, probably would not have done better.[1]

The stress of war was beginning to show on Crittenden. Alfred Pirtle, a Kentucky acquaintance, saw him in July and noted in a letter home that "Gen'l Crittenden was also there, looking pale, thin, and much older than when I saw him last winter." Crittenden may still have been experiencing the lingering effects of the illness that had sidelined him in the spring, but no doubt the stress of leadership was also beginning to take a toll.[2]

Because of Confederate raids on Buell's supply line, the Union army was low on foodstuffs. The men were hungry as they marched back to Kentucky. The hot, dry weather added thirst and heat exhaustion to their tribulations. Due to a bureaucratic mix-up, many men had not received

---

[1] C. P. Wolcott to John J. Crittenden, 25 June 1862, John J. Crittenden Papers, Duke University, Durham NC.

[2] Alfred Pirtle to mother, 5 July 1862, Alfred Pirtle Letters, Filson Club, Louisville.

their pay for over six months. Only a promise of compensation persuaded these men to keep marching. Don Carlos Buell's slowness did not inspire confidence, either. When Buell's soldiers heard the Confederate cannonading at Munfordville and noted that their commander did nothing to relieve the Federal force under John T. Wilder, morale only dropped further. As one soldier complained, "those who were in authority over us will be forgiven by the poor men who had to drag themselves along, and some to be made to hurry up who were totally unfit for marching by the point of the bayonet until they fell cursing those who would kill their men." In the eyes of the soldiers, the army's retreat back to its base made all of the previous year's efforts seem wasted.[3]

On the Kentucky home front, the situation was not much improved. In Louisville, massive fear and confusion reigned as stores closed, and people worried about Bragg's approach. In Lebanon, Maria Knott, mother of a future Kentucky governor, wrote to her son that "there are more than a thousand men encamped before our door, and in all probability before twenty four more hours have passed, many of them will be in eternity or writhing in excruciating pain on the field of battle." Like many Kentuckians, Mrs. Knott assumed that Buell would move rapidly to meet the enemy. She was wrong.[4]

Crittenden's division crossed the Salt River on 24 September and reached Louisville. They had marched 120 miles from Bowling Green in seven days, covering 68 miles during the last three days of the march. The citizens greeted them "with joy and delight" and "vied with each other in doing everything possible for the soldiers." Everyone was in a festive mood.

---

[3] Ashley L. Kerwood, *Annals of the Fifty-Seventh Regiment Indiana Volunteers, Marches, Battles, and Incidents of Army Life by a Member of the Regiment* (Dayton: W. J. Shuey, 1868) 21–122; Thomas J. Wright, *History of the Eighth Regiment Kentucky Volunteer Infantry During its Three Years Campaigns, Embracing Organization, Marches, Skirmishes and Battles of the Command with Much of the History of the Old Reliable Third Brigade Commanded by Hon. Stanley Matthews and Containing Many Interesting and Amusing Incidents of Army Life* (St. Joseph: St. Joseph Steam Printing, 1880) 91–92; John H. Tilford Diary, 15 September 1862, Filson Club.

[4] S. M. Starling to daughter, 5 September 1862, Starling Family Papers, University of Kentucky; S. M. Starling to Ann Mary Payne, 5 September 1862, Western Kentucky University; John H. Tilford Diary, 23 September 1862, Filson Club; Maria I. Knott to J. Proctor Knott, 1 September 1862, Knott Collection, Western Kentucky University.

The soldiers marched up Main Street past the Galt House singing, "We'll hang Jeff Davis on a sour apple tree." More than a few of these soldiers found the local liquor stores and imbibed freely.[5]

Rowdy soldiers were the least of the problems confronting Buell as he reached Louisville. He had to re-supply his army and incorporate the numerous Midwestern volunteers who were entering the army. As Buell prepared to fight a battle for Kentucky, he also had to train an army and completely reorganize the command structure. Since the start of the campaign, the Union commander had had to deal with intense public criticism of his strategic decisions. Buell would do better with reorganization than he would with public relations.

Approximately 20,000 new troops entered Buell's army after its arrival in Louisville. Most of these new volunteers were from the Midwest and had entered when news of Bragg's potential approach to the Ohio River became a reality. These volunteers were an older and more urbane group than their predecessors of 1861, who included a large influx of young, rural Kentuckians. Buell adopted the tactic of mixing the new regiments with the old at a ratio of one to two regiments per brigade. Buell reasoned that exposure to the veteran troops would speed up the new arrivals' acclimation to soldier life. Some raw recruits were still grouped together, but Buell's approach did help the training process.[6]

The Union army also experienced major internal problems. Many officers simply did not like Buell. Opposition centered on the disgruntled officers of the 1st Division (under George H. Thomas), the Indiana

[5] US War Department, comp., *The War of the Rebellion: A Compilation of the Official Records of the Union and Confederate Armies*, 128 vols. (Washington, DC: Government Printing Office, 1880–1901) 1st ser., vol. 16, pt. 2:540; Robert Emmett McDowell, *City of Conflict: Louisville in the Civil War, 1861–1865* (Louisville: Louisville Round Table, 1962) 89; George H. Woodruff, *Fifteen Years Ago: or the patriotism of Will County, Designed to Preserve the Names and Memory of Will County Soldiers, Both officers and Privates—Both Living and Dead; to tell Something of What They Did, and What They Suffered, the Great Struggle to Preserve Our Nationality* (Joliet: Joliet Republican Book & Job Steam Printing, 1876) 225; Kenneth W. Noe, ed., *A Southern Boy in Blue: The Memoir of Marcus Woodcock, 9th Kentucky Infantry, U.S.A.* (Knoxville: University of Tennessee Press, 1996) 100.

[6] William Grose, *The Story of the Marches, Battles, and Incidents of the 36th Regiment Indiana Volunteer Infantry by a Member of the Regiment* (New Castle: Courier Company Press, 1891) 135; Larry J. Daniel, *Days of Glory: The Army of the Cumberland, 1861–1865* (Baton Rouge: Louisiana State University Press, 2004) 118.

regiments, and Alexander McCook's staff. Each of these groups nourished a grudge over something Buell had done or had ambitions to replace him as commander. Of course Buell also had his defenders. Crittenden, Lovell H. Rousseau, James S. Jackson, and Thomas J. Wood supported Buell, as did William B. Hazen, Charles Harker, and William Carlin. Many of these supporters were Kentuckians, like Crittenden, who liked Buell's conservative approach to restoring the Union. Crittenden, who needed the approval of others, probably wished to have peace and calm within the high command. When fellow Kentuckian John M. Harlan criticized Buell in Crittenden's presence, the courtly Crittenden said nothing in response. When rumors of Buell's dismissal began to circulate around the camp, however, Crittenden was one of several generals who sent a telegram to Federal authorities requesting that Buell retain command. Crittenden liked the status quo and only reluctantly consented to a change. Despite his aloofness, Buell had been good to Crittenden and the Kentuckian wanted to return the favor.[7]

An example of the ill humor of the high command occurred on 27 September at a diner party held in Louisville to honor the birthdays of Generals Nelson, Hazen, and James S. Jackson. At the celebration, Senator Crittenden rose and gave a toast to Alexander McCook, "the coming leader of the Army of the Ohio." The toast was ill advised and indiscreet to say the least. Nelson, a strong Buell supporter, took offense with the remark, as did some of Buell's staff. The senator usually did not misspeak so blatantly. This time, however, he exposed a deep wound within the army. For Thomas Crittenden, his father's comments may have laid the seeds of future jealousy and resentment.[8]

On 29 September, the internal bickering within the army reached a crisis. At the Galt House in Louisville, Jefferson C. Davis, one of Nelson's subordinates, shot the general. The shooting, which occurred in the lobby of the hotel, was witnessed by a who's who of Kentucky and Indiana dignitaries. The senator quickly rushed to tell his soldier son. The younger Crittenden ran to his comrade's side. Nelson told Crittenden, "I am

---

[7] Daniel, *Days of Glory*, 128, 130, 131, 135.

[8] McDowell, *City of Conflict*, 98–99; William B. Hazen, *A Narrative of Military Service* (Boston: Ticknor & Comp., 1885) 54.

murdered," and died shortly thereafter. The funeral was held at Christ Church on 2nd Street, and Crittenden was one of several officers serving as pallbearer.[9]

The shooting naturally created uproar within the already divided army. Crittenden, Hazen, William Terrill, and James Jackson demanded Davis's arrest and execution. Not only was Davis not executed, he was never even arrested. Crittenden considered challenging Davis to a duel as a matter of honor to avenge his friend's death, but he did not follow through. Likewise, many of the Kentucky troops were outraged that a Hoosier had shot a Kentuckian. Before more catastrophes could occur, Buell increased the number of guards around the Kentucky and Indiana units.[10]

The press also took interest in the incident. The Indianapolis *Daily Journal* had already reported Nelson's abusive behavior toward Hoosier troops following the disaster at Richmond. Never one to hold back his opinion, Nelson blasted the Hoosiers as the cause of the Union collapse at the battle, and the Hoosiers never forgave him. When the shooting occurred, the paper emphasized Nelson's abusive demeanor and Davis's courteous nature. In order words, the Kentuckian got what he deserved. The Kentucky newspapers naturally took Nelson's position. In this war of words, however, only ink, not blood, flowed.[11]

Nelson had indeed been an abusive commander, and most of his men did not mourn his loss. One soldier described the incident this way: "The soldiers as a general thing seem to be glad the Gen. is shot. He was considered a great tyrant to his men." Few except Buell and Crittenden would miss Nelson.[12]

Nelson's death created an opening for Crittenden. Obviously, Buell needed a new corps commander. Nelson's passing also opened a gap in Kentucky Unionist politics. As the Louisville *Daily Journal* noted several

---

[9] Hambleton Tapp, "The Assassination of General William Nelson" *FCHQ* 9/3 (July 1935): 203; Anonymous, *Louisville Daily Journal,* (1 October 1862): 2.

[10] Kenneth W. Noe, *Perryville: The Grand Havoc of Battle* (Lexington: University Press of Kentucky, 2001) 93; McDowell, *City of Conflict,* 103.

[11] Anonymous, Indianapolis *Daily Journal,* (9 September 1862): 3; Anonymous, Indianapolis *Daily Journal,* (30 September 1862): 2.

[12] John Tilford Diary, 27 September 1862, Filson Club.

months later, "With the exception of one perhaps, Thomas L. Crittenden, he [Nelson] has left no one capable of filling his place." Nelson's admirers wanted Crittenden to deliver an oration at the dedication of a planned monument to the fallen general. Many Kentucky Unionists looked more than ever toward Crittenden as their leader. Crittenden could reap political and military benefits from his friend's untimely death.[13]

Buell had recently consolidated his divisions into corps. George H. Thomas, Alexander McCook, and William Nelson had been designated corps commanders with Crittenden to serve in Thomas's corps. Nelson's murder and the intended replacement of Buell with George H. Thomas called this reorganization into question. Thomas declined the promotion, and Federal authorities had to return army command to Buell. Buell, who had poor personal relations with just about everyone, removed Thomas from corps command and made him his second in command. Thus, Buell now needed two new corps commanders. He decided on Thomas Crittenden as commander of the II Corps and Charles Gilbert as commander of the III Corps.[14]

Buell chose Crittenden for several reasons. Crittenden had not criticized Buell for his strategy in Tennessee and had served reasonably well for months. He was a member of the powerful Kentucky bloc so important to the war effort. Secondly, Crittenden was near at hand and no one better qualified would be able to serve in the upcoming campaign. Loyalty had its rewards.[15]

The II Corps consisted of the 4th Division under William Sooey Smith, the 5th Division under Horatio Van Cleve, and the 6th Division under Thomas J. Wood. Smith, who was once described as "a pleasant and competent commander of the division," had previously served Crittenden as a brigade commander. Wood had been a fellow division commander. A prickly West Pointer, Wood resented Crittenden's political influence in gaining the promotion, and he occasionally erupted in anger over the

---

[13] Anonymous, *Louisville Daily Journal*, (16 February 1863): 4.
[14] *OR*, 1st ser., vol. 16, pt. 1:663, 558.
[15] Noe, *Perryville*, 95.

situation. Van Cleve, an older man, had served at Mill Springs. Of the three divisional commanders, Wood was by far the most talented.[16]

One West Pointer, the very capable William B. Hazen, worried about George Thomas's declining the position as commander of the army. If Thomas refused the position, he reasoned, and Washington authorities continued to push for Buell's removal, the only alternatives would be Alexander McCook or Thomas Crittenden. Neither of these generals should ever command an army, he thought. Hazen need not to have worried, since Federal officials had no plans to promote either man.[17]

In the midst of this chaos in Union army reorganization, Crittenden began his service as a corps commander. Thus far his service was good, and he could lay claim to being one of the better political generals. In an optimistic attitude, the Louisville *Daily Journal* described Crittenden as a "greyhound, straining in the leash" and "a true Crittenden." Kentuckians believed the young general had a bright future ahead.[18]

On 1 October, Buell's columns began to march out of Louisville to meet the enemy. The high command was still in disarray. Personal relations between several of the corps commanders were practically nonexistent, and none of them had any experience commanding a corps in battle. To make matters worse, Buell knew that his job was on the line. Failure would mean his removal.

Crittenden's II Corps began its march from Louisville to Bardstown via the Bardstown Road. One soldier, Marcus Woodcock of the 9th Kentucky, felt that because Crittenden's corps contained so many Kentucky troops, it should have had the honor of taking the vanguard position as the Union army moved out of Louisville. The Union forces skirmished with Confederate cavalry near the Salt River, but by 2 October they had advanced to Mount Washington. Light skirmishing continued until Union forces occupied Bardstown. Many soldiers in the ranks believed that Crittenden's corps would serve as a flanking attack force, so the soldiers redoubled their efforts on the march to accomplish their objective.[19]

---

[16] *OR,* 1st ser., vol. 16, pt. 1:558; Grose, *The Story of the Marches,* 132.

[17] Hazen, *Narrative,* 62.

[18] Anonymous, *Louisville Daily Journal,* (29 September 1862): 3.

[19] Noe, ed., *Southern Boy in Blue,* 101, 102, 107; Kerwood, *Annals of the Fifty Seventh Regiment,* 125; Wright, *History of the Eighth Regiment Kentucky,* 99; Wilbur F. Hinman, *The*

The most complicating factor in the Union command structure was the tense relationship between Buell and his second in command, George Thomas. Since President Lincoln had attempted to replace Buell with Thomas only a week earlier, the Union commander and his second in command were barely communicating. Thomas chose to travel with Crittenden's corps as it left Louisville. Thus, once again Crittenden failed to receive information about major command decisions. Buell's order would go through George Thomas, and Crittenden may or may not receive these orders. In addition, Thomas could overrule any command decision Crittenden might make. Thomas did not appreciate the awkward position, and Crittenden did not care for being left out of the decision-making process once again. The result was a level of inertia for both men that did not encourage aggressive action.[20]

From Bardstown on 4 October, Crittenden's corps marched to Springfield, then from Lebanon toward Danville. The Lebanon Pike was a narrow, rocky, hilly route that local people called the "Wilderness Road." It was a grueling march for the men, many of whom straggled. Confederates had already stripped the land of most of its forage, and very little was left for the Union forces. As one local Unionist gleefully recorded, while the Union army approached the Confederates were "running like scarred rats from a burning barn."[21]

The recent Kentucky drought would play a major role in upcoming events. One soldier described the suffering of men who "take water out of mud holes and drink it as if it was the best water they ever tasted." On 7 October, Crittenden's corps did not find water where they had expected. As a result, they had to march approximately 6 miles to find some. This forced the men to march after dark, and straggling from thirst became a problem. At 3 A.M. on 8 October, orders arrived from Buell to march to Perryville. Crittenden's corps would form the right flank of the Union

---

Story of the Sherman Brigade: The Camp, the March, the Bivouac, the Battles, and How "the boys" Lived During Four Years of Active Field Service (Callianle OH: Wilbur F. Hinman, 1897) 291.

[20] Thomas Van Horne, *The Army of the Cumberland* (1875; repr., New York: Konecky & Konecky, 1966) 145–46.

[21] Noe, *Perryville,* 135–36; Maria I. Knott Diary, 1 October 1862 and 5 October 1862, Knott Collection, Western Kentucky University, Bowling Green.

force on the battlefield. Because of the detour to find water, Crittenden's corps was not in position at dawn.[22]

As morning dawned, the soldiers of the II Corps realized that a battle was imminent. Some were surprised that they did not receive orders to move until 12 o'clock, and they were even more upset when they did not enter the battle until almost sundown. The soldiers could hear cannonading and did not understand why they were not a part of the fighting. The answer to that question lay in the strained relationship between Buell and George Thomas.[23]

The Battle of Perryville was a comedy of errors for both sides. While the average soldier fought well, the high command on both sides failed to function at peak efficiency. Through poor communications the Union army lost an excellent opportunity to inflict heavy losses on the Confederates. Likewise, Thomas Crittenden lost the opportunity to deliver a decisive blow that might have sealed his military fame.[24]

On 8 October Confederates forces attacked A. M. McCook's I Corps in force, inflicting heavy casualties. From Lebanon Pike, Crittenden's force could literally see the unfolding engagement. Only Joe Wheeler's Confederate cavalry stood between them and Perryville. The soldiers in the ranks knew that if they marched forward they could flank the Confederate forces attacking McCook. As one of Crittenden's brigadiers later recorded, "One hour's work and Crittenden's two right divisions could have been in possession of Perryville, upon the transportation line of the army, and at once put a stop to the bloody fighting to our left."[25]

---

[22] John H. Tilford Diary, 7 October 1862, Filson Club; Sergeant E. Tarrent, *The Wild Riders of the First Kentucky Cavalry: A History of the Regiment in the Great War of the Rebellion, 1861–1865, Telling of its Organization; A Description of the Material of Which it was Composed; its Rapid and Severe Marches, Hard Service, and Fierce Conflicts on Many a Bloody Field* (Louisville: R. H. Carothers, 1894) 117–18; John Tuttle Diary, 7 October 1862, University of Kentucky; Van Horne, *Army of the Cumberland*, 146–47.

[23] Noe, *Perryville*, 166.

[24] John J. Hight, *History of the Fifty-eighth Regiment of Indiana Volunteers Infantry: Its Organization, Campaigns, and Battles from 1861–1865* (Princeton: Press of the Clarion, 1895) 101; John Tilford Diary, 8 October 1862, Filson Club.

[25] Hinman, *Sherman Brigade*, 294; Kerwood, *Annals of the Fifty Seventh Regiment*, 133; James A. Barnes, James R. Carnahan, and Thomas H. B. McCain, *The Eighty-sixth Indiana Volunteer Regiment: A Narrative of its Service in the Civil War of 1861–1865* (Crawfordsville IN: Journal Company, 1895) 64; Grose, *Story of the Marches*, 137–38.

As the cannonading began, Crittenden wrongly assumed that it was only an artillery duel and thus was not overly concerned. General Thomas persuaded him to send a staff officer to General Gilbert, commander of the III Corps, to check on the situation on his front. The messenger did not return with Gilbert's answer until about 4 o'clock. Gilbert's reply was almost whimsical when he said that "his children were all quiet and by sunset he would have them all in bed, nicely tucked in, as we used to do at Corinth." Amazingly, Gilbert did not recognize the hard fighting McCook's I Corps were waging in his immediate front.[26]

As the fighting continued, Crittenden and Thomas grew more concerned. Thomas awaited Buell's orders to advance, but such orders never came. The last thing Thomas wanted to do was give advice to Buell about how to fight a battle. Crittenden had the correct military instinct to know that his troops needed to head toward the sound of the guns. The Kentuckian asked for Thomas's permission to initiate a forward movement. Thomas refused, saying, "I know nothing of General Buell's plan and must wait here where he knows I am for orders." If Thomas had taken the initiative and simply informed Buell about what was happening at the front, Perryville could have been a great Union victory. However, Thomas refused to communicate with Buell and simply allowed matters to drift.[27]

Buell, who was still suffering from a riding accident that had occurred only days earlier, eventually learned of the battle in his front. At 4 o'clock he sent orders to Crittenden to hold a division in readiness to reinforce the center if necessary. Crittenden reconnoitered his front to see if the enemy had reinforced his left or was withdrawing; he then reported his findings to Buell. The commander did not send Crittenden any further orders until the battle was essentially over. As a result, the II Corps was only engaged in light skirmishing at Perryville. Crittenden's entire corps had only 12 casualties or less than a 1 percent casualty rate compared to McCook's I Corps, which suffered the loss of nearly a quarter of its men.[28]

---

[26] Noe, *Perryville*, 234–35; Daniel, *Days of Glory*, 154.

[27] Donn Piatt, *George H. Thomas: A Critical Biography* (Cincinnati: Robert Clarke, 1893) 175; Francis F. McKinney, *Education in Violence: The Life of George H. Thomas and the History of the Army of the Cumberland* (Detroit: Wayne State University Press, 1961) 164.

[28] Van Horne, *Army of the Cumberland*, 153; Noe, *Perryville*, 373, 375.

When Buell realized too late that he had missed the opportunity to strike a blow at Bragg's army, he ordered Gilbert and Crittenden's corps forward and planned to renew the battle the next day. As John Tuttle noted in his diary, the soldiers were on the alert throughout the night. Despite their efforts the Confederates slipped away; Bragg, not liking the numerical odds against him, decided to retreat during the night on 8 October. Buell ordered Crittenden to get his men moving after breakfast on 9 October, but Crittenden did not have his men ready. George Thomas criticized Crittenden for his tardiness while Crittenden blamed the signal corps for garbling Buell's orders. Whichever man was to blame, on the morning of October 9 the II Corps was not ready.[29]

Buell believed that Bragg and Edmund Kirby Smith's forces would link up and counterattack him, so he decided to pursue the Confederates very cautiously. Since Thomas still accompanied Crittenden's corps, he held de facto power of command over the operation. Once again, Crittenden awkwardly held the position of a commander without troops.[30]

The soldiers remembered the pursuit of Bragg's army as vividly as the battle of Perryville. The terrain over which the army marched was rough and barren, and many soldiers felt it was more difficult than the battle (the men had done very little at Perryville). One of Crittenden's subordinates remembered the march by saying, "This march, for suffering and hardship, was not surpassed by Valley Forge or Moscow. We had no tents or shelter, no axes to cut wood, was stinted in supplies and poorly clad, many without shoes and clothing about their feet. We marched through frozen slush, snow, and ice leaving bloody footprints wherever we trod." The difficulties of the march did not improve the disposition of the troops, and Buell, as always, bore the blame for their woes.[31]

On 10 October, Crittenden's corps finally advanced cautiously. The soldiers could hear the sound of skirmishing in the distance. However, a major engagement did not occur, so the pursuit continued. On 11 October, three brigades from Crittenden and McCook's corps made a

---

[29] *OR*, 1st ser., vol. 16, pt. 2:597; Noe, *Perryville*, 319; Van Horne, *Army of the Cumberland*, 153; John Tuttle Diary, 8 October 1862, University of Kentucky.

[30] Noe, *Perryville*, 330.

[31] Louis A. Simmons, *The History of the 84th Regt.*, 3 vols. (Macomb: Sampson Brothers, 1866) 1: 20; Grose, *Story of a Regiment*, 140.

reconnaissance in force; they discovered that Bragg was 3 miles south of Harrodsburg and retreating. The next day Crittenden received orders to Danville, where he arrived on 13 October. The following day the troops heard cannonading near Stanford. Wood's division engaged Bragg's rearguard near Stanford on 15 October, but Bragg continued to retreat. By 18 October, the II Corps had advanced through Crab Orchard and Mount Vernon. Skirmishing occurred almost daily throughout the region. Supplies ran low and the men referred to their base as Camp Starvation. Crittenden continued the chase to London and Manchester but then called off further pursuit because of the barren terrain. No longer the mere observer he had been at Perryville, Crittenden played a prominent role in the pursuit.[32]

According to Sam Starling, a relative of Crittenden's adjutant, the Union forces under Crittenden wanted to continue the pursuit. Starling believed that Buell's overly cautious stance hampered Crittenden's pursuit. Crittenden futilely paced back and forth at headquarters when he realized that the Union opportunity to capture Bragg's army had slipped through his fingers. However, victorious Civil War generals rarely pushed pursuits as aggressively as they could have, and complaints were more a boon to the press then a legitimate gripe. Because Crittenden favored an aggressive pursuit, he did not receive public criticism about the meager fruits of Buell's actions.[33]

As Crittenden approached eastern Kentucky, he detached Charles Cruft's 22nd Brigade to destroy the Goose Creek salt works near Manchester. The Confederates needed salt desperately, and the destruction of the works would hinder their war effort. Cruft, a decidedly capable brigade commander, destroyed about 30,000 bushels of salt and thoroughly dismantled the mining equipment in two days' work.[34]

---

[32] Van Horne, *Army of the Cumberland*, 157: Committee of the 73rd Indiana, *History of the Seventy-third Indiana Volunteers in the War of 1861–1865*, Washington, DC: Carnahan Press, 1909) 110, 111; *OR*, 1st ser., vol. 16, pt. 1:1136; John H. Tilford Diary, 10 October 1862, Filson Club.

[33] Sam Starling to Anna Irvin, 17 October 1862, Lewis-Starling Collection, Western Kentucky University; Daniel, *Days of Glory*, 171.

[34] Ebenezer Hannaford, *The Story of a Regiment: A History of the Campaigns, and Associations in the Field, of the Sixth Ohio Volunteer Infantry* (Cincinnati: Ebenezer

Ironically, the Goose Creek salt works, which were owned by Union army officer T. T. Garrard, were located in the heart of Kentucky Unionist territory. Accordingly, Crittenden requested prompt compensation to Garrard and the other owners. The Louisville *Daily Journal* made a similar appeal. The ever politically sensitive Crittenden had no desire to create enemies he would have to contend with after the war.[35]

As the II Corps approached the Appalachian Mountains, Buell ordered a change of plan. The Union forces switched from pursuing Bragg's retreating army to marching back to Nashville, the base for a future move toward Chattanooga. By 23 October Crittenden's forces had retreated to Crab Orchard and Stanford. From there they moved west, arriving at Columbia on 25 October. They reached Edmonton on October 30, Glasgow on 1 November, Scottsville on 5 November, Gallatin on 8 November, and the Cumberland River by 10 November. Union troops entered Nashville on 19 November and began to prepare for their next campaign. As the troops marched toward Nashville, Confederate cavalry aggressively moved to capture Union stragglers. There horsemen became such a problem that Crittenden had to use Union cavalry to prod the stragglers along. Likewise, there were constant rumors of an attack. Sometimes the attacker was purported to be John Hunt Morgan and other times Edmund Kirby Smith or some other Confederate commander. Such rumors kept the anxiety level high.[36]

Throughout the pursuit, several Kentuckians in Buell's army began to notice a change in the attitude of many of the Midwestern soldiers. As Sam Starling noted, "[The Midwesterners] appear to believe that there are no loyal men in our state, that they all are rebels & that they should be so treated." As Kentucky and Kentuckians fell increasingly out of favor with Federal authorities, the political influence of generals like Crittenden waned. Amid this change of public opinion within the army and the

---

Hannaford, 1868) 377; Anonymous, *Louisville Daily Journal,* (1 November 1862): 1; *OR,* 1st ser., vol. 16, pt. 1:1149.

[35] Anonymous, *Louisville Daily Journal,* (1 November 1862): 1; *OR,* 1st ser., vol. 16, pt. 1:1149.

[36] Committee of the 73rd Indiana, *History of the 73rd Indiana,* 111–14; Hinman, *Sherman Brigade,* 316; John H. Tilford Diary, 10 November 1862 and 12 November 1862, Filson Club; Barnes et al., *Eighty-sixth Indiana,* 89.

nation as a whole, Crittenden lost a great deal of political influence. He would have to rely on his military ability for promotion, and sadly he did not possess enough of that valuable quality.[37]

With the battle of Perryville over, recriminations began. Many soldiers in Crittenden's corps disgustedly recorded their commander's failure to order them into the fray. One historian of the 8th Kentucky wrote that "the battle raged indecisively with only a portion of our forces engaged, and our whole corps ready...like eager greyhounds at the leash, praying and pleading to be led on to support our brave battling comrades. But no orders came." Some of the troops thought the generals really did not have the heart to fight the enemy. Many Ohio regiments recorded similar sentiments. There must be treachery in the high command, they thought, blaming Buell for not issuing the appropriate orders and McCook for failing to contact both Buell and the other corps commanders concerning the major Confederate assault on his lines. The soldiers believed that if George Thomas or even Crittenden had been in charge at Perryville, the battle would have been much more advantageous to the Union cause.[38]

Crittenden, however, also came under attack in the press. One story suggested that McCook had requested aid from Crittenden early in the battle but had been denied. Crittenden insisted that he had never received such a request, and McCook and the press did not push the claim. After the battle of Perryville, most believed that Crittenden desired to attack but that others held him back. The troops and the public forgave Crittenden for the failure to act on his own initiative at Perryville.[39]

Not everyone was satisfied with Crittenden's performance. John Beatty, one of Crittenden's subordinates, would later note that he believed Crittenden and others had received promotions for "inconsiderable service in engagements that have long since been forgotten by the public. These

---

[37] Sam Starling to Anna Irwin, 30 October 1862, Lewis-Starling Collection, Western Kentucky University.

[38] Wright, *History of the Eighth Regiment Kentucky*, 100, 101; Whitelaw Reid, *Ohio in the War: Her Statesmen, Her Generals, and Soldiers*, 2 vols. (Cincinnati: Moore, Wilstach & Baldwin, 1868) 2:354, 384, 501; William Ross Hartpence, *History of the Fifty-first Indiana Veteran Volunteer Infantry: A Narrative of its Organization, Marches, Battles, and Other Experiences in Camp and Prison, from 1861 to 1866* (Cincinnati: Robert Clarke, 1894) 88.

[39] Noe, ed., *Southern Boy in Blue*, 103; Daniel, *Days of Glory*, 174.

promotions were not made for the benefit of the service, but for the political advancement of the men who caused them to be made." Beatty also expressed concern over the "petty jealousies existing between the commanders of different army corps and divisions." Many officers agreed that Crittenden's promotion to a level exceeding his ability sparked professional jealousy and hurt army morale. As Crittenden's friend Sam Starling pointed out, around Crittenden or any general for that matter were "flunkeys," individuals who praised the commander in the hopes of earning some preferment or favor. Starling probably worried how Crittenden might respond to these flatterers. Crittenden's affable personality helped ease tension over promotions and even covered some of his military weaknesses. Yet the heat of combat burns away the glitter of personality, leaving only the essence of ability under extreme stress. In such a vortex, Crittenden was found lacking.[40]

The political current claimed Buell before it claimed Crittenden. After the Battle of Perryville, even Kentucky generals like Crittenden, who had long been Buell's primary source of support, had come to realize that Buell had to go. In a story run by the New York *Times*, Crittenden referred to Buell as a "hopeless case." Buell's poor performance at the Battle of Perryville and his slow pursuit of the enemy afterward had sealed his fate. In late November, William S. Rosecrans replaced Buell as commander of the army.[41]

In the Kentucky campaign Thomas Crittenden received incredible opportunities. Through the death of a friend, he gained promotion to corps command. Even more incredibly, at Perryville he had the opportunity to deliver a decisive flank attack. He sensed the opportunity, but he did not receive the orders to make the advance.

Meanwhile a more significant problem had developed. West Pointers sensed Crittenden's mediocre military skills and tended to bypass him in serious military discussions. Buell and Thomas had both ignored Critten-den in issuing orders at different times during the campaign. Such neglect

---

[40] John Beatty, *The Citizen-Soldier; or Memoirs of a Volunteer* (Cincinnati: Wilstach, Baldwin & Co., 1879) 196, 183; Sam Starling to Irvin, 17 October 1862Lewis-Starling Collection, Western Kentucky University, Bowling Green.

[41] Daniel, *Days of Glory*, 174.

further weakened Crittenden's already fragile self-confidence. Crittenden had the correct military instinct at Perryville—better than many West Pointers—but if he was ever going to be a good corps commander he needed to develop a surer sense of his own judgment. Perhaps a new commander would enhance this maturing process. Tennessee battlefields had been kind to Crittenden in the past and they might continue to do so in the future.

8

Stones River:

Glittering Moment

The removal of Don Carlos Buell created new opportunities for Thomas Crittenden and the Union army. The Kentuckian would have to adjust to a new commander with a very different personality and approach to command. Buell was aloof while Rosecrans had a gregarious personality. Buell kept his emotions to himself while Rosecrans freely exploded. Buell projected an aura of calm deliberateness while Rosecrans projected an energetic aura that became almost erratic under pressure.

Most troops responded favorably to the announcement of Rosecrans's appointment. Buell had sunk to such a nadir of unpopularity that almost anyone would have been more acceptable. Rosecrans brought with him a brilliant record in West Virginia and Mississippi, and many soldiers hoped he would lead them to a resounding victory. As usual, the appointment involved politics. Secretary of War Stanton favored offering the position to George H. Thomas again, but Secretary of Treasury Chase favored Rosecrans. Lincoln supposedly said, "Let the Virginian wait." Some still distrusted Thomas's Southern heritage, but the more telling problem was that Thomas had turned down the position only a month earlier.[1]

Almost as soon as he took command Rosecrans had to deal with some delicate issues concerning rank. George H. Thomas, who already resented having not received the offer of command, only grew more resentful because his date of rank predated that of Rosecrans. Federal authorities changed the dating of Rosecrans's rank to meet the objection, and

---

[1] John H. Tilford Diary, 2 December 1862, Filson Club, Louisville; Donn Piatt, *General George H. Thomas: A Critical Biography* (Cincinnati: Robert Clarke, 1893) 198, 199, 201.

Rosecrans made an effort to mollify Thomas's hurt feelings. They had been friends before the war, and Rosecrans gave Thomas the option of serving as second in command or commanding the largest wing of the army. Thomas, who had just suffered through a nightmare as Buell's second in command, chose the position of wing commander. Interestingly, only weeks before Rosecrans received his promotion, he had complained bitterly to his wife that civilians such as Thomas Crittenden received promotions over him. Now that he was Crittenden's superior, his resentment seemed to disappear. Rosecrans personally liked Crittenden but he did not respect his military judgment, as events would eventually prove.[2]

The arrival of Crittenden's corps at Nashville on 18 November 1862 relieved the Nashville garrison of the threat of immediate attack. Smith's division remained at Glasgow until Hazen's brigade could rejoin it after the operation at the Goose Creek salt works. The brigade rejoined the division on 3 November. By 14 November, Smith's division had caught up with the other two divisions at Silver Springs.[3]

Rosecrans set about immediately reorganizing his force. He divided it into the left wing under Crittenden, the center under George H. Thomas, and the right under A. M. McCook. Surprisingly, this force had less West Point domination than any Union army. Crittenden's lack of formal military training did not hurt him at this point in his career.[4]

Crittenden's left wing consisted of Wood's 1st Division comprised of brigades under Milo Hascall, George D. Wagner, and Charles Harker. Harker and Hascall were West Point graduates. Hascall's men described him as "a thorough disciplinarian and a terror to evil doers." The division would perform admirably in the coming campaign.[5]

---

[2] William H. Lamers, *The Edge of Glory: A Biography of William S. Rosecrans* (New York: Harcourt Brace & World, 1961) 75, 182, 183.

[3] Thomas Van Horne, *The Army of the Cumberland* (1875; repr., New York: Konecky & Konecky, 1966) 163, 164, 166

[4] Ibid., 165; Larry J. Daniel, *Days of Glory: The Army of the Cumberland, 1861–1865* (Baton Rouge: Louisiana State University Press, 2004) 193, 194.

[5] Peter Cozzens, *The Battles of Stones River: No Better Place to Die* (Urbana: University of Illinois Press, 1990) 225, 226; Mark M. Boatner II, *The Civil War Dictionary* (New York: David McKay Company, 1959) 375, 383, 883; John J. Hight, *History of the Fifty-eighth Regiment of Indiana Volunteers Infantry: Its Organization, Campaigns, and Battles from 1861–1865* (Princeton: Press of the Clarion, 1895) 49.

John M. Palmer now led the 2nd Division. Sooy Smith had requested a transfer to Grant's army to serve as an engineer. Smith's troops did not bemoan the departure because they had never liked him to begin with. Palmer, an Illinois politician, had no formal military training and detested West Pointers. Although at times he could be difficult to work with, he played an integral part in the coming campaigns. Charles Cruft, William B. Hazen, and William Grose led Palmer's brigades. Cruft and Grose were civilians but they were very capable. Hazen, a West Pointer, was possibly the most talented brigade commander in the army. Palmer described Hazen as "skillful beyond question" though "vain and selfish." The division commander also noted that "It was difficult for those associated with him constantly to do justice to his merits." One regimental historian recalled that Hazen was "an officer qualified in every way for the command assigned him," while another remembered Hazen as the man who turned raw recruits into soldiers by driving his men hard. The talented commander's acerbic personality prevented him from ever receiving the promotions due his remarkable ability.[6]

Horatio Van Cleve led the 3rd Division. An older man with little military ability, he never distinguished himself. Samuel Beatty, James Fyffe, and Samuel Price led his brigades. Fyffe, who was popular with his men, was described as "past the meridian of life but [he] has a heart as young as any boy in the army." Samuel Beatty, on the other hand, had the most ability of the brigade commanders.[7]

Not everyone was pleased with this arrangement. Whitelaw Reid criticized Rosecrans for giving command to two wings of the army to

---

[6] Cozzens, *Battles of Stones River*, 225, 226; Louis A. Simmons, *The History of the 84th Regt.*, 3 vols. (Macomb: Sampson Brothers, 1866) 1: 24; Ebenezer Hannaford, *The Story of a Regiment: A History of the Campaigns, and Associations in the Field, of the Sixth Ohio Volunteer Infantry* (Cincinnati: Ebenezer Hannaford, 1868) 383; John M. Palmer, *Personal Recollections of John Palmer: The Story of an Ernest Life* (Cincinnati: Robert Clarke, 1901) 140; G. W. Lewis, *The Campaigns of the 124th Ohio Volunteer Infantry, with Roster and Roll of Honor* (Akron: Werner Company, 1894) 30; Robert L. Kimberly and Ephraim S. Holloway, *The Forty-first Ohio Veteran Volunteer Infantry in the War of the Rebellion, 1861–1865* (Cleveland: W. R. Smellie, 1897) 9.

[7] Cozzens, *Battles of Stones River*, 225, 226; Hight, *History of the Fifty-eighth Regiment*, 49.

soldiers "scarcely equal to the command of divisions, excepting under the eye of a superior officer who could do their thinking for them."[8]

The removal of Buell in the west and McClellan in the east had clearly shown that Northern public opinion had little patience with slowness or lack of results. The public expected much of their generals, and with limited abilities Crittenden would have a difficult time meeting those expectations. The Federal reverses in Virginia and Mississippi only deepened Crittenden's awareness of the public's high expectations. Rosecrans's army knew that they desperately needed a victory the next time they fought. The opportunity did not take long to materialize.[9]

While the Federals planned for the coming campaign in Nashville, the Confederates made similar plans at Murfreesboro, only 30 miles away. On 9 December 1862, Crittenden sent the 3rd Brigade from Van Cleve's division toward Murfreesboro to gather forage for the army and ascertain Confederate strength. The brigade ran into Wheeler's Confederate cavalry, and after a sharp skirmish the group marched back to Nashville some thirty-five men short.[10]

A general advance began on December 26 when the Federal columns began marching out of Nashville. Crittenden's corps marched along the Murfreesboro Pike with Palmer's division in the lead. As one soldier remembered, the men gave a cheer when the army began to move. The inactivity of the Buell era had ended, and the opportunity to deliver a blow against the enemy had arrived. By nightfall, Crittenden's corps had arrived approximately 4 miles north of La Vergne. Along the way there had been consistent light skirmishing.[11]

---

[8] Lamers, *Edge of Glory*, 185.

[9] John Beatty, *The Citizen-Soldier; or Memoirs of a Volunteer* (Cincinnati: Wilstach, Baldwin & Co., 1879) 189, 193, 194.

[10] Van Horne, *Army of the Cumberland*, 170.

[11] US War Department, comp., *The War of the Rebellion: A Compilation of the Official Records of the Union and Confederate Armies*, 128 vols. (Washington, DC: Government Printing Office, 1880–1901) 1st ser., vol. 20, pt. 2:24–25; Van Horne, *Army of the Cumberland*, 174–76; Committee of the Seventy-ninth Indiana. *History of the Seventy-ninth Regiment Indiana Volunteer Infantry in the Civil War of Eighteen Sixty-one in the United States.* (Indianapolis: Hollenbeck Press, 1899): 57; John H. Tilford Diary, 26 December 1862, Filson Club.

A dense, heavy fog limited visibility on 27 December and the march was not resumed until mid-day, with Wood in the advance position. Haskell's brigade entered La Vergne and captured a bridge over Stewart's Creek. Union soldiers found the region devastated. Confederate soldiers had ransacked and burned houses, so little remained for the Union soldiers to take. Hazen also captured a bridge east of Symrna. That night Wood and Palmer's divisions bivouacked south of Stewart's Creek and Van Cleve's division north of the creek.[12]

On Sunday, 28 December, the army rested. Rosecrans, a deeply religious man, did not want to violate the Sabbath. The delay gave Bragg more time to collect his forces for the coming battle. Although several Union officers thought the Confederates might attack the left wing while divided by Stewart's Creek, such an event did not occur.[13]

The advance continued the next day along the Murfreesboro Pike. Crittenden advanced Wood's division on the east side of the pike with Wagner's brigade in the lead. Meanwhile Palmer's division marched on the west side of the pike with Grose's brigade in the lead. By 3:00 P.M. the men had come within 2 1/2 miles of Murfreesboro and within about 700 yards of Rebel lines. At this point Wood and Palmer informed Crittenden of the situation at their front.[14]

At about this time Crittenden received orders from Rosecrans to occupy Murfreesboro. False rumors of a Confederate abandonment of the town had reached Union headquarters from a report by cavalry commander David Stanley, and Rosecrans wanted to follow up his perceived advantage quickly. Thus, Crittenden ordered Wood and Palmer to advance and occupy the town, but they protested that Confederate forces still occupied Murfreesboro in force. Since Rosecrans's order had not arrived until almost dusk, Wood argued that moving over unknown ground at dark against an entrenched enemy would result in heavy casualties. He pleaded for a delay until daylight. Crittenden refused, probably fearing Rosecrans's wrath if he did not obey orders. Wood came back a short time later with Palmer in

[12] *OR*, 1st ser., vol. 20, pt. 2:247; Van Horne, *Army of the Cumberland*, 177; John H. Tilford Diary, 27 December 1862, Filson Club.

[13] Van Horne, *Army of the Cumberland*, 177; Daniel, *Days of Glory*, 202.

[14] Van Horne, *Army of the Cumberland*, 178; Barnes, *Eighty-sixth Regiment*, 97, 98.

tow. He suggested a least a suspension of orders for an hour in order to receive a clarification from Rosecrans. The division commanders thought that if Rosecrans realized the Confederates had not left Murfreesboro, he would suspend the order.[15]

While Crittenden always wanted to impress and please his superiors he also valued good relations with his subordinates, so he compromised. Wood continued to prepare for an attack while Crittenden awaited clarification from Rosecrans. Fortunately Rosecrans happened by Crittenden's headquarters and, hearing of the dilemma, suspended the order. Unfortunately it was too late for Harker's brigade, which had already begun to move and had suffered a few casualties. Pulling back the troops averted an even greater calamity.[16]

This small incident foreshadowed several dilemmas that significantly impacted the army's future. According to one caustic observer, Rosecrans did not understand conditions on the front. He issued orders based on unrealistic evaluations of the situation. At the same time, the incident showed Crittenden's lack of self-confidence and his inability to make independent decisions. Crittenden would have blindly obeyed the order even if it meant disaster for his divisions. In Crittenden's desire to please superiors, he did not exercise independent judgment. He did not trust his own military instincts, and Wood's direct personality did little to encourage any self-confidence. Corps command required discernment and a degree of independent thinking. Crittenden did not possess either of these qualities.[17]

The Union forces spent 30 December preparing for the coming battle. Rosecrans planned to hold the Confederates with his right wing under McCook and attack with Crittenden's left wing, then flank the Confederate position. Coincidentally, this was also Bragg's plan. The general who opened the battle would have a decided advantage. Unfortunately for Crittenden and the Federals, they were too late. An omen

---

[15] *OR,* 1st ser., vol. 20, pt. 1:448, 449; Van Horne, *Army of the Cumberland,* 178; Palmer, *Personal Recollections,* 143; Kerwood, *Annals of the Fifty-seventh Regiment,* 151; Daniel, *Days of Glory,* 204.

[16] *OR,* 1st ser., vol. 20, pt. 1:448, 449; Daniel, *Days of Glory,* 204.

[17] William F. G. Shanks, *Personal Recollections of Distinguished Generals* (New York: Harper & Brothers, 1866) 148.

of the hard fighting ahead, one of Crittenden's staff died from an exploding shell near the Kentuckian's headquarters. Over the next few days Crittenden would witness many more deaths.[18]

As 31 December dawned, the Confederates attacked McCook's right wing and broke the division of Richard Johnson. Later, Jefferson C. Davis's division and that of Phillip Sheridan also retreated. Rosecrans had to alter his plans quickly and concentrate on saving his army from destruction.

Crittenden, unaware of the disaster on the right wing, had begun to implement his march according to the original plan. By 8:00 A.M., Van Cleve's division had crossed Stones River and was preparing to attack. Wood's division readied to follow suit. Some of Wood's staff noticed that the sound of battle was moving too rapidly and toward the Union rear. They correctly feared that something was amiss. As news of the disaster on the right wing spread, orders arrived for Crittenden to suspend his forward movement and recall Van Cleve's division from across the river. All of Crittenden's corps moved to join Thomas's corps and make a determined stand against the Confederate onslaught.[19]

After learning of the disaster on McCook's front, Rosecrans sent Fyffe's brigade from Van Cleve's division to the rear on the Nashville Road to guard the wagons. The commander then sent Beatty's brigade to the right to link up with L. H. Rousseau's division in Thomas's corps. Shortly thereafter, Rosecrans also sent Harker's brigade from Wood's division. Next he ordered Price's brigade of Van Cleve's division to hold the ford over Stones River; shortly thereafter he added Hascall's brigade from Wood's division. These two brigades would form a type of mobile reserve force in case of emergency—and it looked as if emergencies would appear shortly on this side of the battlefield.[20]

Crittenden soon realized that Rosecrans's behavior on the battlefield differed sharply from Buell's. Rosecrans constantly interjected himself into

[18] Horne, *Army of the Cumberland*, 180, 183; Kenneth W. Noe, ed., *A Southern Boy in Blue: The Memoir of Marcus Woodcock, 9th Kentucky Infantry, U.S.A.* (Knoxville: University of Tennessee Press, 1996) 120.

[19] *OR*, 1st ser., vol. 20, pt. 1:467; Van Horne, *Army of the Cumberland*, 190–91; Daniel, *Days of Glory*, 212.

[20] *OR*, 1st ser., vol. 20, pt. 1:193; Van Horne, *Army of the Cumberland*, 191–93.

command decisions normally made at the corps or division level. At this point in the battle, Crittenden was almost a bystander in the command of his own corps.

By 9:00 A.M. the divisions of Sheridan and Negley had collapsed, and the Confederates seemed on the verge of gaining the Union rear. At this critical moment Palmer's division arrived. Grose and Hazen's brigades, aided by twenty cannon, delivered a galling fire that decimated the advancing Confederates. Their efforts saved the Union position.[21]

Both sides continued to feed more troops into the vortex. Van Cleve had suffered a leg wound and Beatty now commanded the division. Fyffe's brigade of Van Cleve's division and Harker's brigade of Wood's division endured a heavy attack in the late morning. A patchwork line reinforced by artillery held against the assault. The Confederate assault had finally run out of steam. Among Crittenden's troops, Van Cleve's division, particularly Fyffe's brigade, had suffered the most in the morning's fight.[22]

While intense fighting raged on the Union right, the Union center and left made several critical adjustments. George Thomas established a new Union line with his own troops and those of Crittenden. Throughout the morning, Crittenden had effectively moved Palmer and Wood's divisions along with part of Van Cleve's to the center. This movement of troops would be critical during the afternoon fighting. The construction of a new line also gave the Union commander a chance to reform McCook's shattered units. Thomas and Rosecrans received praise for their foresight in strengthening the center, but without Crittenden's efficient movement of the troops their efforts would have been in vain. [23]

While Confederates broke Union lines on the right, they did little on the Union left. John C. Breckinridge, Crittenden's childhood friend, did not want to attack the strong flanking force under Crittenden and only light skirmishing occurred. A strong simultaneous Confederate attack on the Union left could fold the Union up and lead to a complete Union disaster. Apparently, Crittenden projected a sufficient image of strength so that the

---

[21] *OR*, 1st ser., vol. 20, pt. 1:405, 565, 569–72; Van Horne, *Army of the Cumberland*, 194

[22] *OR*, 1st ser., vol. 20, pt. 1:502–03, 574, 597–98; Van Horne, *Army of the Cumberland*, 197.

[23] Van Horne, *Army of the Cumberland*, 196.

Confederate attack did not come until late on the first day, long after the moment of opportunity had passed. Breckinridge's men would pay the price for their delay on the afternoon of the battle's third day.[24]

The key to the Union position that afternoon was a cluster of cedars known as the Round Forest. Hazen's brigade held the position supported by Palmer's other brigades and Wood's division. Rosecrans gave the defense of the Round Forest his "closest attention," sparing no effort or soldier in its defense. Hazen would later recall that Crittenden recognized the importance of the Round Forest and agreed with him that it was necessary to hold the position at all costs. During the afternoon Hazen and his fellow commanders repelled repeated Confederate attacks by Polk's corps. Hazen thereby earned his reputation as the finest brigade commander in the Army of the Cumberland. Bragg finally grew frustrated and around 4:00 P.M. he ordered Breckinridge to cross Stones River and attack the Round Forrest. Breckinridge attacked with the brigades of Adams and Jackson, while Crittenden countered with Wagner and Hascall's brigades in defense. Breckinridge then sent in Palmer and Preston's brigade but they suffered a similar fate. The Confederate assault failed with heavy losses. By nightfall the fighting ceased and both armies had to evaluate their positions.[25]

Although the fighting had ended, the suffering had only begun. One surgeon remembered that wounded soldiers came in as quickly as he could dress wounds. That night's hard freeze did nothing to ease the soldiers' pain or improve their disposition. One Union soldier summed up the battle concisely when he said, "The fight was a hard one and nothing gained on either side." Whichever commander decided to pull his troop back first would concede victory to the other army.[26]

Crittenden could feel proud of his corps after the first day of battle. They had given up little or no ground, and they had inflicted heavy losses on the enemy when attacked. The left wing divisions had been in the thick

---

[24] Ibid., 196.

[25] Van Horne, *Army of the Cumberland*, 196–97; William B. Hazen, *A Narrative of Military Service* (Boston: Ticknor & Comp., 1885) 78.

[26] John H. Tilford Diary, 31 December 1862, Filson Club.

of the fight from the late morning on and had performed admirably. Crittenden and his troops definitely did not feel defeated.[27]

During the night, Rosecrans called a council of war. During the meeting Crittenden openly opposed the idea of retreat, pointing out that a Union withdrawal would discourage the men. He optimistically reported, "My corps is not whipped and we must not fall back." Crittenden also believed that Bragg's army had been more severely crippled by the battle. One regimental history records Crittenden as saying, "We may be able yet to whip the enemy here." The battle could still be won.[28]

Just before daylight on 1 January 1863, Crittenden pulled his lines back about 500 yards to higher ground, yielding the hotly contested territory of the Round Forest. Wood, who had been wounded the previous day, turned his division over to Hascall. As dawn approached, both sides wondered if the enemy would still be in their front. Bragg had expected a Union retreat during the night. Since Union forces had not retreated, he did not know what to do next. [29]

As the second day dawned, Rosecrans also did not quite know what to do. As a result, the armies spent most of the day warily awaiting orders. Lines were strengthened and the wounded tended to as much as conditions allowed. Artillery exchanged fire, but no general assault occurred. Bragg hoped the Federals would realize that they had lost the battle and simply retreat to Nashville. Rosecrans, like Grant at Shiloh, resolutely declined to move. The most significant Federal move took place in the late afternoon when Crittenden moved Van Cleve's division to the east side of Stones River.[30]

---

[27] Ibid., 199.

[28] Thomas Van Horne, The *Life of Major General George H. Thomas* (New York: Charles Scribner's Sons, 1882) 97; Thomas L. Crittenden "The Union Left at Stone's River," in *Battles and Leaders of the Civil War*, 4 vols., ed. Richard U. Johnson and Clarence C. Buel (1887; repr., New York, 1956) 3:633; Piatt, *General George Thomas*, 211; Thomas J. Wright, *History of the Eighth Regiment Kentucky Volunteer Infantry During its Three Years Campaigns, Embracing Organization, Marches, Skirmishes and Battles of the Command with Much of the History of the Old Reliable Third Brigade Commanded by Hon. Stanley Matthews and Containing Many Interesting and Amusing Incidents of Army Life* (St. Joseph: St. Joseph Steam Printing, 1880) 127.

[29] Van Horne, *Army of the Cumberland*, 201–202.

[30] *OR*, 1st ser., vol. 20, pt. 1:195; Van Horne, *Army of the Cumberland*, 202.

The next day Bragg tried to dislodge Van Cleve's division, now commanded by Samuel Beatty, on the left flank of the Union line with an attack by Breckinridge's troops. Beatty's flank was in the air and invited attack. From the high ground near Stones River, Confederate artillery could enfilade the Federal position near the Round Forest. Bragg knew he needed the ground Van Cleve's troops occupied. Beatty and his brigade commanders realized that they occupied a hazardous position and requested that Crittenden provide support. Crittenden promised the cover of his guns and more troops. However, he never attended to the matter.[31]

The terrain did not encourage such an attack. The open area offered no cover for the attacking troops and gave the Federals advance notice of the forthcoming assault. The high ground near the river provided a good defensive position. Breckinridge viewed the attack as a mistake. As Breckinridge's troops rolled forward the unsupported troops of Van Cleve's division, the Federals had to pull back across Stones River.[32]

Foreseeing the danger, Crittenden had ordered his chief of artillery, John Mendenhall, to help defend Beatty's position. The artillerist performed admirably, massing over 50 guns on a knoll overlooking the point of attack. As the guns opened fire they tore huge gaps in the Confederate line, stopping the assault. This was the most decisive use of artillery the western theatre witnessed during the war. As Crittenden later reported, "From a rapid advance they broke at once into a rapid retreat."[33]

After the dramatic failure of Breckinridge's attack, Union soldiers began an unauthorized counterattack to drive in the Confederate right. Elements of Hazen, Harker, and Grose's brigades were among those pursuing Federals. Only nightfall and a driving rain prevented the Federals from doing more damage to the defeated Confederates. The battle was over. Braxton Bragg reluctantly admitted defeat and retreated.[34]

---

[31] Ibid., 203–04; Daniel, *Days of Glory*, 220; *OR*, 1st ser., vol. 20, pt. 1:587.

[32] *OR*, 1st ser., vol. 20, pt. 1:587.

[33] Van Horne, *Army of the Cumberland*, 204; Crittenden, "Union Left at Stones River," in *Battles and Leaders*, 3:633; *OR*, 1st ser., vol. 20, pt. 1:451, 455–459.

[34] Van Horne, *Army of the Cumberland*, 204–205; Committee of the 73rd Indiana. *History of the Seventy-third Indiana Volunteers in the War of 1861–1865*. Washington, DC: Carnahan Press, 1909.; *OR*, 1st ser., vol. 20, pt. 1:195.

The carnage had been immense. One surgeon noted that the battle was "terrible, terrific, and beyond all description." The dazed surgeon added that he had operated on the wounded until 2:00 A.M. Another soldier described the Federal counterattack shortly before nightfall as "the most splendid sight." According to one estimate, Crittenden's corps numbered 12,909 men at Stones River and sustained losses of 650 killed, 3,006 wounded, and 873 missing for a total of 4,529 losses or about 34 percent. It would take time for the Army of the Cumberland to recover.[35]

After the guns fell silent, the Army of the Cumberland and the Northern public could evaluate its performance. Coming after Federal disasters in Virginia and Mississippi, the victory received substantial coverage in the Northern press. Since Crittenden and his troops had performed well in the engagement, the Kentuckian basked in the warm glow of positive public opinion. Soldiers also praised his conduct. Albert Pirtle noted approvingly that Crittenden's corps had been but slightly disorganized throughout the engagement, unlike the chaotic behavior of McCook's soldiers. Another said, "The gallant Crittenden, without betraying the least emotion of excitement, rode among with apparently as much composure as if he was in the midst of a gay procession." Rosecrans also praised his left wing commander: "His heart is that of a true soldier and patriot, and his gallantry, often attested by his companions in arms in other fields, has been witnessed many times in this army, long before I had the honor to command it." The press joined in the praise. The Louisville *Daily Journal* credited the victory to the performance of the "lion-hearted" Crittenden. That the Kentucky press praised Crittenden came as no surprise, but it was not alone. Even twenty years later, after his fall at Chickamauga, the Washington *Post* conceded that the stand of Crittenden's

---

[35] John H. Tilford Diary, 2 January 1863, Filson Club; Albert Pirtle to mother, 4 February 1863, Alfred Pirtle Letters, Filson Club; William F. Fox, *Regimental Losses in the American Civil War, 1861–1865: A Treatise on the Extent and Nature of the Mortuary Losses in the Union regiments, with full and Exhaustive Statistics compiled from the Official Records on file in the State Military Bureaus and at Washington* (Albany: Albany Publishing Company, 1889) 105.

troops at the Round Forest saved the Union army that day. By almost any standard Crittenden had performed well at Stones River.[36]

A few clouds appeared on the horizon, however. Some officers, including Crittenden, disliked Rosecrans's impulsiveness in the heat of battle. Officers complained that "they could not turn their backs on their commands without his ordering a portion of them away." This tendency did nothing to help Crittenden's self-confidence.[37]

Crittenden would also later note that, while Rosecrans had many admirable traits as a commander, his tendency to give too many orders in the heat of battle caused confusion. Others more pointedly noted that the excited general stuttered and became almost incoherent to those around him. The situation created an opportunity for disaster.[38]

With the battle over, the commanders and men relieved stress in any manner they could. On 5 January, Crittenden and several other generals found some alcohol and became drunk. One disgusted general described McCook, Rousseau, and Crittenden as singing "Mary had a Little Lamb," forgetting the horrors of the recent battle. According to the observer, Crittenden was the merriest of the group. Fortunately Crittenden, unlike his elder brother, waited until after the battle to get drunk. Nothing ever came of the incident and Crittenden continued in his command.[39]

Stones River was the highlight of Crittenden's Civil War. On the first day of battle he had efficiently wheeled his corps around to meet the Confederate onslaught. Crittenden's troops had steadfastly held the Round Forest that long, tense afternoon. While others received most of the credit for the troops' performance that fateful day, Crittenden had also played a crucial role. He efficiently moved his troops and had exhibited the intangible strength of character to stubbornly refuse to yield ground. His superiors, his subordinates, and his soldiers all noted his presence and

---

[36] "Stones River Sketch," Alfred Pirtle Writings, Filson Club; Noe, ed., *Southern Boy in Blue*, 123; Francis Hudson Oxx, *The Kentucky Crittenden: The History of a Family Including Genealogy of Descendent in Both Male and Female Lives, Biographical Sketches of its Members, and Their Descent from Other Colonial Lives* (n.p., 1940) 135; Anonymous, *Louisville Daily Journal*, (29 January 1863): 2; Hazen, *Narrative*, x.

[37] Daniel, *Days of Glory*, 217; *OR*, 1st ser., vol. 16, pt. 1:578.

[38] Cozzens, *Battles of Stones River*, 16–17.

[39] Beatty, *Citizen-Soldier*, 211.

courage during those eventful hours. On the third day of battle, Crittenden's foresight in ordering a concentration of artillery overlooking the attack point was worthy of any West Pointer. Had Crittenden resigned his commission at this juncture, he would be remembered as one of the more successful political appointees in the Union army.

9

The Calm before the Storm

After the bloody battle at Stones River, the Federal army spent months recovering and planning for the next campaign. This time of relative quiet was like the calm before a violent storm. Since most remember stormy times more vividly than quiet times, this period of the war has sparked little interest from historians. During this time, Crittenden had an opportunity to develop his administrative skills as a corps commander. He could have left the military and entered politics. Such a move at this point could have enhanced Crittenden's reputation.

The retreat of Bragg pleased the Federals and cemented Rosecrans's reputation among the officers and men of the army. As the days, weeks, and even months passed in relative inactivity, however, problems began to arise. Rosecrans's volatile temper and his sometimes erratic behavior began to create tension among some of the officers. Crittenden liked Rosecrans and got along with him well, but some of Crittenden's subordinates felt differently. John Palmer, who detested West Pointers in general, disliked Rosecrans's official report of the Battle of Stones River. Likewise, John Beatty felt insulted by the commanding general, and Milo Hascall could not stand Rosecrans at all. Others outside of Crittenden's corps—such as A. M. McCook, who disliked the treatment he had received in the official battle report, and L. H. Rousseau, who desired corps command—also had gripes with the commanding general. It took all of Crittenden's affability and charm to keep his disgruntled officers from creating unbearable tension when dealing with Rosecrans. A good politician, Crittenden performed the task well.[1]

As time passed, some Federals began to grow impatient with the inactivity. Slowness had cost Buell his command and in 1863 it began to dampen enthusiasm for Rosecrans. After the collision at Stones River,

---

[1] Larry J. Daniel, *Days of Glory: The Army of the Cumberland, 1861–1865* (Baton Rouge: Louisiana State University Press, 2004) 246–48.

Rosecrans wanted to proceed with caution. One soldier who happened to observe Rosecrans playing chess with Crittenden caustically noted, "I don't suppose he will be looking for Bragg very soon." By springtime, the soldiers were anxious to break the monotony of camp life. They felt ready to take on the enemy even if their generals did not.[2]

As the quiet days passed, the Federals also had time to reflect upon the conduct of their generals during previous campaigns. One newspaper reported that many generals did not know their job and that complacency in high command was a common problem. As one soldier noted, "Our generals are most of them unacquainted with the details of the business of an army, however well they may know how to fight it." General McCook received the bulk of the soldiers' and reporters' criticism. Surprised at both Perryville and Stones River, the critics insisted that he should have known better. John Beatty described McCook as a "chucklehead" who was "very green or deficient in the upper story." McCook's men disliked him as well. The situation was different for Crittenden, whose pleasant personality ameliorated criticisms. During these quiet days, Crittenden suffered relatively little harsh criticism.[3]

Rosecrans used the quiet time to reorganize his army. He eliminated the left wing, center, and right wing arrangement by placing Crittenden in command of the XXI Corps, Thomas in charge of the XIV Corps, and McCook in command of the XX Corps. During these months, Rosecrans often reviewed the troops and waited to gather sufficient supplies for a march toward Chattanooga.[4]

---

[2] William Blair to wife, 18 May 1863, William W. Blair Letters, Indiana Historical Society, Indianapolis; John H. Tilford Diary, 31 March 1863 and 12 April 1863, Filson Club, Louisville.

[3] Anonymous, *Louisville Daily Journal*, (4 May 1863): 1; Alfred Pirtle to mother, 7 February 1863 and 5 April 1863, Alfred Pirtle Letters, Filson Club; John Beatty, *The Citizen-Soldier; or Memoirs of a Volunteer* (Cincinnati: Wilstach, Baldwin & Co., 1879) 235–36.

[4] ; US War Department, comp., *The War of the Rebellion: A Compilation of the Official Records of the Union and Confederate Armies*, 128 vols. (Washington, DC: Government Printing Office, 1880–1901) 1st ser., vol. 23, pt. 2:36; Thomas J. Wright, *History of the Eighth Regiment Kentucky Volunteer Infantry During its Three Years Campaigns, Embracing Organization, Marches, Skirmishes and Battles of the Command with Much of the History of the Old Reliable Third Brigade Commanded by Hon. Stanley Matthews and Containing Many*

As the army waited, Crittenden became aware of a delicate political situation. In 1861 the Army of the Cumberland had had a large and powerful Kentucky contingent in the ranks. Crittenden had received his position primarily due to his Kentucky connections. After Perryville, the composition of the army changed to include a much larger Midwestern element. Kentuckians had not welcomed news of the Emancipation Proclamation with much enthusiasm. They had enlisted to restore the Union as it existed in 1860, not to begin a crusade to end slavery. As a result, Kentuckians did not enlist in large numbers after 1862, and as the war progressed Kentuckians on the home front and in the army became more critical of Federal policy. Other soldiers were not pleased.

During the early months of 1863, this new attitude toward Kentuckians found expression in many subtle ways. For example, one Ohioan noted of Kentucky troops that "As a general thing, they are not much to us, and might as well be home as here." John Beatty noted that a Major H. F. Kalfus of the 5th Kentucky resigned his commission on 1 March 1863 in protest over the Emancipation Proclamation. Beatty felt Kalfus was a "crossroads" politician who would be a "lion among his half-loyal neighbors when he returns home." In another incident, Kentucky troops noted with disgust that following a speech to the troops by T. Buchanan on 15 March, cheers were offered up for Indiana and Ohio but not for Kentucky. Kentuckians had fallen out of favor with the Midwesterners.[5]

At the same time, rumors also circulated claiming that Senator Crittenden had lost the confidence of the citizens of Kentucky because he was behind the times. If the Crittenden patriarch no longer held a Kentucky power base, and if Midwesterners viewed Kentuckians as half loyal, then Thomas Crittenden's future with the Army of the Cumberland might be in danger. The general needed to mend his political fences.[6]

Interesting and Amusing Incidents of Army Life (St. Joseph: St. Joseph Steam Printing, 1880) 147.

[5] George Landrum to sister, 6 February 1863, George W. Landrum Letters, Ohio Historical Society, Columbus; Beatty, *Citizen-Soldier*, 223, 226; Anonymous, *Louisville Daily Journal*, 20 March 1863.

[6] Anonymous, *Louisville Daily Journal*, (24 March 1863): 4.

In March Crittenden went back to Kentucky, supposedly to confer with General Burnside of the Department of the Ohio about coordinating the moves of Burnside's forces against Knoxville with those of Rosecrans against Chattanooga. The militarily and politically incompetent Burnside was not popular among Kentuckians. Many Kentuckians in the Army of the Cumberland already looked to Crittenden as their leader, and there were rumors that an independent command in Kentucky would soon open up. As the Louisville *Daily Journal* later wrote, "If the President is going to give any Kentucky general an independent command to defend Kentucky from invasion the command will be given to Gen. Crittenden as his name and well known ability and prudence would be equal in itself to a host." Burnside kept his command, however, and Crittenden did not return home even though with his political gifts he could have dealt with the Kentucky home front more effectively than the beleaguered Burnside could. As the Louisville *Daily Journal* noted, "Kentucky regards with deep interest the career of this distinguished and brilliant soldier."[7]

Another intriguing possibility simultaneously presented itself. The Union party of Kentucky nominated Crittenden for the position of lieutenant governor on a ticket with Thomas Bramlette, another former Union army officer. Crittenden immediately asked his friend John M. Harlan to withdraw his name from nomination, saying that he did not desire any civil office. The press agreed with the decision, commenting, "Kentucky did not desire that gallant officer should be withdrawn from the field of labor in which he has reflected such distinguished honor upon his native state." Perhaps Crittenden thought politics could wait until after the war or perhaps his meager self-confidence was not up to a political campaign. He would easily have won the election and parlayed his achievements into even greater laurels later. Unfortunately, he did not heed the call of politics at this time. The opportunity to run for office as a conquering military hero was never as favorable again.[8]

During his Kentucky visit, Thomas had the opportunity to spend time with his family. The senator, worn from years of public service, was

---

[7] Anonymous, Louisville *Daily Journal*, (23 March 1863): 3; Anonymous, *Louisville Daily Journal*, (6 April 1863): 3; Anonymous, *Louisville Daily Journal*, (25 April 1863): 4.

[8] Anonymous, *Louisville Daily Journal*, (20 March 1863): 2.

in declining health and would die within a few months. This was Thomas's last opportunity to impress his father with his many accomplishments. He could also visit with his Confederate-sympathizing sisters and hear news of George's situation. Unfortunately, the Crittendens did not record their conversations or share with others the details of Thomas's visit.

During the continuing military lull, Crittenden had the opportunity to deal with the more mundane aspects of military command. Many of the married Civil War soldiers requested leave to visit families. Crittenden did not want to project an image of softness, so he denied most requests. Crittenden also dealt with subordinate officers who were maneuvering for his recommendations whenever their states raised new regiments. Naturally, Kentuckians frequently appealed to Crittenden to intercede on their behalf with officials back home.[9]

The most challenging issue Crittenden faced during this timeframe concerned army discipline. One particularly trying incident involved Private Richard Hembree of the 58th Indiana, who had been sentenced to death for desertion. His regimental commander, James T. Embree, and his brigade commander, George P. Buell, both pleaded for clemency. Wood, the division commander, opposed commutation of the sentence. Crittenden, owing to his civilian background, favored mercy for those found guilty of desertion. He decided to delay the sentence, saying, "I recommend that further time be given in this case. The prisoner pled guilty and was convicted. An ignorant man may have distanced himself from many extenuating circumstances; may have thought it a trivial offense and refused to put in any defense; and may at the same time, have had testimony to mitigate the penalty of death." Crittenden, a good lawyer, wanted to give the accused every possible chance of saving himself. According to the regimental historian, the man was later pardoned. Firing squads alienated soldiers while leniency won their favor. Crittenden wanted to keep his men and potential future voters happy.[10]

---

[9] Wright, *History of the Eighth Regiment Kentucky*, 108; Alfred Pirtle to Father, March 1, 1863, Alfred Pirtle Letters, Filson Club.

[10] John J. Hight, *History of the Fifty-eighth Regiment of Indiana Volunteers Infantry: Its Organization, Campaigns, and Battles from 1861–1865* (Princeton: Press of the Clarion, 1895) 136, 140, 142.

When the cold days of winter yielded to the warmth of spring, soldiers in the army expected to move against the enemy. When news of Hooker's crossing of the Rappahannock reached Tennessee, hopes rose that the Army of the Cumberland would deliver a similar blow against the enemy on their front. The only fighting they saw, however, was an occasional skirmish. Rosecrans would not move until he felt completely ready.[11]

Federal authorities applied political pressure on Rosecrans to move, but he refused. On 8 June, Rosecrans called a council of war to assess his generals' opinions about a move against the enemy. At the council Crittenden vehemently opposed a premature advance. He said that an advance against Bragg would result in a "bloody battle at Shelbyville" that, in turn, would only result in the Federals being "cooped up at Tullahoma" with only "one wretched mountain country road" to depend on for supplies. Crittenden went on to suggest that Rosecrans should not move without a force of at least 100,000 infantry and 6,000 to 10,000 cavalry. The Kentuckian concluded that Secretary of War Stanton, who was demanding action, was "either crazy or bent upon the destruction of this army." The generals agreed with Crittenden.[12]

The Kentuckian may very well have said what he thought Rosecrans wanted to hear. Crittenden had a good relationship with Rosecrans, and he must have known his commander's thinking. Crittenden normally did not speak before he sensed how others might perceive his comments. His willingness to vocalize his thoughts here broke with past tendencies. The general seemed to be gaining a degree of self-confidence in his abilities and apparently felt at ease addressing Rosecrans and others. Perhaps he was becoming an effective corps commander.

As pressure for Rosecrans to move intensified, the commanding general had to respond. A memo from Rosecrans's chief of staff, James Garfield, had begun to circulate. It refuted the rationale of not moving against the enemy. Rosecrans and the other generals were not pleased. Crittenden warned Garfield, "It is understood, sir, by the general officers

---

[11] John H. Tilford Diary, 3 May 1863, Filson Club; Wright, *History of the Eighth Regiment Kentucky*, 148.

[12] *OR*, 1st ser., vol. 23, pt. 2:403; Larry J. Daniel, *Days of Glory: The Army of the Cumberland, 1861–1865* (Baton Rouge: Louisiana State University Press, 2004) 261.

of the army that this movement is your work. I wish you to understand it is a rash and fatal move, for which you will be held responsible." The angry Crittenden believed that Garfield had betrayed their beloved commander.[13]

On 23 June, Rosecrans finally began his campaign against Bragg. Rosecrans intended to feint an attack toward Shelbyville while concentrating Crittenden and Thomas's corps for a flanking march toward Manchester. If Thomas and Crittenden could reach the Confederate rear without detection, they would force the Confederate army to yield its position and retreat toward Chattanooga. The key to the campaign was the ability of Thomas and Crittenden's troops to gain control of Hoover's Gap.[14]

Crittenden played a significant role in this campaign, Rosecrans having designated him to deliver a flank attack as he had at Stones River. To enhance the prospects of success, Rosecrans added Thomas's corps to this flank attack. Van Cleve's division remained at Murfreesboro on garrison duty, while Wood and Palmer's division advanced along the McMinnville Road approaching Manchester.

Marches rarely go exactly as planned, and Crittenden's troops bogged down. Wood and Palmer's divisions got a late start and did not communicate with each other, causing a traffic jam to develop at the Bradyville-Cripple Creek intersection. The delay cost Crittenden's force valuable time. Adding to the soldiers' difficulties was the constant rain that made the roads almost impassable. One soldier recalled that it rained for fourteen consecutive days. Crittenden's forces marched through a region known locally as the "Barrens," and the rugged terrain made the task even more difficult. Still, by 27 June the vanguard of the corps had reached within 4 miles of Manchester. Rosecrans's plan had worked to perfection. The Confederates had not expected an attack at Hoover's Gap and had only lightly defended it against Thomas's attack. The Federals had maneuvered Bragg out of his position and forced the Confederate general to retreat toward Chattanooga just as Rosecrans had hoped.[15]

---

[13] Daniel, *Days of Glory*, 264.

[14] *OR*, 1st ser., vol. 23, pt. 1:404–05; Van Horne, *Army of the Cumberland*, 223.

[15] *OR*, 1st ser., vol. 23, pt. 1:523–24; G. W. Lewis, *The Campaigns of the 124th Ohio Volunteer Infantry, with Roster and Roll of Honor* (Akron: Werner Company, 1894) 31–33; John H. Tilford Diary, 28 and 29 June 1863, Filson Club.

The Federal army was so exhausted, however, that on 28 June it was not able to march quickly against Tullahoma. The rainy weather had taken its toll. Wood had marched 25 miles in five days, and the men simply could not move any faster. On 29 June, Bragg's army slipped away. Rosecrans had forced the Confederates out of Middle Tennessee, but the Confederate army had escaped to fight another day. Crittenden and the Army of the Cumberland would soon regret their missed opportunity.[16]

The Federals entered Tullahoma on 30 June, and Rosecrans halted the advance to regroup and await supplies. Many of the soldiers had suffered from exposure during the constant rains, and Crittenden fielded requests for furloughs. As before, he refused. Perhaps news that his father was dying soured his characteristically genial demeanor, or perhaps he was simply maintaining his consistently tough position on leaves. Still, he allowed himself a three-week leave of absence to care for his dying father and tend to other family matters. He turned over command of his corps to John M. Palmer, and no doubt Thomas Wood resented that another non-West Pointer received preferment. Wood had far more military talent than Palmer, and he deserved the honor of command.[17]

Crittenden was welcomed home with a great deal of praise for his military conduct. The Louisville *Daily Journal* noted that Crittenden's career had "been very brilliant in the past" and that it "promises to be yet more brilliant in the future." The editor proudly noted, "we could hardly wish him a brighter destiny on earth." If Crittenden entered Kentucky politics after the war, it certainly seemed that he would meet with a great deal of success.[18]

While Crittenden attended to family matters in Kentucky, the Army of the Cumberland prepared to move against Chattanooga. Unfortunately for Rosecrans, the preparations for the campaign proceeded far too slowly. On 6 August, the commanding general held another council of war. Crittenden had returned from Kentucky, and he and the other generals

---

[16] *OR*, 1st ser., vol. 23, pt. 1:407–08, 524.

[17] Ebenezer Hannaford, *The Story of a Regiment: A History of the Campaigns, and Associations in the Field, of the Sixth Ohio Volunteer Infantry* (Cincinnati: Ebenezer Hannaford, 1868) 438; Lewis, *Campaigns of the 124th Ohio*, 41–43; Mark M. Boatner II, *The Civil War Dictionary* (New York: David McKay Company, 1959) 617.

[18] Anonymous, *Louisville Daily Journal*, (10 August 1863): 3.

agreed with Rosecrans about the dangers of a premature advance. Rosecrans decided against a direct assault on the Confederate army, instead planning to operate against Bragg's lines of communication.[19]

On 15 August, the Federal army moved out of Tullahoma. Crittenden's XXI Corps had eighteen days' rations on hand and was ready for action. Wood's division marched from Hillsborough via Pelham to the Sequatchie Valley. Palmer's division marched from Manchester to Dunlop, and Van Cleve's division minus one brigade marched from McMinnville to Pikeville. Rosecrans intended to make Bragg believe that the Confederate's position had been turned from the north.[20]

Crittenden's corps advanced along a broad front, giving the impression that they intended to cross the Tennessee River at Blythe's Ferry about 45 miles north of Chattanooga. To carry out the deception, the brigades of Hazen and Wagner were detached from the corps and joined by the brigades of Minty and Wilder. Hazen commanded this force, which consisted of between 6,000 and 7,000 men. While Bragg worried about Crittenden's corps to his north, Rosecrans had McCook and Thomas approach Chattanooga from the southwest. By ruse and deception, Crittenden's men convinced Bragg that their movement north of Chattanooga was the major Union thrust and could not be ignored. Besides, Bragg simply could not risk a possible linking of Crittenden's force with those of Burnside coming from Knoxville. While Bragg concentrated on Hazen's detachment, Crittenden moved the bulk of his corps down the Sequatchie Valley to Battle Creek and on 2 September crossed the Tennessee River. From there, Crittenden's corps followed the Memphis and Charleston Railroad through the Tennessee River Gorge to Wauhatchie.[21]

As his corps crossed the Tennessee River, Crittenden met with Rosecrans and the other corps commanders at Bridgeport. Although speed was of the essence if Rosecrans's plan was to work, Crittenden did not seem

---

[19] John H. Tilford Diary, 12 August 1863, Filson Club; Van Horne, *Army of the Cumberland*, 233; *OR*, 1st ser., vol. 23, pt. 2:594, 597.

[20] *OR*, 1st ser., vol. 30, pt. 1:50; *OR*, 1st ser., vol. 30, pt. 3:29.

[21] *OR*, 1st ser., vol. 30, pt. 1:52; Stephen Woodworth, *Chickamauga: A Battlefield Guide* (Lincoln: University of Nebraska Press) p. 4; *OR*, 1st ser., vol. 30, pt. 3:36; *OR*, 1st ser., vol. 30, pt. 1:50–52; Van Horne, *Army of the Cumberland*, 235.

worried. If Bragg decided to attack Hazen's detachment or Burnside's approaching force from Knoxville, he could destroy the smaller Federal forces, then turn against the remainder of Rosecrans's army and destroy it. Crittenden believed that "If Bragg should make a dash at Burnside and Burnside retire slowly, declining the fight, I think we can destroy his army." Crittenden had confidence that Hazen and his soldiers could keep the deception going until the Federal army was in Bragg's rear. The next few days would tell if Crittenden's men deserved this confidence.[22]

It took the Federal forces a few days to move into position. On 6 September, Crittenden received orders to advance along the Memphis and Charleston Railroad to the base of Lookout Mountain. He immediately ordered Wood's division to advance. Wood, however, ignored the order because he did not want his men needlessly exposed to enemy fire as they entered Lookout Valley. The prickly division commander, fearing heavy casualties from skirmishers he observed to his front, used the excuse that Crittenden had not stated the time of the advance. When Crittenden sent two staff officers to ascertain why Wood had not obeyed the order, Wood exploded, telling the staff officers that they did not have "one tenth" of Wood's experience, nor military education. Wood, no doubt frustrated over civilian Crittenden and even Palmer's promotion over him, angrily vented his feelings. Crittenden, probably biting his tongue, told Wood that the order came from Rosecrans and required unquestioned obedience. Crittenden conceded that he could accept questioning of his orders, but orders coming directly from the commanding general required immediate compliance. Crittenden also told Wood that his delay had hindered the army's progress and pointedly made reference to sharp skirmishing that produced no casualties. This criticism generated another round of letters from Wood.[23]

The tense situation worsened. Rosecrans exploded at Crittenden for his failure to endorse the order as army regulations required. Crittenden, assailed by both his superior and his subordinates, apologized: "I acknowledge the correctness of the reproof and it shall not occur again, be I well or ill, sleepy or awake, in or out of bed." Rosecrans also chastised

---

[22] *OR*, 1st ser., vol. 30, pt. 3:305.
[23] *OR*, 1st ser., vol. 30, pt. 3:414–16, 419–25, 455–58.

Wood. Still steaming, Wood accused Crittenden of slandering him, but Rosecrans did not agree. At this point, Crittenden wanted to let the matter rest and hoped for a return of peace and calm. Throughout the entire situation, Crittenden had showed considerable poise. His political skills aided his handling of the crisis.[24]

Although Wood was not the army's most affable commander, he was capable. One regimental historian observed that Crittenden had been "unkind" to Wood. According to his argument, Crittenden held superior rank only due to family connections and should have listened to Wood, who was on the ground and a professional soldier.[25]

Meanwhile, on 7 September, Hazen's detachment made a bold reconnaissance in force in front of Lookout Mountain, maintaining the ruse that the main Federal thrust was coming from the north. The reconnaissance drew heavy fire from the defenders, although some Federals thought the Confederates were preparing to retreat.[26]

In fact, the Confederates did retreat and, on 9 September, the XXI Corps occupied Chattanooga without a fight. Crittenden detached Wagner's brigade to garrison the city and advanced with his main force to Ringgold. Hazen's detachment north of Chattanooga rejoined the pursuing Federals. Rosecrans had captured a major Confederate city without suffering huge casualties. Crittenden's corps had performed well in creating the ruse of an attack from the north, but not everyone agreed. John Connelly of the 123rd Illinois remarked, "we went ahead of his corps and cleared the way in his front so that his infantry has moved along without seeing a single rebel soldier except those we sent back as prisoners." No matter, Crittenden had completed his assignment as well as anyone could have asked.[27]

On 10 September the excited Federals continued their pursuit, one soldier recalling that "the boys are anxious to meet the foe." Palmer's

---

[24] Ibid.

[25] Hight, *History of the Fifty-eighth Regiment*, 173.

[26] Van Horne, *Army of the Cumberland*, 236–37.

[27] *OR*, 1st ser., vol. 30, pt. 3:479, 481; Van Horne, *Army of the Cumberland*, 237, 239; William B. Hazen, *A Narrative of Military Service* (Boston: Ticknor & Comp., 1885) 117; Paul M. Angle, ed., *Three Years in the Army of the Cumberland: The Letters and Diary of Major James A. Connelly* (Bloomington: Indiana University Press, 1959) 119.

division led Crittenden's corps, Rosecrans having Crittenden reconnoiter the area around Ringgold. The Federals did not expect Confederate troops in the region and were somewhat surprised by the skirmishing that occurred along the way. What the Federals did not know was that the Confederates were trying to spring a trap on the ever-widening Federal columns and thus defeat them piecemeal.[28]

On 11 September, the XXI Corps advanced from Ringgold against the Confederates with Palmer and Van Cleve's divisions in the lead. Before they could get very far, Rosecrans recalled them. Crittenden also detached Harker's brigade to reconnoiter toward Lee & Gordon's mill. He reported sharp skirmishing to Wood, who then sent George P. Buell's brigade to support Harker's move. By nightfall, these brigades had reached Lee & Gordon's mill and reported numerous Confederate campfires in the distance. The Union commander decided to let his army fan out over a wide arc as they pursued the fleeing Confederates.[29]

The following day Rosecrans ordered Van Cleve and Palmer's division toward Lee & Gordon's mill to support Wood. Crittenden recalled his advance units under John Wilder and belatedly began a concentration. He saw no reason to worry or make haste. Crittenden did not realize there were Confederates in force on his front, believing instead that the Rebels were fleeing. By the night of 12 September, the entire XXI Corps was concentrated at Lee & Gordon's mill. [30]

The Confederates had previously missed an opportunity to attack the XIV Corps at McLemore's Cove, and now they moved Polk and Walker's corps against Palmer at Pea Vine church. Only the slowness of the Confederate movement prevented the destruction of Palmer's division and the entire XXI Corps. By the time Polk moved to attack Palmer's division, Crittenden had concentrated the whole corps. The battle never materialized.

---

[28] John H. Tilford Diary, 11 September 1863, Filson Club; Van Horne, *Army of the Cumberland*, 240–42.

[29] *OR*, 1st ser., vol. 30, pt. 1:603–04; Van Horne, *Army of the Cumberland*, 242–43.

[30] *OR*, 1st ser., vol. 30, pt. 3:563–71, 577–78, 580–81; John M. Palmer, *Personal Recollections of John Palmer: The Story of an Ernest Life* (Cincinnati: Robert Clarke, 1901) 172; Van Horne, *Army of the Cumberland*, 245–46.

Bragg and many of the Confederate soldiers regretted this lost opportunity.[31]

It was about this time that reports first reached the Federals of the transfer of Longstreet from Virginia to Tennessee. Unfortunately, Rosecrans did not believe the reports. Instead, he asserted the more optimistic reports of Crittenden and others who did not believe that Longstreet was present. Over time Crittenden had perfected the ability to say and do things that pleased those in authority. So, once again, the Kentuckian expressed what Rosecrans wanted to hear. As late as 17 September, Crittenden refused to believe reports of Longstreet's presence. When General Minty reported Longstreet's presence to Rosecrans, Crittenden told Rosecrans, "Longstreet is in Virginia." Crittenden further promised "to whip every rebel within twenty miles of us." Within a few days the Kentuckian would have the chance to fulfill this boast.[32]

On 13 September, one of Van Cleve's brigades advanced to Lafayette, where two Confederate corps lay in wait. This aggressive move by Crittenden disconcerted Confederate General Leonidas Polk, who not only did not attack despite two-to-one odds his favor, but actually asked for reinforcements from Bragg. Bragg moved Buckner's troops to aid Polk in the attack. Rosecrans called Van Cleve's brigade back before the Confederates could spring their trap. As one early historian noted, Crittenden's aggressive stance delayed an overwhelming Confederate attack that could have destroyed the separated corps. The optimistic Crittenden did not realize his dilemma. He still did not believe that the Confederates were massing for a counterattack.[33]

Rosecrans ordered Van Cleve and Palmer to march to junction with Thomas's corps at Bailey's Crossroads; he left Wood at Lee & Gordon's mill. The two divisions made slow progress. Until 16 September the isolated XXI Corps faced attack and destruction. Over 60,000

---

[31] *OR*, 1st ser., vol. 30, pt. 2:44–45; Van Horne, *Army of the* Cumberland, 245–46; Albert B. Kirwan, ed., *Johnny Green of the Orphan Brigade: The Journal of a Confederate Soldier* (Lexington: University of Kentucky Press, 1956) 92.

[32] Daniel, *Days of Glory*, 311–13.

[33] *OR*, 1st ser., vol. 30, pt. 1:604–05; Van Horne, *Army of Cumberland*, 246–47; Donn Piatt, *General George H. Thomas: A Critical Biography* (Cincinnati: Robert Clarke, 1893) 387.

Confederates opposed Wood, who could only call on the brigades of Whittaker and Mitchell in Steedman's division for support. If forced to retreat, Wood had orders to hold the road to Chattanooga at all costs. If Bragg could get his subordinates to attack as ordered, the XXI Corps and the Army of the Cumberland were doomed.[34]

On 14 September, Crittenden marched into the Chattanooga valley with Palmer and Van Cleve's division. Finally he and Rosecrans perceived their danger and began a hasty concentration, Rosecrans ordering Van Cleve's division back to Crawfish Springs and Palmer's to Owen's ford. By 17 September, the Union corps were in supporting distance of each other. Only the final touches remained before the greatest battle and turning point of Crittenden's life.[35]

The lull after Stones River had given Crittenden the opportunity to learn the administrative side of corps command. While personally brave and very likable, the Kentuckian really had no administrative talent. He disliked the mundane tasks of filing reports and following up on problems or complaints from soldiers. Because Crittenden disliked personal confrontations and desired acceptance, he tended to avoid distasteful decisions and had a lax attitude toward disciplining the troops. West Pointers such as Wood disdained such character traits in Crittenden and other political appointees.

Crittenden had several admirable qualities, however. Up to this point in his career, he had shown bravery under fire and had exhibited a strong desire to confront the enemy. In both the Tullahoma and Chattanooga campaigns, Crittenden had maneuvered his men well enough to accomplish their assigned tasks. During the Tullahoma campaign, he had moved his corps slowly, but the horrible weather was more to blame than any hesitancy on Crittenden's part. During the Chattanooga campaign, Crittenden's forces had provided a very effective feint for the Federal forces, enabling an almost bloodless capture of the key Confederate city.

Perhaps the most encouraging aspect of Crittenden's career was his developing self-confidence. In councils of war and in correspondence, he openly and aggressively stated his opinion. The need for his father's

---

[34] *OR*, 1st ser., vol. 30, pt. 1:604–05; Van Horne, *Army of Cumberland*, 247.

[35] Van Horne, *Army of the Cumberland*, 248–49.

approval had disappeared with the senator's death. The Kentuckian also gained influence with the commanding general, and thus his star was on the ascent. Unfortunately, Crittenden had not learned enough as a brigade and division commander earlier in the war. A more thorough military training at that point would have made his corps command experience more enlightening.

10

Chickamauga: Career Crisis

On 18 September 1863, Crittenden and the Federal army as a whole finally sensed the predicament Rosecrans's hasty advance following the capture of Chattanooga had caused them. The Federals hastily concentrated their forces before Braxton Bragg could attack them piecemeal. The campaign became a race to see which army could execute orders more promptly. On the Federal side, Rosecrans worried about the exposed Federal left under Crittenden. If the Confederates turned Crittenden's position, they could block the Federal line of retreat to Chattanooga and destroy the Union army. Thus, Rosecrans planned to move Thomas's corps to the left of Crittenden to strengthen the area. At the same time, the Confederates planned to attack Crittenden before the Federals could strengthen that flank.[1]

Despite the obvious crisis, Rosecrans could not resist the temptation to tinker with the alignment of his troops. He moved Van Cleve's division to the left of Wood's and later moved Palmer's to the left of Van Cleve's. Palmer did not receive the orders quickly and as a result he had to make a night march to get into position. As the troops marched, some of the officers of the 41st Ohio happened to march by Rosecrans's headquarters; when the officers dropped by headquarters to greet their colleagues, they noted that Rosecrans barely spoke. The commander and Palmer did not get along well and the tensions of the coming battle had not improved their relationship. The soldiers hated the night march. As one later recalled, "dust was shoe deep and it came up filling our nostrils with dirt and our

---

[1] Thomas Van Horne, *The Army of the Cumberland* (1875; repr., New York: Konecky & Konecky, 1966) 256.

souls with indignation." Despite the griping, Palmer's troops were in position by morning.[2]

While the Federals maneuvered, the Confederates attempted to launch an attack against Wood's position. As usual, Bragg had problems getting his subordinates to carry out his orders. As the Confederates advanced, the Union cavalry brigades of Minty and Wilder held Reed's and Alexander's bridges and delayed the Confederate advance for most of the day. Only late in the day did the Confederates cross Chickamauga Creek, and by then it was too late for them to follow up their gains.[3]

Crittenden had little time to rejoice in the Confederate failure. Rumors were moving through the Federal camp that Longstreet's corps had arrived on the battlefield. One anxious soldier recorded in his diary, "expect hard fighting tomorrow."[4]

Crittenden's mission on 18 September was to keep Bragg from crossing Chickamauga Creek. Despite superb efforts by Minty and Wilder, Crittenden failed in that mission. The Union cavalry had to yield ground to overwhelming Confederate infantry numbers. More importantly, Crittenden failed to inform Rosecrans of the Confederate gains on his front during the day.[5]

As 19 September dawned, Crittenden received orders to hold his position. The Kentuckian feared that Bragg was massing forces in his front for an enormous assault on his position. Within a short time, Minty reported to Crittenden that Confederates had massed to Crittenden's left in the XIV Corps sector. To evaluate the situation, Crittenden ordered

---

[2] US War Department, comp., *The War of the Rebellion: A Compilation of the Official Records of the Union and Confederate Armies*, 128 vols. (Washington, DC: Government Printing Office, 1880–1901) 1st ser., vol. 30, pt. 1:605, 336–37; Robert L. Kimberly and Ephraim S. Holloway, *The Forty-first Ohio Veteran Volunteer Infantry in the War of the Rebellion, 1861–1865* (Cleveland: W. R. Smellie, 1897) 53.

[3] Van Horne, *Army of the Cumberland,* 252.

[4] G. W. Lewis, *The Campaigns of the 124th Ohio Volunteer Infantry, with Roster and Roll of Honor* (Akron: Werner Company, 1894) 52; John H. Tilford Diary, 18 September 1863, Filson Club, Louisville.

[5] Francis F. McKinney, *Education in Violence: The Life of George H. Thomas and the History of the Army of the Cumberland* (Detroit: Wayne State University Press, 1961) 230.

Palmer's division to reconnoiter with Grose's brigade. At this point, the two forces collided and the climatic battle of Chickamauga began.[6]

Engaged heavily, the XIV Corps requested aid from Crittenden. In a rare moment of decisive action, Crittenden sent Palmer's division to Thomas's aid immediately without waiting for permission from Rosecrans. Crittenden realized that he did not have time to go through normal military channels. Palmer's division and Johnson's division from Thomas's corps struggled for over an hour against the Confederate division of Frank Cheatham. They held. Years later, Johnson thankfully noted the timely and helpful arrival of Crittenden's troops.[7]

As Palmer fought with the XIV Corps, another problem developed in the Union lines. A gap remained between Crittenden's and Thomas's corps. If the Confederates struck at that point, disaster awaited the Union army. To fill the gap Rosecrans moved two brigades, Beatty's and Dick's, from Van Cleve's division and Davis's division from McCook's corps. Almost as soon as the Federal units moved, the Confederates attacked. As the battle raged, other units joined the struggle—first Harker's brigade from Wood's division and then Sam Bradley's brigade from Sheridan's division. Later, Buell's brigade from Wood's division, Beatty's brigade from Van Cleve's division, and Laiboldt's brigade from Sheridan's division arrived. The Union lines held. The traditional corps and divisional command structure had broken down. One division from both Crittenden and McCook were fighting with Thomas. The ad hoc command structure created confusion on an already chaotic battlefield. [8]

As the Confederates continued to hammer away at Thomas's position on the Federal left, Crittenden saw an opportunity to deliver a devastating flank attack from his position near the Viniard farm. He probably remembered the lost opportunity at Perryville. A flank attack would throw

---

[6] Van Horne, *Army of the Cumberland*, 253–54.

[7] Van Horne, *Army of the Cumberland*, 256–57; Donn Piatt, *General George H. Thomas: A Critical Biography* (Cincinnati: Robert Clarke, 1893) 395; Ebenezer Hannaford, *The Story of a Regiment: A History of the Campaigns, and Associations in the Field, of the Sixth Ohio Volunteer Infantry* (Cincinnati: Ebenezer Hannaford, 1868) 454; Richard W. Johnson, *Memoir of Major General George H. Thomas* (Philadelphia: J. B. Lippincott, & Co., 1881) 98.

[8] Van Horne, *Army of the Cumberland*, 262; 257–60.

the Rebels completely off balance and perhaps turn the tide of the battle. Crittenden sought Rosecrans's permission, probably hoping the commander would give him troops from McCook's corps to augments his own force. Rosecrans, however, did not agree with Crittenden's assessment of the situation. He refused to authorize the assault.[9]

Instead of delivering a crushing blow on the enemy, Crittenden had to wait in position until the Confederates finally attacked him in the late afternoon. Crittenden behaved splendidly in the fight. One report noted his bravery in rallying the troops, describing how he had recklessly exposed himself during the fight. In fact, he barely escaped capture. Still, his lines held.[10]

It had been a long day for both sides. Crittenden's troops were tired and short of ammunition. One soldier recorded that Chickamauga was "much more severe than Stones River" and that "neither side seemed to have gained any" during the fighting. Both sides probably hoped the other would give up and retreat, just as Bragg had withdrawn at Stones River. In the morning, however, the conflict began anew on an even greater scale.[11]

As the next morning dawned, the Federals expected the Confederates to continue hammering at the Union left under Thomas. Thus, Rosecrans wanted to continue strengthening this sector. General Thomas did nothing to discourage this concentration on his front, and Crittenden's remaining force would continue to serve as a reserve force in case of emergency.[12]

Rosecrans planned to relieve Negley's division in Thomas's sector and replace it with Wood's division and Barnes's brigade of Van Cleve's division. However, Wood's orders to move never reached him. Eventually a staff officer appeared and asked why Wood had not moved to relieve Negley's position. Wood replied that he had no orders to move and would remain until he received such orders. When Rosecrans learned of the delay, he castigated Wood for not following orders. Needless to say, the prickly Kentuckian thus was not in a good mood.[13]

---

[9] *OR,* 1st ser., vol. 30, pt. 1:608.

[10] *OR,* 1st ser., vol. 30, pt. 1:448.

[11] Lewis, *Campaigns of the 124th Regiment,* 59; John H. Tilford Diary, 19 September 1863, Filson Club.

[12] *OR,* 1st ser., vol. 30, pt. 1:57; Van Horne, *Army of the Cumberland,* 265.

[13] *OR,* 1st ser., vol. 30, pt. 1:355–56.

Shortly thereafter, Rosecrans issued one of the most ill-fated orders of the war. Always tinkering with the alignment of his troops, Rosecrans ordered Wood to close up his division to the division of Reynolds. The problem was that Wood's division was not in line next to Reynolds's division, it was next to Brannan's division. To comply with Rosecrans's order, Wood would have to pull his division out of line, march behind Brannan's division, and close up to Reynolds's division. Rosecrans had become confused about the alignment of his forces and had misspoken when he issued the order. One of his staff officers should have caught the error, or Crittenden could have modified the order before its delivery. Because of the confusing command structure and the stress of the battle, Crittenden did not realize the potentially disastrous impact of the order and thus did not countermand it. Wood could have taken it upon himself, realizing that this was an unwise order, and delayed complying with it until he received clarification. He could have ridden over to Crittenden, only 100 yards away, and asked him to countermand the order or to delay its implementation until the situation could be resolved. Wood was already in a foul mood; he was angry at Crittenden for his actions during the capture of Chattanooga and at Rosecrans for his treatment that morning. Instead, he acted spitefully and complied with the order.[14]

As Wood's division pulled out, it created a 600-yard gap in the Federal line. At almost the same moment, Longstreet's corps attacked the Federals in the exact area Wood had vacated. Jefferson C. Davis quickly moved two of his brigades into the gap but they were not enough. Within a short period, Buell's brigade of Wood's division, Lytle and Bradley's brigades from Sheridan's division, Wilder's brigade of cavalry, and Beatty and Dick's brigades of Van Cleve's division all gave way to the Confederate onslaught. Rosecrans and McCook were in the area when the breakthrough occurred, and they were caught up in the fleeing force. The Union right collapsed.[15]

Crittenden attempted to stem the tide with massed artillery as he had on the third day at Stones River. He told his artillery chief, Major John Mendenhall, "We will go to the batteries and we will yet drive those fellows

---

[14] *OR*, 1st ser., vol. 30, pt. 1:59.
[15] Van Horne, *Army of the Cumberland*, 268.

back and hold them in check." Mendenhall's batteries held the Rebels back for about a half-hour, but the Federals did not have enough guns or infantry support to hold them indefinitely. When the artillerist requested permission to retreat, Crittenden replied, "You are not to retire at all, but hold your position." The cannoneers could not hold, and they eventually lost seventeen guns. According to family tradition, in the midst of the disaster Crittenden personally helped man the guns and did not give up his positions until almost overtaken by skirmishers.[16]

The excitable Rosecrans, believing that all was lost, hurried to Chattanooga to organize the city's defense. By leaving his army in the midst of crisis, he forfeited much of his reputation among contemporaries and historians alike. By late afternoon, Crittenden would join Rosecrans in Chattanooga, with similar consequences for his reputation.[17]

The situation was not as bleak as Rosecrans, Crittenden, and others first believed. Only two brigades of Van Cleve's division had fled during the Rebel breakthrough. Crittenden's remaining brigades were still with Thomas on the Federal left. If Crittenden had followed Wood to Thomas's position and helped Thomas manage the battle on Snodgrass Hill, the Kentuckian could have salvaged much of his reputation. In that sector of the battlefield, the fighting still raged.[18]

Crittenden, however, raced to Chattanooga. He later had to explain his actions. The Kentuckian argued that he had believed Rosecrans and McCook were either dead or captured by the enemy. Therefore, he thought it best to go to Chattanooga to organize the defense. In the late afternoon, Crittenden had learned that Rosecrans was alive and at Chattanooga, so he believed he should report there for orders.[19]

When Rosecrans learned that Thomas still held the field, his hopes revived. Thomas was placed in command of all forces still on the

---

[16] OR, 1st ser., vol. 30, pt. 1:984; Francis Hudson Oxx, *The Kentucky Crittenden: The History of a Family Including Genealogy of Descendent in Both Male and Female Lives, Biographical Sketches of its Members, and Their Descent from Other Colonial Lives* (n.p., 1940) 139.

[17] OR, 1st ser., vol. 30, pt. 1:612; Van Horne, *Army of the Cumberland,* 269.

[18] Piatt, *General George H. Thomas,* 420–22; Van Horne, *Army of the Cumberland,* 282–83.

[19] OR, 1st ser., vol. 30, pt. 1:984–985.

battlefield. McCook and Crittenden were ordered to Rossville to help move unorganized troops to Chattanooga and assist Thomas's force as it retreated. According to an early army historian, Rosecrans told McCook and Crittenden, "Gentlemen this is no place for you. Go at once to your commands at the front." The day might yet be redeemed.[20]

Crittenden made several major mistakes that day. The most obvious was his decision to leave the battlefield and head toward Chattanooga rather than follow the sound of the guns and join Thomas's heroic stand. In a later court of inquiry, some of Crittenden's staff officers testified that they had urged the general to remain on the battlefield to safeguard his reputation. Crittenden expressed no concern for his reputation, only a desire to do his duty as a soldier. Most in the public defined that duty as staying on the field as long as the troops were still fighting. Crittenden's explanation for leaving may have been plausible, but it certainly was not convincing. Crittenden's background as a lawyer and politician came to fore but did not serve him well in the crisis. [21]

Retreating, Crittenden encountered Colonel John Parkhurst, Thomas's provost. After the Rebel breakthrough, Parkhurst had been actively attempting to round up stragglers and organize them into a useable force. Parkhurst suggested that Crittenden assume command of these scattered forces and lead them to the aid of Thomas. Crittenden declined the request, saying that Parkhurst was doing a good job on his own. This story made it appear as though Crittenden had abandoned Thomas to his fate. This surely was not what Crittenden intended to convey, but the image he projected was negative.[22]

After the battle, Crittenden seemed stunned. As some of his troops fled the battlefield, aides noted the general insisting that he had done all he could. The Kentuckian seemed to have lost his will to continue the fight. While no one else saw Crittenden crying about the day's events, as Van Cleve had, the Kentuckian was dejected at the turn of events.[23]

---

[20] *OR*, 1st ser., vol. 30, pt. 1:612; Henry Cist, *The Army of the Cumberland* (New York: Charles Scribners & Sons, 1882) 226.

[21] *OR*, 1st ser., vol. 30, pt. 1:984–985.

[22] *OR*, 1st ser., vol. 30, pt. 1:611, 984–85.

[23] *OR*, 1st ser., vol. 30, pt. 1:984–985; William B. Hazen, *A Narrative of Military Service* (Boston: Ticknor & Comp., 1885) 127.

Although Crittenden received a great deal of condemnation for his actions, he had some supporters. One of his divisional commanders, John Palmer, later recalled that one of the major problems at Chickamauga was that Rosecrans had tinkered with the corps command structure. By the time of the fateful Rebel breakthrough, Crittenden and McCook were corps commanders practically without any command. Thus, orders arrived at divisional headquarters directly from the commanding general without the corps commanders having had any opportunity to modify them as circumstances at the front dictated. The Federal disaster occurred because Wood received orders directly from Rosecrans without Crittenden having any impact. If Crittenden had only delayed the implementation of Wood's order, he could have averted disaster. On the second day of Chickamauga, Crittenden was a man without a force. Palmer expected more decisive action from Crittenden than the Kentuckian probably could have mustered, but Palmer was correct in asserting that Rosecrans's command style did nothing to make the task easier.[24]

During the night of 20 September, Crittenden and McCook rejoined Thomas's force as Thomas retreated toward Chattanooga, Crittenden and McCook reassuming command of their scattered forces. In the confusion of the moment, it was difficult to locate commanders and units. Palmer later recalled that he could not find Crittenden that night. One Federal commander, William B. Hazen, suggested rounding up Union stragglers and marching back to the strong position at Snodgrass Hill to renew the battle the next day. However, the defeated army's confusion, the nighttime conditions, and the force's low morale prevented such an outcome. Rather, the Federals waited for the victorious Rebels to move against their position at Chattanooga.[25]

The scene in the Union camp showed an army on the verge of destruction. One soldier recorded, "wagons and horses were running everywhere, everyone taking care of themselves, woods were full of men, some were trying to rally the stragglers, but such was impossible, for the

---

[24] John M. Palmer, *Personal Recollections of John Palmer: The Story of an Ernest Life* (Cincinnati: Robert Clarke, 1901) 186–87.

[25] Van Horne, *Army of the Cumberland,* 277; Palmer, *Personal Recollections,* 180; Hazen, *Narrative of Military Service,* 135.

army was now utterly demoralized. Part of our troops still fought hard and kept the enemy in check, troops were now falling back to Chattanooga." The soldier noted that Chickamauga was the "severest battle of the war" and went on to admit that his division had been in a "disgraceful retreat." The diarist disgustedly reported that the Confederates "flanked us at every point and it seemed as though the entire army would be captured." Many others shared this bleak assessment.[26]

After the shooting ceased, the commanders tallied the battle's cost. The XXI Corps entered the battle with 11,180 men and suffered 322 killed, 2,382 wounded, and 699 missing for 3,403 total casualties, or about 31 percent. Within the corps, Palmer's division had suffered the most severe losses.[27]

Crittenden's career had taken an incredible turn at Chickamauga. On the first day, he had performed brilliantly and could rightfully claim the honor of being one of the most capable political appointees of the war. By the second day, Crittenden reputation lay in shambles. His record of personal bravery and his earlier successes disappeared from the consciousness of most Union supporters. After the battle, it was only a matter of time before a court of inquiry investigated the disaster and assessed blame for the setback. Before Chickamauga, Crittenden had bypassed criticism and seemed to lead a charmed life. The same could not be said of the Kentuckian after Chickamauga.

Since the second day of Chickamauga so overshadows the first in the minds of historians, they have often overlooked it. Crittenden's failures on the second day have colored evaluations of his performance on the first day. For instance, William G. Shanks, a newspaper reporter, caustically portrayed Crittenden as an incompetent general in his reports, and Shanks believed that Crittenden should have attacked the Confederates in the afternoon while Thomas was being attacked. According to Shanks's memoirs, "All that was at one time needed to have secured us a great victory was to

---

[26] John H. Tilford Diary, 20 September 1863, Filson Club.

[27] William F. Fox, *Regimental Losses in the American Civil War, 1861–1865: A Treatise on the Extent and Nature of the Mortuary Losses in the Union regiments, with full and Exhaustive Statistics compiled from the Official Records on file in the State Military Bureaus and at Washington* (Albany: Albany Publishing Company, 1889) 106; Van Horne, *Army of the Cumberland*, 284.

have someone to tell Crittenden that it was his manifest duty to charge with Thomas." The reporter ridiculed Crittenden for not attacking simply because Rosecrans had not issued the orders. The reporter did not know that Crittenden had requested permission for such an attack and that Rosecrans had denied the request. Unfortunately for Crittenden, the image Shanks portrayed was the one most familiar to the public following the battle.[28]

Recent historians have been kinder to Crittenden. In many ways, the first day of Chickamauga was Crittenden's best performance as a corps commander. In the morning, Crittenden had sensed the danger to the XIV Corps and had promptly responded to Thomas's call for reinforcements before receiving Rosecrans's approval. In the official report of the battle, the commander approved of the move and commended Crittenden for his good judgment. Having saved Thomas's forces that morning, during the afternoon Crittenden proposed what was probably Rosecrans's best opportunity to turn the battle decisively in the Union's favor. Another such opportunity never presented itself.[29]

After the first day, Crittenden seemed to have grown into his position as corps commander. He had discerned battlefield conditions and exercised prudent independent judgment during a crisis. The Kentuckians had cooperated with a colleague in a moment of need without quibbling over unnecessary matters of military etiquette. Crittenden had also proposed a viable plan of attack that could have produced great benefits to the Federal cause. Few West Pointers would have performed better than Crittenden that day. Perhaps Crittenden would make a fine corps commander. All he needed was a little luck and further time to develop his skills and self-confidence. Unfortunately, by the second day of Chickamauga Thomas Crittenden's luck had run out.

---

[28] William F. G. Shanks, *Personal Recollections of Distinguished Generals* (New York: Harper & Brothers, 1866) 266–67.

[29] Larry J. Daniel, *Days of Glory: The Army of the Cumberland, 1861–1865* (Baton Rouge: Louisiana State University Press, 2004): 314–337.

11

Turmoil after the Storm

On the night of 20 September, the defeated Army of the Cumberland stumbled back to Chattanooga in a foul mood. As one soldier poignantly remembered, "never in the history of the Army of the Cumberland had the spirit of its officers and men been more depressed," adding, "we also lost what was more than losing a battle, we had lost confidence in our commander." In the aftermath of the battle, the extremely popular Rosecrans watched his reputation fall sharply. Troops in Crittenden's XXI Corps had their own personal reasons for shame. The officers deeply resented their corps commander for abandoning the troops during the midst of battle.[1]

Before dealing with command failures, the Union army had to solve the real problem of defending Chattanooga from the expected Confederate attack. In the chaotic situation, units mixed in a helter-skelter pattern. Marcus Woodstock of the 9th Kentucky could not even find his division until the next day. Eventually, as order returned, Rosecrans prepared for Chattanooga's defense. Crittenden's forces would hold the Union left. Fortunately for Crittenden and the Union forces, Bragg decided to besiege the city rather than attack it. The Confederate commander had his own old scores to settle within the Confederate high command structure. The Confederate respite gave the Federals time to evaluate their recent disaster and assess blame.[2]

---

[1] Lewis, *Campaigns of the 124th Regiment*, 78; Louis A. Simmons, *The History of the 84th Regt.*, 3 vols. (Macomb: Sampson Brothers, 1866) 1:114; Francis F. McKinney, *Education in Violence: The Life of George H. Thomas and the History of the Army of the Cumberland* (Detroit: Wayne State University Press, 1961) 276.

[2] Kenneth W. Noe, ed., *A Southern Boy in Blue: The Memoir of Marcus Woodcock, 9th Kentucky Infantry, U.S.A.* (Knoxville: University of Tennessee Press, 1996) 215; US War Department, comp., *The War of the Rebellion: A Compilation of the Official Records of the*

The Union camp filled with rumors about the previous battle and forthcoming changes within the army. Several candidates emerged as scapegoats for the debacle of Chickamauga, but only Federal authorities in Washington could make the decisions that would destroy reputations and careers. As Alfred Pirtle recalled, "Great changes in the Army of the Cumberland are said to be contemplated, where we are drifting who can tell?"[3]

Crittenden faced several significant charges. Both newspaper reporters and Federal officials derided his performance on that fateful second day. The first major critic was William Shanks, a journalist working for the New York *Herald*. Shanks, who had early accompanied Rosecrans and the Army of the Cumberland, had long held a poor opinion of Crittenden, even since Perryville. He observed of Crittenden and McCook, "These men were not capacitated by nature or education for the position they held. Not one of them had any iron in his nature—neither were deep reasoners or positive characters. They were of that class of men who 'intended to do well' but without any fixed or unswervering principle to guide them, vacillated and procrastinated until the great motive and propitious time for action had passed."[4]

After Chickamauga, Shanks denigrated Crittenden's character and intelligence. He referred to Crittenden as "a country lawyer with little legal and no military ability." The reporter believed that Crittenden was "never, on the battlefield, had an opinion of his own, or ever assumed any responsibility that he could possibly avoid." Finally, Shanks attacked Crittenden's intelligence, saying, "The place which that clever gentleman, but very poor soldier, Thomas L. Crittenden, filled, was properly Tom Wood's." Wood "furnished him [Crittenden] with all the military brains, and formed for him all the military character he ever had."[5]

The reporter just as savagely attacked McCook and Rosecrans. Shanks referred to McCook as "an overgrown school-boy without dignity" He also

---

Union and Confederate Armies, 128 vols. (Washington, DC: Government Printing Office, 1880–1901) 1st ser., vol. 30, pt. 1:196.

[3] John H. Tilford Diary, 9 October 1863; Alfred Pirtle to mother, 7 October 1863, Alfred Pirtle Letters, Filson Club, Louisville.

[4] William F. G. Shanks, *Personal Recollections of Distinguished Generals* (New York: Harper & Brothers, 1866) 249.

[5] Ibid., 249, 266, 295.

pointedly noted that Rosecrans could not censure Crittenden or McCook for abandoning the battlefield since they had simply followed his example. Rather, the commanding general attempted to make Wood and Negley the culprits for the Federal disaster at Chickamauga. As Shanks correctly noted, Crittenden and McCook's troops were just as good as Thomas's, but their men had no faith in them because neither were men of "inspiring presence."[6]

Crittenden had more to worry about than a caustic journalist. Washington had sent nosey informants to the Army of the Cumberland. Charles A. Dana, a newsman and war department official, accompanied the army during the campaign. His primary responsibility was to gather information about the army's condition and report back to Secretary of War Stanton. In sum, he was a spy for Stanton, who wanted to remove Rosecrans from command. His account of the campaign would be the one the president and cabinet believed. Thus, Crittenden should have made great efforts to placate this man. As the son of a powerful Kentucky senator, Crittenden should have clearly realized the political implications of Dana's reports to Washington. Crittenden, however, never cultivated the newsman nor ever made his list of army favorites.

Dana sent numerous reports to Washington stressing the need to remove useless officers such as Crittenden. Secondly, he reported on "good evidence" that Palmer, Wood, and Hazen did not want to serve under Crittenden after he deserted his troops. According to Dana, they talked to him about their attitude. Dana believed that Rosecrans's reluctance to break with Crittenden and McCook stemmed from the commander's belief that to criticize their behavior was to criticize his own. Finally, Dana reported that Crittenden had a reputation for not paying attention to detail and for not riding his lines to assess battlefield conditions. The implication was that, if Crittenden had taken the time to consider the impact of the infamous Wood order, he could have averted the Federal disaster. With such damning information reaching the highest authorities in Washington, Crittenden's career faced destruction.[7]

---

[6] Shanks, *Personal Recollections*, 249, 289, 79.

[7] *OR*, 1st ser., vol. 30, pt. 1:197–99, 204.

Secretary Stanton agreed with Dana's assessment, noting, "[McCook] and Crittenden both made pretty good time away from the fight to Chattanooga, but Rosecrans beat them both." Perhaps more cutting were comments made by Crittenden's colleagues. According to Palmer, Rosecrans had essentially destroyed the corps command structure at Chickamauga because he had no confidence in the command skills of either Crittenden or McCook. Another officer, Emerson Opdycke, noted that "McCook is more to blame than Crittenden, because he has always failed, and he left his troops before Crittenden." He went on to suggest that Crittenden "has just enough sense to keep still, say nothing, and do little. His troops have made him." Crittenden's previous achievements disappeared from public memory.[8]

As the days passed, it became apparent that Crittenden and McCook had become Chickamauga's Federal scapegoats. Although early reports concerning the total shattering of Crittenden's corps and his abandonment of the troops had proved false and were even retracted by some newspapers, the initial negative image remained firmly etched in the minds of the Union public. One of the few bright spots for Crittenden during these dark days was that most blamed McCook more than they blamed him. As Whitelaw Reid wrote, "[McCook] displayed, as he always did, fine personal bravery, but few after this battle believed in his capacity to handle so large a command." Crittenden's amicable personality had apparently softened the criticism against him, but still the future looked bleak.[9]

The Kentuckian did not have to wait long for Federal authorities to decide his fate. On 9 October, McCook and Crittenden were relieved of command and the XX and XXI Corps merged into the new IV Corps under Gordon Granger. Camp rumor said the pair had lost their jobs due

---

[8] Tyler Dennett, ed., *Lincoln and the Civil War: In the Diaries and letters of John Hay* (1939; repr., New York: DaCapo, 1988) 93; William H. Lamers, *The Edge of Glory: A Biography of William S. Rosecrans* (New York: Harcourt Brace & World, 1961) 382; Emerson Opdycke to wife, 14 October 1863, Emerson Opdycke Papers, Ohio Historical Society, Columbus; Whitelaw Reid, *Ohio in the War: Her Statesmen, Her Generals, and Soldiers,* 2 vols. (Cincinnati: Moore, Wilstach & Baldwin, 1868) 1:807.

[9] *OR*, 1st ser., vol. 30, pt. 1:201–02, 204; Daniel, *Days of Glory*, 348; Anonymous, *Louisville Daily Journal,* (30 September 1863): 1; Anonymous, Indianapolis *Daily Journal,* (25 September 1863): 2.

to "unsatisfactory conduct." On the day of their dismissal, a correspondent named Henry Villard talked with the two men. The reporter found both "in a bitter and depressed state of mind." They wanted to give their account of their actions at Chickamauga. Crittenden's excuse was that he technically had no command left when Rosecrans moved Wood's division and thus felt "duty bound" to report to Rosecrans at Chattanooga for further orders. Although correct, this explanation did not satisfy the public. Crittenden demanded a court of inquiry be called to clear his name, declaring that he would "resign rather than draw pay for not working."[10]

On 10 October, Crittenden turned over command of his troops to the new commander. Two days later, he bade his corps farewell. His statement read as follows:

> The General Commanding announces with sorrow that the name of this corps has been stricken from the army rolls, and that he has been relieved from duty and ordered to report to Indianapolis that his conduct in the late battles of Chickamauga may be investigated.
>
> The General Commanding regrets the separation from his command—not the investigation. Investigation—the closest scrutiny—however it may affect him can only brighten your fame. Your deeds at Chickamauga, as at Stones River, will hand down to posterity your honored names.
>
> You have honored me! The mighty hand of the 21st Army Corps has graven the name of its commander on famous pages of the past. And the slanderer's tongue cannot revoke the past, future honors await you. May God bless you.

Crittenden did have a great affection for the men of the XXI Corps, and they returned it. Many soldiers expressed surprise and regret over the

---

[10] *OR*, 1st ser., vol. 30, pt. 4:210–13; Hinman, *The Sherman Brigade*, 447; Henry Villard, *memoirs of Henry Villard: Journalist and Financier, 1835–1900*, 2 vols. (Boston: Houghton Mifflin, 1904) 2:186–89; Lamers, *Edge of Glory*, 386.

loss of their old commander. They believed that Crittenden's reputation and career had suffered unjust attack.[11]

Crittenden agreed with these assessments. He told one regiment, "Toward the government I have no ill-feeling, but toward traducers and slanderers, perhaps I have." He went on to declare, "I go to clear myself from these base insinuations, and, when my character is unspotted, I may, perhaps, be again among you." No doubt Crittenden hoped to be restored to command after his name was cleared.[12]

In his official report of the battle, Crittenden commended the men and officers of the corps. He praised his divisional and brigade commanders as well as his staff officers. Instead of shifting blame to the division commanders, he praised them. For example, Crittenden did not condemn Van Cleve for the shattering of two of his brigades by Longstreet's onslaught, nor did he attack Wood for his ill-considered divisional move. The only regret to which Crittenden referred was Rosecrans's tampering: "It is a source of much regret to me that circumstances made it impossible, with any regard to the interest of the service, for my corps to act as a unit in these battles. The pride of the corps was such, that I think its attack would have been irresistible, and an attack upon it, fatal to the enemy." Crittenden personally liked Rosecrans, and he did not push the matter. Besides, others had already noted this command weakness in Rosecrans.[13]

On 12 October, Crittenden attended the presentation of the regimental flag to the 9th Indiana at Chattanooga. The regiment had originally intended that General William Nelson preside at the ceremony, but

---

[11] Francis Hudson Oxx, *The Kentucky Crittenden: The History of a Family Including Genealogy of Descendent in Both Male and Female Lives, Biographical Sketches of its Members, and Their Descent from Other Colonial Lives* (n.p., 1940) 140; John H. Tilford Diary, 10 October 1863, Filson Club; Thomas J. Wright, *History of the Eighth Regiment Kentucky Volunteer Infantry During its Three Years Campaigns, Embracing Organization, Marches, Skirmishes and Battles of the Command with Much of the History of the Old Reliable Third Brigade Commanded by Hon. Stanley Matthews and Containing Many Interesting and Amusing Incidents of Army Life* (St. Joseph: St. Joseph Steam Printing, 1880) 202; Joseph R. Reinhart, *History of the Sixth Kentucky Volunteer Infantry, U.S.: The Boys Who Feared No Noise* (Louisville: Bluegrass Press, 2000) 230.

[12] Anonymous, *Louisville Daily Journal*, (7 December 1863): 1.

[13] *OR*, 1st ser., vol. 30, pt. 1:612.

because of his death in Kentucky the previous year the honor fell to Crittenden. He bade the regiment farewell and encouraged the soldiers to finish the work they had begun. A reporter commented:

> Although General Crittenden by his acknowledged ability as a commander, and by his kind and gentlemanly spirit toward all under his command, had already secured the universal good will and esteem of both officers and men, yet the depth of feeling, the manifest honest purpose of heart, and, withal, the very happy manner in which these brief farewell words were spoken, seemed to produce without exception, in both officers and men of the 9th, the deep conviction that their former estimate of the man had been far short of the real merits of his character."

Crittenden still had a core of supporters, but they did not have the power to keep him in his command.[14]

Crittenden's Kentucky friends did not forget him in his time of need. The Kentucky legislature passed a resolution requesting an investigation of Crittenden's behavior at Chickamauga and expressed its firm belief that the inquiry would vindicate his reputation. Although the action helped to rouse Crittenden's low spirits, it did not persuade the Federal authorities in Washington. Many Federal officials had long doubted Kentucky's commitment to the Union cause; they would not give a Kentucky Unionist leader the benefit of a doubt over his questionable conduct at Chickamauga. Crittenden had no powerful political connections, and he had to face the crisis on his own. His father was no longer there to advise him or come to his aid. Crittenden experienced a loneliness he had never experienced. Only his elder brother George, who had suffered negative publicity after Mill Springs, could have understood the pain the second Crittenden son felt.[15]

The state's leading newspaper, the Louisville *Daily Journal*, continued to express the opinion of most Kentucky Unionists that Crittenden did not deserve the criticism he had received. On 5 October, the paper noted that one man alone could not staunch the rout of a large number of troops and

---

[14] *Louisville Daily Journal,* (24 October 1863): 1.

[15] *OR*, 1st ser., vol. 30, pt. 1:618.

Crittenden did not deserve censure for failing to rally the troops. The paper attacked Shanks's veracity and pointed to other reporters who had offered a more favorable opinion of Crittenden. The paper reported on Crittenden's bravery on the field of battle and added approvingly that Generals Rosecrans and Garfield commended the Kentuckian for acting energetically to stem the rout. The editor went on to claim that some of Crittenden's critics were reporters far removed from the camp and who had themselves fled the battle ingloriously. The editor concluded of Crittenden, "All he demands is justice henceforth."[16]

The controversy refused to die down. During November and December 1863, the *Daily Journal* continued to publish reports defending Crittenden's actions. One report noted his bravery and near capture in attempting to rally the troops. Doubts as to the Federal authorities' motives also continued. Kentucky Unionists did not blame Crittenden for the Chickamauga debacle.[17]

The disgraced Kentuckian also received support from fellow officers. General Palmer, his most outspoken defender, insisted that the Federal government's treatment of Crittenden was unfair. In a pique of disgust, he offered his resignation:

> I tender my resignation because of the late order of the war department which abolishes the 21st army corps and orders its late commander, Major-General Crittenden before a Court of Inquiry, it implies, and will be understood by the country as implying, the severest censure upon the conduct of the officers and men lately composing the corps.
>
> The order is in its circumstances, without example in the military history of the country. No corps, before this, has been deprived of its commander and stricken out of existence within a few days after a great battle in the midst of important military operations, and in the face of the enemy. By this sudden decisive,

---

[16] Anonymous, *Louisville Daily Journal*, (29 September 1863): 2; Anonymous, *Louisville Daily Journal*, (5 October 1863): 3; Anonymous, *Louisville Daily Journal*, (14 October 1863): 2; Anonymous, *Louisville Daily Journal*, (16 October 1863): 2.

[17] Anonymous, *Louisville Daily Journal*, (10 November 1863): 2.

sweeping order, the government has given to the misrepresentation of its fugitives from the battlefield the weight of its own apparent endorsement, slander is dignified into history, and henceforth refutation is impossible.

The disgruntled Illinois general still admired Crittenden and believed that the consolidation of McCook's and Crittenden's corps was humiliating.[18]

Crittenden also received support from the ranks. One soldier remembered their commander's farewell, reflecting, "The men parted from Crittenden with general regret, his kind manners and thoughtful regard for their comfort having made him personally popular with all." Marcus Woodstock of the 9th Kentucky recalled that Crittenden was a "brave and efficient officer" and observed that "The mere fact of a man losing a battle was a poor plea upon which to have him arraigned before a court of inquiry in defense of his character as an officer." Many held similar attitudes. A sense of injustice pervaded the Army of the Cumberland.[19]

Likewise, Crittenden earned the support of his commander. Following the battle Rosecrans told him, "Every action of yours in the battle of Chickamauga met my cordial approbation." Rosecrans believed that Wood or Negley deserved more censure than Crittenden. After Rosecrans's hasty retreat to Chattanooga, however, he lost his credibility. Although Rosecrans's praise helped soothe Crittenden's wounded feelings, it did little to change public opinion.[20]

On 21 October, after his removal from command, Crittenden returned to Louisville. He enjoyed his respite in the friendly confines of his home state but grew more restless over the delay in the beginning of his court of inquiry. The *Daily Journal* noted that Crittenden was "impatient under the inexcusable delay"; but that he was in good spirits and expected vindication. The editor believed that the government should "not withhold

---

[18] John M. Palmer, *Personal Recollections of John Palmer: The Story of an Ernest Life* (Cincinnati: Robert Clarke, 1901) 190, 192; Oxx, *Kentucky Crittendens*, 140.

[19] Ebenezer Hannaford, *The Story of a Regiment: A History of the Campaigns, and Associations in the Field, of the Sixth Ohio Volunteer Infantry* (Cincinnati: Ebenezer Hannaford, 1868) 482; Noe, ed., *Southern Boy in Blue*, 225–26.

[20] Lamers, *Edge of Glory*, 386–87.

from this gallant officer the poor justice of a speedy and full investigation."
While waiting, Crittenden organized his legal defense.[21]

The court of inquiry began on 9 January 1864 and consisted of
David Hunter, George Caldwalder, and J. S. Wadsworth. None of these
men had Kentucky or western connections, nor were they overly
sympathetic to Crittenden. The court first convened in Nashville on 29
January 1864 but quickly moved to Louisville and met there until 23
February.[22]

During the court's deliberations Crittenden wanted to make several
key points. First, he insisted he had done all that was humanly possibly to
rally the troops after the critical breakthrough at Chickamauga. Secondly,
Crittenden wanted the court to realize that, with the transfer of Van Cleve
and Wood, he had no troops to command. Third, he also wanted the court
to hear of his efforts to make connection with Thomas's troops on
Snodgrass Hill.[23]

After nearly two months of hearings, the court rendered its opinion
on 23 February. Concerning Crittenden's performance on the first day of
Chickamauga, the court stated: "The evidence adduced respecting General
Crittenden's operation on that day not only shows no cause for censure,
but on the contrary, that his whole conduct was most creditable." The court
praised Crittenden's "watchfulness and prompt and judicious support of
troops engaged." As for Crittenden's performance on the second day of
Chickamauga, the court concluded:

> For the disaster which ensued he is by no means responsible...It
> is amply proven General Crittenden did everything he could, by
> example and personal exertion to rally and hold his troops, and to
> prevent the evils resulting such a condition of affairs, but without
> avail.
>
> Believing that by his presence on the field nothing more could
> be effected, he left for Rossville, where he learned little else than the
> commanding general had gone to Chattanooga, he repaired thither,

---

[21] *OR*, 1st ser., vol. 30, pt. 1:2971; Anonymous, *Louisville Daily Journal*, (14 October
1863): 3; Anonymous, *Louisville Daily Journal*, (9 November 1863): 3.

[22] *OR*, 1st ser., vol. 30, pt. 1:971.

[23] *OR*, 1st ser., vol. 30, pt. 1:974–96.

where one of his brigades was stationed. In the opinion of the court, General Crittenden is not censurable for this act.[24]

Crittenden no doubt believed his long nightmare was over. Perhaps he would receive another corps command somewhere in the Union army. Unfortunately, Union public opinion did not forgive Crittenden as easily as the court of inquiry.

Despite the favorable findings of the court, the Kentuckian's public reputation lay in tatters. Public criticism shaped by Shanks and Dana denigrated Crittenden's character as well as his intelligence. Federal authorities and fellow generals were reluctant to give him another opportunity to prove Shanks and Dana wrong. The Kentuckian had not expected this outcome. In fact, for the rest of his life the shame and pain of Chickamauga never left Crittenden.

---

[24] *OR,* 1st ser., vol. 30, pt. 1:996.

12

The Virginia Interlude

Thomas Crittenden desperately desired reunion with his old command, but Federal authorities refused to comply with his wish. Instead of rapidly returning to the field, Crittenden spent several months just waiting. During this time, he returned home and enjoyed socializing with family and friends, perhaps realizing his need for the support and comfort of family.[1]

Crittenden's first opportunity to return to active command came during his court of inquiry. Several leading Union generals, including Grant, Rosecrans, Thomas, and John Schofield, were in Louisville attending a conference on Union strategy. Crittenden met with the men and expressed a desire to return to duty. Using his keen political skills, he planted a seed for future germination. Several months later, his opportunity arrived.[2]

In the eastern theatre, there was an opening in the IX Corps. On 10 May 1864, Thomas G. Stevenson, commander of the corps' 1st Division, had received a fatal head wound, creating the need for an immediate replacement. On 11 May, Crittenden received the appointment as divisional commander. This appointment was Crittenden's opportunity to redeem his reputation and renew his military career. Yet it also presented several problems for the eager Kentuckian.[3]

---

[1] Eliza Lee to Patrick Joyes, 28 March 1864, Joyes Family Papers, Filson Club, Louisville.

[2] Robert Emmett McDowell, *City of Conflict: Louisville in the Civil War, 1861–1865* (Louisville: Louisville Round Table, 1962) 159.

[3] US War Department, comp., *The War of the Rebellion: A Compilation of the Official Records of the Union and Confederate Armies*, 128 vols. (Washington, DC: Government Printing Office, 1880–1901) 1st ser., vol. 36, pt. 1:909; Charles F. Walcott, *History of the Twenty-first Massachusetts Volunteers in the War for the Preservation of the Union, 1861–1865, with Statistics of the War and Rebel Prisons* (Boston: Houghton Mifflin and Co., 1882) 320.

The first problem Crittenden faced was acceptance by the easterners. During this period, the Appalachian Mountains were the dividing line between east and west. Relatively few western troops served in the Army of the Potomac, and almost all commanders had eastern backgrounds. Theodore Lyman, one of General Meade's staff officers, offered a typical eastern observation when he said of Crittenden, "He is the queerest-looking party you ever saw, with a thin staring face, and hair hanging to his coat collar—a very wild appearing major general, but quite a kindly man in conversation, despite his terrible looks." It would require a great deal of effort and some battlefield success for Crittenden to gain acceptance among this new group of fellow officers.[4]

A second dilemma Crittenden confronted in Virginia was the ticklish issue of rank. Due to his political connections and early success in the war, he outranked many generals in the East due to his early promotions. In fact, the only Union generals there who outranked him were Grant and Burnside. An officer's date of rank established their seniority and was therefore extremely important. The solution was for Crittenden to serve under Burnside in the IX Corps. Still, the issue of rank would rear its ugly head within a few months.[5]

Ambrose Burnside posed another potential problem for Crittenden. Burnside had unsuccessfully commanded Union troops in Kentucky during 1863. He had declared martial law, sentenced Kentucky citizens, and meddled in Kentucky politics. Crittenden was one of several prominent Kentucky Unionists who frequently heard complaints about Burnside's ineptitude. Because of such grumbling, the Louisville *Daily Journal* and others had pushed for Burnside's replacement with Crittenden. Nothing had ever come of the demand, but Burnside was aware of its existence. During Rosecrans's Chattanooga campaign and Burnside's Knoxville efforts, Crittenden had inadvertently gotten Burnside into trouble. When the Federals captured Chattanooga, Crittenden had wired Burnside that Bragg's forces were in full retreat. As a result,

---

[4] George R. Agassiz, ed., *Meade's Headquarters, 1863–1865: letters of Colonel Theodore Lyman from the Wilderness to Appomattox* (Boston: Atlantic Monthly Press, 1922) 116–117.

[5] William Marvel, *Burnside* (Chapel Hill: University of North Carolina, 1991) 362.

Burnside moved to crush lingering Confederate resistance in East Tennessee and did not move toward Chattanooga to cooperate with Rosecrans's pursuit of the Confederate army. Within a few weeks, the Battle of Chickamauga showed how desperately Rosecrans needed Burnside's troops. Burnside took a great deal of criticism for not cooperating with Rosecrans, but he had only acted on Crittenden's overoptimistic view of the situation. Burnside could have made Crittenden pay dearly for his previous actions, but he never held Crittenden's previous actions against him and the two men worked well together.[6]

Unfortunately, Burnside and the IX Corps did not have the best reputation in the Union army. Burnside had suffered one of the worst Union defeats of the war at Fredericksburg, and the IX Corps had not performed well either. The 1st Division, which Crittenden was to command, reflected many of the problems on the eastern front. Casualties had decimated the ranks and taken many capable officers, and by 1864 new troops of less than stellar quality had replaced the losses. As a result, Crittenden's division consisted of many new recruits of untested ability. Crittenden's 1st Brigade, originally led by Colonel Stephen Weld, now consisted of the 35th Massachusetts, the 56th Massachusetts, the 57th Massachusetts, the 59th Massachusetts, the 4th US, and the 10th US. The incompetent James Ledlie replaced Weld, who had died in battle shortly after the arrival of Crittenden, as a brigade commander. Crittenden's 2nd Brigade, commanded by the almost equally incompetent David Leasure, consisted of the 3rd Maryland, the 21st Massachusetts, and the 100th Pennsylvania. During the campaign Joseph Sudsburg replaced Leasure. The 2nd Maine and 14th Massachusetts batteries provided artillery support. Later, Crittenden received reinforcements in the form of a provisional brigade under Elisha G. Marshall. This provisional brigade consisted of the 2nd New York Rifles (dismounted), the 14th New York Heavy Artillery, the 24th New York Cavalry (dismounted), and the 2nd Pennsylvania Provisional Heavy Artillery. These troops joined Crittenden shortly before beginning operations at Cold Harbor. The quality of the troops and officers fell far short of Crittenden's former comrades in the

---

[6] *OR*, 1st ser., vol. 30, pt. 3:770; Marvel, *Burnside*, 287.

West. There Crittenden had also depended on Thomas J. Wood for advice, but in the East he would have no such luxury.[7]

One recent campaign historian described Crittenden's division as "cursed with perhaps the most inept leaders in the Army of the Potomac." Soldiers of the time did not have a much higher opinion of the division. One soldier said, "our division is in a terrible state of discipline and organization." Given Crittenden's previous record of slackness in administrative details and Burnside's long recognized failings as a commander, Crittenden should have expected little in the way of success.[8]

A final difficulty Crittenden struggled to overcome concerned his attitude. He had been a corps commander and before the second day of Chickamauga had boasted a respectable record. He had held a prominent position, while many of his new colleagues were leading regiments or brigades. Crittenden's new assignment was clearly a demotion, and the proud Kentuckian no doubt realized this fact. According to Crittenden family tradition, he never felt at home in the East and resented having not received a new command equivalent to his former position.[9]

Interestingly, too, Crittenden arrived in the eastern theatre during some of the most intense fighting of the war. General Grant, recently promoted to lieutenant general, had decided to accompany Meade's Army of the Potomac during the campaign. Grant's strategy consisted of continually attempting to turn Lee's flank and cut Lee off from his line of retreat. Lee, a brilliant tactician, made Grant's turning movements extremely costly for Federal troops. From 7 May through 20 May, in the Wilderness campaign, the two armies collided repeatedly. In the midst of this vortex of battle, Crittenden arrived to assume command of the 1st Division of the IX Corps.

---

[7] Gordon C. Rhea, *The Battles for Spotsylvania Court House and the Road to Yellow Tavern, May 7–12, 1864* (Baton Rouge: Louisiana State University Press, 1997) 341; Gordon C. Rhea, *Cold Harbor: Grant and Lee, May 26–June 3, 1864* (Baton Rouge: Louisiana State University Press, 2002) 406; Marvel, *Burnside,* 366–67.

[8] Rhea, *Cold Harbor,* 257; William G. Gavin, ed., *Campaigning with the Roundheads: The History of the Hundredth Pennsylvania Veteran Volunteers Infantry Regiment in the American Civil War, 1861–1865* (Dayton: Morningside, 1989) 447.

[9] Francis Hudson Oxx, *The Kentucky Crittenden: The History of a Family Including Genealogy of Descendent in Both Male and Female Lives, Biographical Sketches of its Members, and Their Descent from Other Colonial Lives* (n.p., 1940) 140.

Crittenden assumed command on the night of 11 May, just before Grant carried out a major attack the following morning. During the previous days, Grant had forced the Confederates into a line that jutted outward and created a salient that invited attack. This salient, known as the mule shoe, was the focus of the assault on 12 May. Grant planned to attack the apex of the salient with Hancock's II Corps reinforced by Wright's VI Corps on the left flank. Burnside's corps would attack the right flank. If the attacks occurred simultaneously, the Confederate line would hopefully give way, resulting in a major breakthrough that might end the war.

Hancock's II Corps attacked and achieved a spectacular advance in the Battle of the Bloody Angle. However, Burnside's corps did not move in unison. This gave the hard-pressed Confederates precious time to construct a new line and prepare for the second wave of assaults. By the time Burnside committed Crittenden's division to the attack, it was too late for success. Crittenden's troops, unlike those of the II Corps that morning, did not have tactical surprise, so Crittenden's attack failed. Burnside's tardiness in ordering the attack and Crittenden's unfamiliarity with both his forces and the terrain contributed to the Union woes that day. Crittenden's fresh start had not begun well.[10]

Crittenden received little criticism for his failure. Perhaps other officers realized that many of his problems that day were beyond his control and did not deserve censure. Burnside did not criticize Crittenden in his report of the battle, and most press coverage faulted Burnside, not Crittenden, for failing to make the troops move earlier. Burnside made a convenient target for those who wanted to criticize the slow Union advance, and thus Crittenden thankfully received little attention for his poor performance.[11]

On 16 May and 18 May, Grant attacked the Confederate lines again with Crittenden's troops. On both occasions, the Federals quickly discovered that the Confederates still manned their works in strength and

---

[10] *OR*, 1st ser., vol. 36, pt. 1:909–10; Marvel, *Burnside*, 363.
[11] *OR*, 1st ser., vol. 36, pt. 1:909–10.

that any assault was futile. Luckily for Crittenden's troops, both attacks ended quickly before the casualties mounted.[12]

Grant eventually perceived the uselessness of another frontal assault on Lee's lines and began a turning movement, hoping to gain the North Anna River and cut Lee off from his base at Richmond. Lee made a countermove, planning a trap for the aggressive advancing Federals. He placed his troops in a roughly inverted V formation near the probable crossings of the North Anna River. When the Federals advanced, they faced a withering fire from the defenders and were not able to support each other or easily retreat back across the river. It was a superb Confederate tactical plan, and only Lee's illness prevented the Confederate trap from causing more damage.

Burnside's IX Corps, in particular Crittenden's division, played a prominent role in the North Anna campaign. On 23 May, Burnside reached the North Anna River at Telegraph Bridge and Jericho Mills. Another river crossing known as Ox Ford, near Quarles Mill between these two locations, would provide a crossing for Burnside's troops. Grant planned for Burnside's corps to cross the river at Ox Ford and to link up with those already across the River.

There were problems, however. First, the terrain at Ox Ford made a crossing difficult. The slope of the riverbank made it physically difficult for troops to cross the river. Secondly, unknown to the Federals, A. P. Hill's III Corps were waiting to obstruct the Federal movement.[13]

Burnside dutifully obeyed orders and sent Crittenden's division across the ford first, with James Ledlie and some of his 1st Brigade units in the lead. Crittenden expected Ledlie to establish a beachhead and wait for the remainder of the division to cross. Ledlie, apparently drunk, decided to attack the strong Confederate position in his front. With only 1,500 men, he planned to attack A. P. Hill's entire corps. Toward that end, he indignantly sent a messenger back to Crittenden demanding reinforcements to make the assault. Crittenden, no doubt in shock, advised caution. He replied, "Tell General Ledlie not to charge unless he sees a sure thing. I am afraid it will be a failure and result in bringing on a severe

---

[12] Gordon C. Rhea, *To the North Anna River: Grant and Lee, May 13–25, 1864* (Baton Rouge: Louisiana State University Press, 2000) 121, 136–38.

[13] Marvel, *Burnside*, 370

engagement, which we are in no condition to meet right now, as a large part of my division is still on the other side of the river with the rest of the corps. Tell him to use the utmost caution." Caution was something Ledlie did not possess. The drunken general ordered an assault, and his troops were decimated. One recent historian of the battle estimated that Ledlie lost around 450 men.[14]

Upon hearing the sound of battle, Crittenden rode to the front and assumed command. He pulled the troops back before the Confederates could do more damage. Many of the men in the brigade knew that Ledlie's drunkenness had cost them dearly, but in his report Burnside credited the irresponsible officer with bravery. Ledlie was not punished for his actions and Crittenden may well have wondered about the quality of the corps.[15]

The Ox Ford incident brought no glory or honor to Crittenden's already tarnished reputation. Although the fiasco was the fault of an irresponsible subordinate, Crittenden should have noticed Ledlie's unfitness for command before beginning the operation. Once again, Crittenden's carelessness toward mundane administrative details had come back to haunt him. In the West, subordinates like Wood, Palmer, or even Van Cleve would never have let Crittenden down so badly, but he had no such luxury now. Crittenden needed capable, faithful subordinates if he was going to restore his reputation. Apparently, his fellow officers in the IX Corps utterly lacked such qualities.

After the Ox Ford fiasco, Grant modified his command structure to provide better communication and efficiency. Burnside would now receive orders directly from Meade. At the same time, Meade placed Crittenden's division under the temporary command of G. K. Warren and the V Corps. Crittenden's division was nearer that corps than the remaining divisions of the IX Corps.[16]

Unlike Burnside, Crittenden had problems with the new structure. He had commanded a division when Warren had only led a regiment. Crittenden already looked upon division command as a demotion, and

---

[14] *OR*, 1st ser., vol. 36, pt. 1:912–13; Marvel, *Burnside*, 370–71; Rhea, *To the North Anna River*, 339, 342.

[15] Marvel, *Burnside*, 371.

[16] *OR*, 1st ser., vol. 36, pt. 1:170.

serving under a junior in rank only added insult to injury. Never one to coddle those around him, Warren did nothing to ease the situation. He did not care about Crittenden's feelings. In the midst of this upsetting situation, Crittenden turned to Burnside for advice. Burnside had just suffered a similar slight in relation to Meade, and Crittenden no doubt wondered what advice Burnside could offer. Burnside replied, "I fully appreciate your feelings in the matter to which you refer, but under all circumstances I would as a friend advise you to remain where you are. If you wish I will ask General Grant to relieve you, but I really think it would be a mistake." For the moment, Crittenden heeded Burnside's advice. On 25 May, when Warren visited Crittenden's position to inspect the lines, the affable Crittenden bit his tongue and graciously received Warren and his staff. One of Warren's staff officers noted that Crittenden was "very pleasant and did not visit his dissatisfaction on Warren."[17]

While Crittenden's temper simmered, the war continued. Lee's ingenious formation at the North Anna River stymied further Federal advance along that line. As Grant evacuated his untenable position at Ox Ford, Crittenden's division served as a rearguard force for the withdrawal. This movement required a great deal of skill and coordination—both of which Crittenden lacked.[18]

On 30 May at about 11 A.M., Crittenden received orders to link up with Griffin's division of the V Corps. Crittenden began to move only to have Burnside tell Crittenden and Potter's divisions to change their axis of march to the more threatened point of the Confederate attack between Griffin and Crawford's divisions near the Shady Grove Road. As a result, Crittenden's division did not arrive until late in the day, too late to have any impact. This only worsened Crittenden's relations with Warren. On 31 May, Warren blamed Crittenden for endangering the V Corps when he was slow to relieve them.[19]

Crittenden's division moved slowly through the dense undergrowth and swampy terrain. When it arrived in position, it built crude breastworks. Warren acted as if Crittenden's troops were a permanent part

---

[17] Rhea, *To the North Anna River*, 35; *OR*, 1st ser., vol. 36, pt. 3:228–29.

[18] *OR*, 1st ser., vol. 36, pt. 3: 228–229.

[19] *OR*, 1st ser., vol. 36, pt. 3:404, 409; Marvel, *Burnside*, 380.

of the V Corps. Warren would do no favors for Crittenden. Crittenden's prospects for success with the army seemed bleak.[20]

The breastworks that Crittenden's men built had a major problem. The swampy terrain forced the troops leave a gap between their division and Griffin's division in the V Corps. Such an opening provided an invitation for the Confederates to attack, which they did on 1 June under Rodes and Gordon. During the attack, one soldier disgustedly remarked that Crittenden did not seem to care about the enemy penetration and did nothing to counter it.[21]

The Battle of Cold Harbor provided the final impetus for Crittenden's demise and quick departure from the Army of the Potomac. On 2 June, Crittenden's division marched with no cavalry screen. Crittenden could have used his pickets to serve this function, but instead he called them in. The Confederates, seeing an opportunity, created a wedge between the IX Corps and the V Corps. The situation might have escalated had there been more Confederate troops available to exploit the breakthrough. Since this was not the case, the Union lines held. Crittenden's division suffered heavy losses of approximately 440 men, and Warren blamed Crittenden. In fact, Burnside was more responsible for the loss than Crittenden. He had pulled Crittenden out of line without informing Warren. This order had created the gap, and the abrupt relocation of Crittenden's division probably disconcerted the normal Union cavalry screen.[22]

Tired of the incompetence below and the attacks from above, Crittenden asked to be relieved. On 7 June, Federal authorities accepted his request. The incompetent Ledlie replaced him and soon led the division into disaster at Petersburg.[23]

Crittenden still hoped for another command, preferably in the West with his old colleagues. Unfortunately, his poor battlefield performance with the IX Corps and his outburst with Warren over rank did not help to resurrect his career. Consequently, Crittenden waited for an assignment

[20] *OR*, 1st ser., vol. 36, pt. 3:33–41, 358–59.
[21] Rhea, *Cold Harbor*, 256; Gavin, *Campaigning with the Roundheads*, 448.
[22] *OR*, 1st ser., vol. 36, pt. 1:544, 913; Rhea, *Cold Harbor*, 296, 300, 493.
[23] *OR*, 1st ser., vol. 36, pt. 1:544, 913.

that never came. The popular Kentuckian could have used his political skills to good effect had he received an assignment that required political finesse not military genius. Sadly, this was not to be. Thomas L. Crittenden, who had personally sacrificed so much for the Union effort, spent the last six months of the war as a civilian.[24]

Crittenden's stint with the Army of the Potomac clearly had not enhanced his reputation. Surrounded by subordinates, superiors, and troops of uneven quality at best, Crittenden could only fail. His old XXI Corps had superb veteran troops ably led by qualified officers. Even Van Cleve, probably the weakest commander in Crittenden's old command, was a genius compared to the officers in Crittenden's new one. Only extra attention to detail and a little luck could have saved Crittenden from the predictable failings of this weak command. The disgruntled Kentuckian's lack of aggressiveness and his new streak of misfortune prevented a happy outcome.

---

[24] Oxx, *Kentucky Crittendens,* 141.

13

Reconciliation after the Storm

After Appomattox and the coming of peace, the Crittenden siblings had to decide how to work out their personal relationships. The senator had died during the war, estranged from his eldest children. Would the siblings continue that estrangement or attempt to find ways to reconcile? As time passed, the brothers and sisters chose to return as much as possible to their lives as they had been before the cannons roared. Many other families in Kentucky and the border state region had similar postwar experiences.

Although most Kentuckians had supported the Union cause in 1861, as the war progressed many had grown increasingly critical of Lincoln's policies. By 1865, Confederate sympathy was strong in Kentucky. Most Kentucky Unionists expressed satisfaction with the war's outcome and chose not to dwell on the past. For Unionists such as Thomas Crittenden, reconciliation should come as quickly as possible.[1]

The Crittenden siblings had been close before the war, but the conflict put great stress on their relationship. Despite the family divisions, they had maintained some degree of contact with each other even during the war. For instance, unionist Thomas mentioned in a letter to his pro-Confederate sister Ann Mary of having recently seen his Confederate-sympathizing sister Cornelia in Kentucky. In another instance, Thomas inquired from Ann Mary if she had heard anything from Confederate-sympathizing George. Although surviving correspondence is sparse, both Confederate and Union Crittenden siblings interacted during the war. Family ties, though nearly torn asunder by war, remained intact.[2]

---

[1] Thomas Speed, *The Union Cause in Kentucky* (New York: G. P. Putnam & Sons, 1907) ix-x.

[2] Thomas L. Crittenden to Ann Mary Coleman, 11 August 1864, John J. Crittenden Papers, Duke University, Durham NC; Thomas L. Crittenden to Harry I. Todd, 5 January 1867, Todd Collection, Kentucky Historical Society, Frankfort. Unfortunately, neither Thomas nor George were prolific correspondents. Among the siblings, only Ann Mary

One humorous example of family reconciliation occurred in 1872. Thomas had an appointment at the White House to see his former commander, Ulysses Grant. Upon arriving, he saw his sister Ann Mary waiting to see the president first. Years earlier, Ann Mary had translated for the president some German works on the campaigns of Frederick the Great. Thomas jokingly questioned why "rebels" got to see the President before good Unionists. Since the two Crittendens could joke about their past differences, some reconciliation must have occurred.[3]

Ann Mary's scholarly interests helped create an avenue of reconciliation. The eldest daughter had always had an extremely close relationship with her father and no doubt deeply regretted their separation during the last months of his life. As a means of reconciling with her departed father, she decided to write an adoring biography. Pursuant to that goal, she requested input from her siblings—letters, anecdotes, and other memories of their father. The siblings gladly responded, perhaps realizing that the memory of their father united them in a powerful way. Ann Mary's work paid off. In 1871 J. B. Lippincott published *The Life of John J. Crittenden*. The siblings expressed their satisfaction with the family matriarch's work. Not surprisingly, Ann Mary did not include Crittenden family letters that highlighted deep divisions within the family. She probably realized that publicizing old scars would not serve family unity. Ann Mary had made peace with her father's memory and had contributed in a tangible way to the siblings' reconciliation.[4]

---

preserved much of her correspondence with her father and siblings. In the surviving family correspondence, a great deal of writing concerned family news and expressed the siblings' concern for and interest in one another. This did not change from prewar to postwar correspondence.

[3] Francis Hudson Oxx, *The Kentucky Crittenden: The History of a Family Including Genealogy of Descendent in Both Male and Female Lives, Biographical Sketches of its Members, and Their Descent from Other Colonial Lives* (n.p., 1940) 147.

[4] George B. Crittenden to Ann Mary Coleman, 1 May 1870, John J. Crittenden Papers; and Kitty Crittenden to Ann Mary Coleman, 4 January 1872, John J. Crittenden Papers, Duke University. Many of the papers Ann Mary used in the preparation of her manuscript are included in the Crittenden collection at Duke. She omitted many family letters in the manuscript, and one can probably surmise that she edited her family letters before allowing them to pass to posterity. Since the other Crittenden siblings did not preserve much family correspondence, much of what we do know of the family's inner workings come to us through Ann Mary's filtered lens.

In 1873, another unexpected opportunity developed for family reconciliation. Ann Mary's daughter Cornelia had married John Marriott. When Cornelia died, she left behind two young children. John Marriott, who was very ill himself and had suffered heavy financial losses in the Panic of 1873, died within a year, leaving the children orphaned. Ann Mary offered a proposal to her brother Thomas. Ann Mary would raise the daughter if Thomas would raise the son. Thomas loved his grandnephew, named Crittenden Marriott, and raised him as his own. That Ann Mary was able to allow her Unionist bother to raise her grandson suggests that the deep wounds of the war must have completely healed.[5]

The next example of family reconciliation concerned the third son, Robert. Content to remain in the background and enjoy the benefits of his family connections, he had never excelled in either business or politics. In 1885, when creditors sued Robert for debt, Ann Mary's son-in-law Patrick Joyes proposed a solution. Ann Mary, Joyes, and Thomas would split the amount owed and pay the legal expenses for their younger brother. Thomas replied to Joyes proposal, saying, "I am hard up for money, but I will pay my proportion of the expenses." Unfortunately, even with his siblings' help, Robert never recovered from his losses.[6]

The Crittenden siblings clearly chose the path of restoration rather than continuing to fight the war. During the conflict both George and Thomas had suffered humiliating disasters. Both had endured scathing criticism from the press. Both needed the love and support of their families to soothe the wounds of Civil War. Perhaps the reality that both brothers had failed militarily eased the path to reconciliation since they needed each other. As the healing process began, each sibling had to rebuild his or her life from the chaos of war. As before the war, some had better fortune than others.

---

[5] Oxx, *Kentucky Crittendens,* 152. Crittenden Marriott adored his Uncle Thomas and passed down to his children Thomas's achievements and personal stories. His daughter married Francis Oxx, who undertook a Crittenden family genealogy that gave a prominent position to the accomplished Thomas. Oxx's work somewhat counterbalances Ann Mary's editing. Combining both sources provides a better perspective on the Crittenden family dynamics.

[6] Patrick Joyes to Thomas L. Crittenden, 5 January 1885; and Thomas L. Crittenden to Patrick Joyes, 5 November 1885, Joyes Family Papers, Filson Club.

George, the firstborn, returned to Kentucky after Appomattox. Many Kentuckians did not hold his humiliating defeat at Mill Springs against him. Despite his loss, Kentucky's growing Confederate spirit actually helped win George favor upon his return. Bearing the Crittenden name and possessing Southern loyalties, he could have entered politics and might have done well. Yet he chose otherwise. Unlike his younger brother Thomas, he did not have many political skills or ambitions. George preferred to stay out of the spotlight and enjoy his remaining years among friends and family. Since the affable and handsome George Crittenden never married, these friends and family were of the utmost importance.

George served as the state librarian at Frankfort for several years after the war. Like many of the Crittendens, he enjoyed cultivating the mind and now had time to enjoy such pursuits. George seemed happy in the postwar era. One colleague summed up George's postwar life when he said, "He lived many years after the war, and enjoyed the goodwill and respect of all who knew him." After retiring as state librarian, George moved to the home of his sister Cornelia in Danville. While there in November 1880, he died. The family held the funeral in the Frankfort home of George's stepbrother Harry I. Todd. Afterward, the family buried George in the family plot in Frankfort Cemetery.[7]

Cornelia remained in Danville following George's death. She died in 1890, and unlike the rest of the Crittenden siblings her body remained in Danville. Cornelia's strong ties to Centre College overcame family loyalty. As was true of much of her life, she remained somewhat distanced from her siblings.[8]

Ann Mary remained active in a variety of affairs. She read widely and frequently gave presentations on American history to groups near Washington, DC. Her European stay helped her become fluent in German, and she translated several historical works on Frederick the Great for President Grant. The president and Mrs. Grant enjoyed Ann Mary's company and

---

[7]   Http://sunsite.unc.edu/pub/academic/histo...literary/civilwar-usa/d-H-Maaury–06,txt accessed 11 November 1999.

[8]   Oxx, *Kentucky Crittendens*, 192.

she frequently wished the White House.[9]

Ann Mary also continued to manage her varied business interests. One of her sons in law, Patrick Joyes, served as her primary financial advisor. As matriarch of a large and powerful family, Ann Mary frequently gave advances to cover financial difficulties. One of the more frequent petitions for aid came from her younger brother Robert. In 1877, Ann Mary had to sign a bond for Robert, and in 1885, she joined Thomas and Joyes in settling one of Robert's debts. Robert never learned financial responsibility. Ann Mary, like her indulgent father, would not make Robert pay for the consequences of his irresponsibility.[10]

Ann Mary moved back to Louisville, where she died in 1891. Robert died in Frankfort in 1898. Both were buried in the Crittenden family plot at Frankfort Cemetery.[11]

Eugene, after chasing John Hunt Morgan during the Civil War, remained in the army. He served until his death in Arizona in 1874. He died at Camp Barrie, and according to family tradition his men loved him dearly. The youngest daughter, Sarah Lee Watson, died in 1887 in Frankfort.[12]

Of all the Crittenden siblings, Thomas had the most distinguished postwar career. He returned to Kentucky in 1865 and quickly became involved in Kentucky politics. Kentucky politics divided three major ways. The Radical Republicans supported or accepted Lincoln's Civil War policies, including emancipation, and looked forward to Kentucky's future industrialization. The second group called themselves Conservative Unionists. They supported the Union as it existed in 1860 and opposed many of Lincoln's wartime policies. The third group consisted of the returning Confederates. Once they reentered Kentucky politics, they held the balance of power between the first two groups. Crittenden became a

---

[9] Ulysses S. Grant to Ann Mary Coleman, October 3, 1866; Oxx, *Kentucky Crittendens*, 147; The John J. Crittenden Papers at Duke University has Ann Mary's notes from some of her presentations.

[10] Robert H. Crittenden to Ann Mary Coleman, July 6, 1877, John J. Crittenden Papers, Duke; Patrick Joyes to Thomas L. Crittenden, January 5, 1885, John J. Crittenden papers, Duke.

[11] Oxx, *Kentucky Crittendens*, 192.

[12] Ibid., 192.

leader of the Conservative Party and supported the reconstruction policies of President Andrew Johnson.[13]

Crittenden's political ambitions ran into difficulties almost immediately. He wanted the 1866 elections to serve as referendum on the Unionist position of 1861. The Conservatives said they "stood squarely behind Johnson" and called for "the earnest and disinterested support of all Union men of Kentucky in all conflicts with both extremes." Crittenden expected the Unionist majority of 1861 to asset itself and for his party to dominate the upcoming elections. The returning Confederates, however, painted the Conservative Unionists as closet Radical Republicans. Thus, in the 1866 elections Crittenden's party failed to win many votes. Because of Crittenden's personal appeal, that year he did win the position of state treasurer. He quickly realized that his future political prospects were poor. Crittenden was a politician without a large following. He needed a new career.[14]

Crittenden resigned his position as treasurer in June 1866, after only five months in office, to accept an appointment as army colonel. He would serve with the 32nd Infantry regiment near Tucson, Arizona. Crittenden sailed to San Francisco, arriving on the West Coast seasick, and then made the journey to the Arizona territory. The department commander, Irwin McDowell, greeted the Kentuckian with the utmost respect and courtesy.[15]

Service in the Arizona territory did not have the best reputation among the military. As Crittenden confided to his brother-in-law Harry Todd, "I believe that it is generally conceded that I have the most disagreeable command in the land, but I am more than contented." As time passed, his opinion of the region changed. In a few months, Crittenden wrote to his friend Orlando Brown, "The climate I am pleased to say is generally misunderstood & slandered. I cannot conceive of a more delightful climate than this, since we reached here." He added, "but for the

---

[13] Hamleton Tapp and James C. Klotter, *Kentucky's Decades of Discord: 1865–1900* (Frankfort: Kentucky Historical Society, 1977) 16; E. Merton Coulter, *Civil War and Readjustment in Kentucky* (Chapel Hill: University of North Carolina press, 1926) 305.

[14] Coulter, *Civil War and Readjustment*, 305, 309; Oxx, *Kentucky Crittendens*, 141.

[15] Oxx, *Kentucky Crittendens*, 141; Thomas L. Crittenden to Harry I. Todd, 5 January 1867, Todd Collection, Kentucky Historical Collection, Frankfort.

Indians this territory would soon become populous." He foresaw a bright future for the region.[16]

Crittenden faced many problems in Arizona, one being the Apache Indians. Shortly after his arrival, Crittenden wrote to Todd, "I expect to be held accountable for every outrage committed by the Indians in any part of the territory." He also remarked that "the rascals don't mean to let me have any rest here." Crittenden noted that once the Indians reached the mountains, it was difficult to catch them. As many other commanders had already learned, pursuit was an exercise in futility.[17]

Crittenden also struggled with homesickness for his beloved Kentucky. He confided to Brown, "I sometimes feel that I am too far away ever to get back to old Ky," adding that "this only [happens] in a melancholy mood which occasionally gets hold of me." He lamented over lost friends. The homesick Crittenden then asked Brown to write him a long letter saying, "I am so wrapped up in Kentucky & Ky people that it goes very hard with me to hear of them so seldom."[18]

Crittenden asked for news of Kentucky politics. Reflecting on the recent political setbacks his party had suffered, he noted, "Time does not always cure vice but never fails to correct mistakes in judgment. Our noble state has suffered enough & I hope that she will choose good & wise men to manage her affairs." Kentucky would always be near and dear to Crittenden's heart, for as he said, "God bless Kentucky is my prayer on all occasions." Crittenden had entered Kentucky politics at the wrong time in 1866 and with the wrong party. If he had entered in 1863, he would have been more successful.[19]

Crittenden also expressed a newfound interest in spiritual affairs. He stated, "But if these afflictions do drive man to seek more earnestly the

---

[16] Thomas L. Crittenden to Harry I. Todd, 5 January 1867, Todd Collection, Kentucky Historical Society; Thomas L. Crittenden to Orlando Brown, 16 June 1867, Orlando Brown Papers, Filson Club.

[17] Thomas L. Crittenden to Harry I. Todd, 5 January 1867, Todd Collection, Kentucky Historical Society; Thomas L. Crittenden to Orlando Brown, 16 June 1867, Orlando Brown Papers, Filson Club.

[18] Ibid.

[19] Thomas L. Crittenden to Orlando Brown, 16 June 1867, Orlando Brown Papers, Filson Club.

friendship of the only true friend who cannot die, then we are indeed but blessed in disguise." Crittenden now turned to the Bible for guidance and he expressed a hope that Brown would also read the Bible often. With the zeal of a new convert, he asked Brown why he rebelled against God. Crittenden's devout sister Cornelia would have approved of her younger brother's new attitude.[20]

In the aftermath of Chickamauga, Crittenden had lost much of his carefree outlook for the future. This battle, combined with the poor performance in Virginia and recent political defeats in Kentucky, had broken his pride. After spending most of his life trying unsuccessfully to meet his father's expectations, in middle age he now sought to please his heavenly father. He had substituted one heavy psychological burden for another, but this one was much less difficult.

Crittenden's Arizona command kept him busy. He told a friend, "It seems to me that my days of leisure are over, I have more to think of & more to do with my little command than when I had an army of 20,000 men in the field." Crittenden expected to stay in the army until retirement and hoped to become an "accomplished officer."[21]

The Kentuckian had little expectation of promotion. He admitted that the "authorities and I had a very different estimate upon my services" but professed no unhappiness about the situation. He added, "If my father were alive [he would] be mortified by it." The younger Crittenden had pride in his position, feeling he had earned it completely on his own without family aid. He believed that his accomplishments were "indestructible" and that truth "would break thru mountains of lies, flatterer, & traductions." Thus, Crittenden felt free of his father's expectations, and he believed that time would eventually clear his Civil War reputation.[22]

Crittenden remained in the Arizona territory until transfer to the Dakota territory in the 1870s. He served with the 17th Infantry regiment originally stationed at Fort Rice. Later he moved to Fort Abercrombie.

---

[20] Ibid.

[21] Thomas L. Crittenden to Orlando Brown, 16 June 1867, Orlando Brown Papers, Filson Club.

[22] Ibid.

While in the northern plains, Crittenden experienced a new climate and a new terrain, and he liked the experience. At one point, he sent some buffalo hides back to friends in Kentucky, commenting that he rather enjoyed buffalo meat. He also experienced a very different climate. While the Arizona territory was known for its blazing summer heat, the Dakota territory was notorious for its frigid winters. In one letter to Kentucky, Crittenden's wife Kitty noted that the temperature was 34 degrees below 0. Little wonder that Crittenden later suffered from rheumatism.[23]

While Crittenden enjoyed his tour of duty in the Dakota territory, his men also enjoyed their commander. The soldiers at Fort Rice composed a ditty about the Kentuckian's dogs. They called it "General Crittenden at Fort Rice Reviewing His Bodyguard previous to a Descent on the Sioux Indians." The ditty mocked Crittenden's large, loud collection of hounds and their propensity to bark during visits by dignitaries. Apparently, Crittenden had not lost his old affability.[24]

Unfortunately, Crittenden would also have reason to mourn his stay in the Dakota territory. His son John J. Crittenden wanted to follow his father's example. He had frequently stayed with his father during the Civil War and apparently felt an attraction to military life. Thus, in 1871 the young man gained entry to West Point, but he did not do well at the academy. His mother confided in a letter to Ann Mary, "We can't help feeling anxious about John J.'s January examination—We do not think he'll fail but it is possible. He writes that he has been studying hard (and I believe that he has) and does not fear being deficient." Mrs. Crittenden had reason to fear for her son's welfare. Young John never excelled at the academy and in 1874 suffered expulsion for a deficiency in philosophy.[25]

---

[23] Oxx, *Kentucky Crittendens*, 152; Thomas L. Crittenden to Harry I. Todd, 2 November 1871, Todd Collection, Kentucky Historical Society; Kitty Crittenden to Ann Mary Coleman, 4 January 1872, John J. Crittenden Papers, Duke University; Thomas L. Crittenden to Patrick Joyes, 5 January 1885, Joyes Family Papers, Filson Club; Jack D. Welsh, *Medical Histories of Union Generals* (Kent: Kent State University Press, 1997) 82.

[24] Anonymous, "General Crittenden at Fort Rice Reviewing his Bodyguard Previous to a Descent on the Sioux Indians," Thomas L. Crittenden Letters, Kentucky Historical Society, Frankfort.

[25] Oxx, *Kentucky Crittendens*, 152–53; Kitty Crittenden to Ann Mary Coleman, 4 January 1872, John J. Crittenden Papers, Duke University.

Saddened by his failure, young Crittenden went to the Dakota territory to confer with his father. While there, he had an unfortunate accident when a cartridge stuck in a breech-loading shotgun he was using. When he attempted to remove the cartridge it exploded, puting out one of his eyes and injuring the other. Despite his poor performance at the academy and this recent accident, young John still wanted to pursue a military career. He utilized his father's numerous contacts to receive a commission in 1875 as a second lieutenant in the 20th Infantry regiment.[26]

Young John had learned from his father's military career that opportunity for promotion did not come along very often. Like most of the Crittenden family, he sought opportunities for recognition and promotion. In 1876 an opportunity presented itself. The government planned a major expedition against the Sioux Indians and young John, thinking it might be his best chance for recognition, volunteered to participate. Thus, he asked his father to intercede for him and obtain a transfer to the 7th Cavalry, which would play a prominent role in the upcoming campaign. Thomas Crittenden and his siblings had always benefited from the senator's helpful intercession during their earlier years, so it only seemed natural for Thomas to intercede on his son's behalf. His efforts succeeded, and John J. received his transfer to the 7th Cavalry just before the start of the infamous Little Bighorn campaign.[27]

According to family tradition, when John left to serve with Custer his father told him, "My boy do your duty! Never retreat! Die, if need be with your face to the foe!"[28] Another family tradition stated that as John J. rode away with his unit, Crittenden Marriott, the general's adopted son, ran after his brother so far that General Crittenden had to send a detachment from the fort to return his younger son. Marriott may have sensed the disaster to come.[29]

---

[26] Anonymous, Frankfort *Tri-Weekly Yeoman*, (4 November 1874):3; Oxx, *Kentucky Crittendens*, 152–53.

[27] Oxx, *Kentucky Crittendens*, 152–53.

[28] Francis Oxx married the daughter of Crittenden Marriott. When Oxx wrote his Crittenden genealogy, he learned many of the stories about Thomas L. and John J. from Crittenden Marriott's personal accounts of his childhood.

[29] Ibid., 153.

At the Little Bighorn, the Sioux destroyed Custer's force and young John was among the numerous dead. According to family tradition, Thomas told the soldiers that he wished his son buried where he fell on the battlefield. As a result, John J.'s grave was located some distance from most of the other graves on the battlefield.[30]

In 1880, a Sioux warrior sold a watch to a mixed blood named Gladieux, the Indian claiming that he taken the watch from a soldier he had killed at Little Bighorn. An officer then purchased the watch from Gladieux and an investigation of the manufacturer's records discovered that the watch had been young John's. Naturally, for sentimental reasons Thomas wanted the watch returned. When commanding General William T. Sherman heard of the situation, he ordered the return of the watch. The watch would be all that remained of the Crittenden's only son.[31]

Crittenden's later years were bittersweet. His career separated him from all of his old Kentucky acquaintances, while the loss of his son shattered his hopes for the future. One old family friend reported his concern for Crittenden: "I am truly sorry for Tom & wife, he is a noble tenderhearted generous man and it is a pity he has to suffer in his old age. I have been wanting to write to him for some time, but really I don't know what to say to him in the way of consolation in his troubles." One of Crittenden's few joys in his later years was his adopted son, Crittenden Marriott. Marriott also attempted to follow Crittenden's example and pursue a military career. He entered Annapolis but had to leave because of poor eyesight. He spent most of his life as a writer and always held his adopted father in the highest esteem.[32]

Crittenden retired from the army in 1881 and moved to New York City. He continued to play an active role in civic affairs. In 1883, for example, he returned to Louisville, Kentucky, to deliver the keynote address at the unveiling of a statute honoring his old commander Zachary

---

[30] H. H. Crittenden, comp., *The Crittenden Memoirs* (New York: G. P. Putnam's Sons, 1936) 507–508; Oxx, *Kentucky Crittendens*, 156.

[31] Oxx, *Kentucky Crittendens*, 158–61.

[32] John B. Bibb to Mary Starling Payne, 10 March 1878, Lewis-Starling Collection, Western Kentucky University, Bowling Green; Oxx, *Kentucky Crittendens*, 166.

Taylor. He gave a stirring address to the crowd. Apparently, the old charisma still remained.[33]

In 1888, the old general decided to visit Mexico City. He hoped the warm climate would help his rheumatism and gout. Perhaps he also wanted to revisit the days of his Mexican War command, when it seemed that a bright future lay ahead of him.[34]

The old general usually attempted to stay clear of disputes between generals concerning their wartime performance. In 1888, at a conference of the Society of the Army of the Cumberland, Thomas J. Wood presented a paper praising the Army of the Cumberland and lauding the skills of George H. Thomas. He said nothing of the controversial order at Chickamauga or his former corps commander, Thomas L. Crittenden. Apparently, Wood had not forgotten Crittenden's criticisms of him in the days before Chickamauga. Crittenden, who had seen enough division for one lifetime, chose to remain silent on the matter. Before the next reunion of the Army of the Cumberland in Chattanooga, he received an invitation to speak about the controversy surrounding the Battle of Chickamauga. He could have taken issue with Wood but decided to refrain from stirring up more heated debate. Crittenden declined the invitation, explaining, "I regret that I cannot attend the reunion. However misrepresented and misunderstood, the battle of Chickamauga illustrated the discipline & courage of our army in as marked a manner as any one of the bloody battles of the war." Unfortunately few Civil War generals took this path, and the professional faultfinding continued unabated until the death of the contending generals.[35]

One of the few public comments Crittenden made during the postwar era concerning his war service emerged in an article he wrote for Richard B. Johnson and Clarence L. Buel's *Battles and Leaders* series. The article dealt with his role on the third day at Stones River. Since most agreed that Crittenden had performed admirably there, the article excited little

---

[33] Oxx, *Kentucky Crittendens*, 162.

[34] Welsh, *Medical Histories of Union Generals*, 82.

[35] Thomas G. Wood, "1888 Presentation Before Society of the Army of the Cumberland," Thomas J. Wood Papers, Filson Club; Thomas L. Crittenden to William J. Colburn, 12 September 1889, Thomas L. Crittenden Letters, University of Kentucky, Lexington.

controversy. The general never sought nor had the opportunity to write an article about his controversial performance at Chickamauga. Perhaps given his already damaged reputation it was better to appear above the tumultuous debate.

The old general finally succumbed to death on 23 October 1893 at Staten Island, New York. An honor guard led by O. O. Howard led his body through New York City for its return to Frankfort. A delegation that included his foster son Crittenden Marriott and nephews H. C. Watson and J. Watson escorted the body to its final resting place at Frankfort Cemetery. Thomas lay in the Crittenden family plot near his father and most of his siblings in the cemetery he had helped create so many years earlier.[36]

After years of living in the shadow of their illustrious father, Thomas and his siblings had found peace. No more comparisons of their achievements with that of their father. No more paternal nudges to achieve and gain honor for the family name. Sibling rivalries disappeared in the peace of a final resting place.

---

[36] Oxx, *Kentucky Crittendens*, 141; Alfred Pirtle, comp., *The Union Regiments of Kentucky* (Louisville: Courier-Journal Printing Comp., 1897) 55.

Epilogue

If one visits the Frankfort cemetery today and views the headstones of Senator Crittenden and his family, it may appear as though no traces of the deep divisions of the Civil War era remain. In the peaceful surroundings, all seems calm. In the mid-nineteenth century, however, the Crittendens, like many border state families, endured tragedy. How does the Crittenden family story deepen our understanding of such conflict, and of the senator and his children?

The senator was an undoubtedly talented and hardworking man who achieved much in his lifetime. However, an often forgotten aspect of his early years may provide the key to understanding his family life. The senator's father, Major Crittenden, had achieved a great deal before his early death. Thus, the senator never experienced a nurturing supportive father. As an adult, he strived to add to the family reputation and equal his father's deeds without having ever experienced the nurturing side of parenthood. Later, as a parent the senator sought to instill in his children a desire to do as he had done, to work hard and add honor to the Crittenden name. Although the Senator Crittenden made the effort to be supportive, he simply had no model for how to offer that support. For the senator, support became indulgence in the face of his children's vices, as was the case with George. Unintentionally, the senator became for his sons a demanding patriarch whose mixture of pressure and indulgence influenced his children differently.

George did not act like an eldest child. In many families, the firstborn assumes parent-like responsibilities and leads the other siblings. Wanting to please the parent, the eldest is often a perfectionist. The senator had high expectations for George, but George could not live up to his father's dreams. George did not want to assume responsibility, did not want to lead, and definitely had no perfectionist leanings. It seemed as if he did everything he could to dishonor the family and disappoint his father. He constantly made costly mistakes that his father had to correct. George realized that supporting the Confederacy was something his father could never repair. In many ways, his support of secession was a complete declaration of independence. Whatever George achieved would be by his own ability and if it rankled his father, George did not really care. In ways beyond the gray uniform he wore, he was truly a rebel.

George's almost self-destructive personality did not enhance his military career. Heavy drinking impaired his judgment and made him appear ridiculous at times. Likewise, George's dislike of assuming responsibility did not bode well for his career as a commander of a significant force. Command requires assuming leadership and making decisions. It also necessitates accepting responsibility for mistakes. George had always made mistakes, but his father's indulgence had always found excuses for his failures. George had never had to bear the responsibility for his actions. Thus, after Mill Springs, he was not prepared for the criticism and ridicule he suffered. As a general, George Crittenden was a disaster waiting to happen.

Ann Mary's relationship with her father was different. The senator placed great pressure on his sons to excel, but this corrosive pressure was not present in his relationship with his eldest daughter. The senator's first wife died when Ann Mary was eleven and he remarried when she was thirteen. As a result, Ann Mary assumed many of the household's matriarchal duties. Her father often confided in her about her younger siblings. Ann Mary was probably the most talented of the senator's children. Like her father, she was hardworking and driven to enhance the family reputation. A well-educated woman of means, Ann Mary prized her independence. Seeing the impact of her father's pressure on her brothers only strengthened her desire to retain a degree of independence. The Civil War gave Ann Mary the opportunity to voice her independence of mind. Yet that independence came with a cost, and estrangement from her father was the price Ann Mary paid.

Cornelia distanced herself from the Crittenden family by immersing herself in the work of her husband at Centre College. Deeply religious, she gently chided her father for his secular worldview. Apparently not a condemning person, she welcomed her alcoholic brother to spend his last years with her.

Thomas had perhaps the most complex relationship with the family. Thomas was the middle son but often acted more like the eldest child. George's failures only placed more pressure on Thomas. The senator recognized Thomas's ability and did not want his second son to fail.

Unlike George, Thomas wanted to please his father. If George was a rebellious child, then Thomas was a compliant one. Thomas's marriage to his stepsister only deepened his dependence on the senator's approval.

Thomas's need for his father's approval laid the basis for his failure as a politician and a general. Since Thomas sought the support of others before he acted, he often lacked self-confidence. Thomas had political skills and ambitions, but before his father's death he did not pursue them aggressively. On the battlefield, he often had good instincts. His desire to attack at Shiloh and Perryville showed a fighting instinct. His concentration of artillery on the third day of Stones River and his movement of troops on the first day of Chickamauga demonstrated sound judgment. However, he never trusted his instincts, a tendency that arose perhaps from critical West Pointers like Wood serving under him or perhaps from the aloof Buell never praising his work as a divisional commander. In fact, the lack of self-confidence stemmed from Crittenden's desire to attain his father's approval before he acted.

The younger sons, Robert and Eugene, responded to parental pressure by failing. Robert was financially irresponsible throughout his life, while Eugene followed George's pattern of drinking and gambling his life away. Robert depended on the charity of his siblings. Eugene seemed headed down that same self-destructive path when disease prematurely took his life.

The senator provided his children with great privileges as a part of Kentucky's leadership class, but he also expected the children to assume greater responsibilities. However, the siblings were either not prepared or not willing to assume those responsibilities. The result was a family tragedy.

The Crittenden family divisions bring to fore several significant issues. Obviously the rifts illustrated the personal traumas of a deep familial conflict. Beyond that, they showed the impact family dynamics such as birth order and parental expectations have on character development. George and Robert reacted to the pressure with self-destructive behaviors while Thomas constructed a poor self-image due to lack of confidence. Perhaps a broader study on the family dynamics of divided border-state families would further illuminate the situation.

Another issue raised by the Crittendens concerned the role of politics in military promotion. The careers of George and Thomas showed the folly of depending solely on political connections for career advancement. Thomas, who had sound military instincts, faced professional jealousies from West Pointers. While by no means a brilliant commander, he deserved better treatment from his contemporaries and from historians.

In the postwar era, the careers of George and Thomas mirrored those of their comrades. Although on the victorious side, Thomas's political party lost the 1866 elections and he sadly left his native state. Kentucky Unionists would see their former Confederate foes consistently win Kentucky elections for the next generation. Likewise George, defeated and disgraced during the war, returned as a hero and lived in peace in his native Kentucky until his death. The Crittenden experience reflected the political reality of postwar Kentucky.

Realizing that a house divided against itself cannot stand, the Crittendens made peace with each other and with their father's high expectations. Hopefully, posterity's expectations for these siblings will not be as demanding and impossible to fulfill as those of the senator. The siblings deserve the lifting of that heavy burden and history's appreciation for them in their own right.

Bibliography

PRIMARY SOURCES

Archival Material

John J. Crittenden Papers, Special Collections, Duke University, Durham, North Carolina.

Orlando Brown Papers, Filson Club, Louisville, Kentucky.

Don Carlos Buell Papers, Filson Club, Louisville, Kentucky.

John J. Crittenden Papers, Filson Club, Louisville, Kentucky.

Thomas L. Crittenden Letters, Miscellaneous file, Filson Club, Louisville, Kentucky.

Dabney-Joyes Family Papers, Filson Club, Louisville, Kentucky.

Joyes Family Papers, Filson Club, Louisville, Kentucky.

Kentucky Mounted Gunmen Volunteer Regiment, Miscellaneous file, Filson Club, Louisville, Kentucky.

Humphrey Marshall Letters, Filson Club, Louisville, Kentucky.

David Meriwether Memoirs, Filson Club, Louisville, Kentucky.

Alfred Pirtle Journal, Filson Club, Louisville, Kentucky.

Alfred Pirtle Letters, Filson Club, Louisville, Kentucky.

Alfred Pirtle Writings, Filson Club, Louisville, Kentucky.

James Fowler Simmons Papers, Filson Club, Louisville, Kentucky.

Speed Family Papers, Filson Club, Louisville, Kentucky.

John H. Tilford Diaries, Filson Club, Louisville, Kentucky.

Todd Family Collection, Filson Club, Louisville, Kentucky.

Bibb-Burney Papers, Kentucky Historical Society, Frankfort.

Orlando Brown Papers, Kentucky Historical Society, Frankfort.

John J. Crittenden Papers, Kentucky Historical Society, Frankfort.

Robert H. Earnest Papers, Kentucky Historical Society, Frankfort.

Fall Family Papers, Kentucky Historical Society, Frankfort.

Todd Family Collection, Kentucky Historical Society, Frankfort.

John J. Crittenden Papers, Library of Congress, Washington, DC.

William W. Blair Letters, Ohio Historical Society, Columbus.

George W. Landrum Letters, Ohio Historical Society, Columbus.

Jeremiah T. Boyle Letters, Special Collections, University of Kentucky, Lexington.

Thomas L. Crittenden Letters, Special Collections, University of Kentucky, Lexington.

Samuel Woodson Price Papers, Special Collections, University of Kentucky, Lexington.

Starling Family Papers, Special Collections, University of Kentucky, Lexington.

John Tuttle Diary, Special Collections, University of Kentucky, Lexington.

Jacob Weaver Davis Papers, Special Collections, Western Kentucky University, Bowling Green, Kentucky.

Jefferson Dean Letters, Special Collections, Western Kentucky University, Bowling Green, Kentucky.

Green Family Collection, Special Collections, Western Kentucky UniversityBowling Green, Kentucky.

Knott Family Collection, Special Collections, Western Kentucky University Bowling Green, Kentucky.

Lewis-Starling Collection, Special Collections, Western Kentucky University, Bowling Green, Kentucky.

Temple Family Collection, Special Collections, Western Kentucky University, Bowling Green, Kentucky.

Underwood Family Collection, Special Collections, Western Kentucky University, Bowling Green, Kentucky.

Wickersham Family Papers, Special Collections, Western Kentucky University, Bowling Green, Kentucky.

Official Documents

Atlas to Accompany the Official Records of the Union and Confederate Armies. Washington, DC: Government Printing Office, 1891–1895.

Hill, Sam E. *Report of the Adjutant General of the State of Kentucky: Mexican War Veterans.* Frankfort: John D. Woods, 1889.

Kentucky Documents, 1860–1865. Frankfort: State Printing Office, 1860–1865.

Terrill, W. H. H. *Indiana in the War of the Rebellion: Report of the Indiana Adjutant General.* 1869. Reprint, Indianapolis: Indiana Historical Society, 1960.

U.S. War Department. *The War of the Rebellion: A Compilation of the Official Records of the Union and Confederate Armies.* 128 volumes. Washington, DC: 1880–1902.

Newspapers

Frankfort *Tri-Weekly Yeoman*

Indianapolis *Daily Journal*

Louisville Daily Journal

New York *Times*

New York *Tribune*

Books and Articles

Agassiz, George R., editor. *Meade's Headquarters, 1863–1865: Letters of Colonel Theodore Lyman from the Wilderness to Appomattox*. Boston: Atlantic Monthly Press, 1922.

Angle, Paul M. *Three Years in the Army of the Cumberland: The Diary of Major James A. Connelly*. Bloomington: Indiana University Press, 1959.

Barnes, James A., James R. Carnahan, and Thomas A. B. McCain. *The Eighty Sixth Indiana Volunteer Infantry: A Narrative of its Service in the Civil War of 1861–1865*. Indianapolis: Journal Company, 1895.

Beatty, John. *The Citizen-Soldier; or Memoirs of a Volunteer*. Cincinnati: Wilstach, Baldwin & Co., 1879.

Byrne, Frank L. *The View from Headquarters: The Civil War Letters of Henry Reid*. Madison: State Historical Society of Wisconsin, 1965.

Clay, Cassius Marcellus. *The Life of Cassius Marcellus Clay: Memoirs, Writings, and Speeches Showing His Conduct in the Overthrow of American Slavery, the Salvation of the Union, and the Restoration of the Autonomy of the States*. 1896. Reprint, New York: Negro Universities Press, 1969.

Coleman, Ann Mary. *The Life of John J. Crittenden*. 2 volumes. Philadelphia: J. B. Lippincott, 1871.

Committee of the Seventy-ninth Indiana. *History of the Seventy-ninth Regiment Indiana Volunteer Infantry in the Civil War of Eighteen Sixty-one in the United States*. Indianapolis: Hollenbeck Press, 1899.

Committee of the 73rd Indiana. *History of the Seventy-third Indiana Volunteers in the War of 1861–1865*. Washington, DC: Carnahan Press, 1909.

Crittenden, Thomas L. *Obituary Address Delivered Upon the Occasion of the Re-interment of the Remains of Gen. Charles Scott, Major William T. Barry, and Captain Bland Ballard and Wife in the Cemetery at Frankfort, November, 1854*. Frankfort: State Printer, 1855.

Dana, Charles. *A Recollection of the Civil War*. New York: D. Appleton, 1898.

Davis, Jefferson. *Rise and Fall of the Confederate Government*. 2 Volumes. New York: D. Appleton, 1881.

Davis, William C., and Meredith L. Swentor, editors. *Bluegrass Confederate: The Headquarters Diary of Edward Guerrant*. Baton Rouge: Louisiana State University Press, 1999.

Dennett, Tyler, editor. *Lincoln and the Civil War: In the Diaries and Letters of John Hay*. New York: DaCapo, 1988.

Fitch, John. *Annals of the Army of the Cumberland: Comprising Biographies, Descriptions of Department, Accounts of Expeditions, Skirmishes, Battles, also its Police record of Spies, Smugglers, and Prominent Embassaries, Together with Anecdotes, Incidents, Poetry, Reminiscences, etc. and Officers related to the Battle of Stones River.* Philadelphia: J. B. Lippincott, 1863.

Gavin, William G., editor. *Campaigning with the Roundheads: The History of the Hundredth Pennsylvania Veteran Volunteer Infantry Regiment in the American Civil War, 1861–1865.* Dayton: Morningside, 1989.

Grose, William. *The Story of the Marches, Battles, and Incidents of the 36th Regiment Indiana Volunteer Infantry by a Member of the Regiment.* New Castle: Courier Company, 1891.

Hannaford, Ebenezer. *The Story of a Regiment: A History of the Campaigns, and Associations in the Field, of the Sixth Ohio Volunteer Infantry.* Cincinnati: Ebenezer Hannaford, 1868.

Hartpence, William R. *History of the Fifty-first Indiana Veteran Volunteer Infantry: A Narrative of its Organization, Marches, Battles and Other Experiences in Camp and Prison; From 1861 to 1866.* Cincinnati: Robert Clarke, 1894.

Hazen, William B. *A Narrative of Military Service.* 1885. Reprint, Huntington: Blue Acorn, 1993.

Hight, John J. *A History of the Fifty-eight Regiment of Indiana Volunteer Infantry: Its Organization, Campaigns, and Battles from 1861 to 1865.* Princeton IN: Press of the Clarion, 1985.

Hinman, Wilbur F. *The Story of the Sherman Brigade: The Camp, the Marches, the Bivouac, the Battles, and how "the boys" Lived During Four Years of Active Field Service.* Alliance OH: Wilbur F. Hinman, 1897.

Johnson, Richard U. and Clarence C. Buel, editors. 4 volumes. *Battles and Leaders of the Civil War.* New York:

Johnson, Richard W. *Memoir of Maj. Gen. George H. Thomas.* Philadelphia: J. B. Lippincott, 1881.

Kerwood, Ashley L. *Annals of the Fifty-seventh Regiment Indiana Volunteers: Marches, Battles, and Incidents of Army Life by a Member of the Regiment.* Dayton: W. J. Shuey, 1868.

Kimberly, Robert L. and Holloway, Ephraim S. *The Forty-first Ohio Veteran Volunteer Infantry in the War of the Rebellion, 1861–1865.* Cleveland: W. R. Smellie, 1897.

Kirwan, Albert D., editor. *Johnny Green of the Orphan Brigade: The Journal of a Confederate Soldier.* Lexington: University of Kentucky Press, 1956.

Lewis, G. W. *The Campaigns of the 124th Regiment Ohio Volunteer Infantry with Roster and Roll of Honor* Akron: Werner Comp., 1894

Noe, Kenneth W., editor. *A Southern Boy in Blue: The Memoir of Marcus Woodcock 9th Kentucky Infantry U.S.A.* Knoxville: University of Tennessee Press, 1996.

Palmer, John M. *Personal Recollections of John Palmer: The Story of an Earnest Life.* Cincinnati: Robert Clarke Comp., 1901.

Rerrick, John A. *The Forty-fourth Indiana Volunteer Infantry: History of its Services in the War of the Rebellion and a Personal Record of Its Members.* La Grange IN: John A. Rerrick, 1880.

Saunders, James Edmonds. *Early Settlers of Alabama.* New Orleans: L. Graham & Sons, 1899.

Shanks, William F. G. *Personal Recollections of Distinguished Generals.* New York: Harper & brothers, 1866.

Simmons, Louis A. *The History of the 84th Regt.* 3 volumes. Macomb: Sampson Bothers, 1866.

Smith, John T. *A History of the Thirty-first Regiment of Indiana Volunteer Infantry in the War of the Rebellion.* Cincinnati: Western Method Book Concern, 1900.

The Biographical Encyclopedia of Kentucky of the Dead and Living Men of the Nineteenth Century. Cincinnati: J. M. Armstrong & Comp., 1878.

Tarrant, Sergeant E. *The Wild Riders of the First Kentucky Cavalry: A History of the Regiment in the Great War of the Rebellion, 1861–1865, Telling of the Origins and Organization; A Description of the Material of Which it was Composed; its rapid and Severe Marches, Hard Service, and Fierce Conflicts on many a Bloody Field.* Louisville: R. H. Carothers, 1894.

Taylor and His Generals: A Biography of Major-General Zachary Taylor; and Sketches of the Lives of Generals Worth, Wool, and Twiggs; With a Full Record of the Various Actions of their Divisions in Mexico up to the Present Time; Together with a History of the Bombardment of Vera Cruz, and a Sketch of the Life of Major-General Winfield Scott. Philadelphia: E. H. Butler & Comp., 1847.

Villard, Henry. *Memoirs of Henry Villard: Journalist and Financier, 1835–1900.* 2 volumes. Boston: Houghton Mifflin, 1904.

Walcott, Charles F. *History of the Twenty-first Regiment Massachusetts Volunteers in the War for the Preservation of the Union 1861–1865, with Statistics of the War and of Rebel Prisons.* Boston: Houghton Mifflin, 1882.

Woodruff, George H. *Fifteen Years Ago: or the Patriotism of Wills County, Designed to Preserve the Names and Memory of Will County Soldiers, Both Officers and Privates—Both Living and Dead; to tell Something of What they did, and of What they Suffered, in the Great Struggle to Preserve our Nationality.* Joliet: Joliet Republican Book & Job Steam Printing, 1876.

Wright, Thomas J. *The History of the Eighth Regiment Kentucky Volunteer Infantry During the Three Years Campaigns Embracing Organization, Marches, Skirmishes and Battles of the Command with Much of the History the Reliable Third Brigade Command by Honorable Stanley Matthews and Containing Many Entertaining and Amusing Incidents of Army Life.* St. Joseph MO: St. Joseph Steam Printing, 1880.

SECONDARY SOURCES

Books

Andrews, J. Cutler. *The North Reports the War.* 1955. Reprint, Pittsburgh: University of Pittsburgh Press, 1985.

Bauer, K. Jack. *The Mexican War, 1846–1848.* New York: Macmillan, 1974.

———. *Zachary Taylor; Soldier, Planter, Statesman of the Old Southwest.* Baton Rouge: Louisiana State University Press, 1985.

Beach, Damian. *Civil War Battles, Skirmishes and Events in Kentucky.* Louisville: Different Drummer Books, 1995.

Bowers, John. *Chickamauga and Chattanooga: The Battles that Doomed the Confederacy.* New York: HarperCollins, 1994.

Brown, Kent Masterson, editor.. *The Civil War in Kentucky: Battle for the Bluegrass State.* Mason City IA: Savas Publishing Comp., 2000.

Buell, Thomas B. *The Warrior Generals: Combat Leaders in the Civil War.* New York: Crown, 1997.

Cist, Henry. *The Army of the Cumberland.* New York: Charles Scribner's sons, 1882.

Clark, Thomas D. *A History of Kentucky.* Lexington: John Bradford Press, 1960.

———. *Kentucky: Land of Contrast.* New York: Harper & Row, 1968.

Clift, Glenn G., compiler. *Kentucky Marriages, 1797–1865.* 1938. Reprint, Baltimore: Genealogical Publishing Comp., 1966.

———, compiler. *Kentucky Obituaries, 1787–1854.* 1938. Reprint, Baltimore: Genealogical Publishing Comp., 1979.

Cooling, Benjamin F. *Fort Donelson's Legacy: War and Society in Kentucky and Tennessee, 1862–1863.* Knoxville: University of Tennessee Press, 1997.

Cooling, Benjamin Franklin. *Fort Henry and Donelson: The Key to the Confederate Heartland.* Knoxville: University of Tennessee Press, 1987.

Connelly, Thomas L. *Army of the Heartland: The Army of Tennessee, 1861–1862.* Baton Rouge: Louisiana State University Press, 1967.

Coulter, E. Merton. *Civil War and Readjustment in Kentucky.* Chapel Hill: University of North Carolina Press, 1926.

———. *William G. Brownlow: Fighting Parson of the Southern Highlands.* Chapel Hill: University of North Carolina Press, 1937.

Cozzens, Peter. *No Better Place to Die: The Battle of Stones River.* Urbana: University of Illinois, 1990.

———. *This Terrible Sound: The Battle of Chickamauga.* Urbana: University of Illinois Press, 1993.

Crittenden, H. H., compiler. *The Crittenden Memoirs.* New York: G. P. Putnam's Sons, 1936.

Daniel, Larry J. *Days of Glory: The Army of the Cumberland, 1861–1865.* Baton Rouge: Louisiana State University Press, 2004.

———. *Shiloh: The Battle that Changed the Civil War.* New York: Simon & Schuster, 1997.

Davis, William C. *Breckinridge: Statesman, Soldier, Symbol.* Baton Rouge: Louisiana State University Press, 1974.

———. *Jefferson Davis: The Man and His Hour.* Baton Rouge: Louisiana State University Press, 1991.

———. *The Orphan Brigade: The Kentucky Confederates Who Couldn't Go Home.* New York: Doubleday, 1980.

Dyer, John P. *From Shiloh to San Juan: The Life of Fighting Joe Wheeler.* Baton Rouge: Louisiana State University Press, 1941.

Engle, Stephen D. *Don Carlos Buell: Most Promising of All.* Chapel Hill: University of North Carolina Press, 1999.

Eubank, Damon R. *The Response of Kentucky to the Mexican War, 1846–1848.* Lewiston: Edwin Mellon Press, 2004.

Faragher, John Mack. *Daniel Boone: The Life and Legend of an American Pioneer.* New York: Henry Holt, 1992.

Forgie, George B. *Patricide in the House Divided: A Psychological Interpretation of Lincoln and His Age.* New York: Norton, 1979.

Forer, Lucille, with an introduction by Henry Still. *The Birth Order Factor: How Your Personality is Influenced by Your Place in the Family.* New York: Pocket Books, 1976.

Fox, William F. *Regimental Losses in the American Civil War, 1861–1965: A Treatise on the Extent and nature of the mortuary Losses in the Union Regiments, with full and Exhaustive Statistics, Compiled From the Official Records on File in the State Military Bureaus, and at Washington.* Albany: Albany Publishing Comp., 1889.

Glenn, Nettie Henry. *Early Frankfort Kentucky, 1786–1861.* Frankfort: Kentucky Historical Society, 1986.

Grimsley, Mark. *The Hard Hand of War: The Union Military Policy toward Southern Civilians 1861–1865.* Cambridge: Cambridge University Press, 1995.

Hafendorfer, Kenneth A. *Mill Springs: Campaign and Battle of Mill Springs.* Louisville: KH Press, 2001.

———. *Perryville: Battle for Kentucky.* Utica KY: McDowell Publications, 1981.

Harrison, Lowell H. *The Civil War in Kentucky.* Lexington: University Press of Kentucky, 1975.

———. *Lincoln of Kentucky.* Lexington: University Press of Kentucky, 2000.

Hess, Earl J. *Banners to the Breeze: The Kentucky Campaign, Corinth and Stones River.* Lincoln: University of Nebraska Press, 2000.

Hood, Fred J., editor. *Kentucky: Its History and Heritage.* St. Louis: Forum Press, 1978.

Horn, Stanley F. *The Army of Tennessee.* Indianapolis: Bobbs-Merrill Comp., 1941.

Hughes, Nathaniel Cheairs Jr., and Gordon D. Whitney. *Jefferson Davis in Blue: The Life of Sherman's Relentless Warrior.* Baton Rouge: Louisiana State University Press, 2002.

Johnson, Adam R. *The Partisan Rangers of the Confederate States Army.* Louisville: Geo. C. Fetter Comp., 1904.

Johnson, J. Stoddard. *Kentucky,* in *Confederate Military History.* 1899. Reprint, no place: Blue and Gray Press, 1976.

Johnson, L. F. *The History of Franklin County, KY.* Frankfort: Roberts Printing, 1912.

Kirwan, Albert D. *John J. Crittenden: The Struggle for the Union.* Lexington: University of Kentucky Press, 1962.

Kramer, Carl E. *Capital on the Kentucky: A Two Hundred Year History of Frankfort & Franklin County.* Frankfort: Historic Frankfort, 1986.

Lamers, William M. *The Edge of Glory: A Biography of General William S. Rosecrans, U.S.A.* New York: Harcourt, Brace, & Word, 1961.

Leman, Kevin. *The New Birth Order Book: Why You Are the Way You Are.* Grand Rapids: Revell, 1998.

Marvel, William. *Burnside.* Chapel Hill: University of North Carolina Press, 1991.

Marszalek, John F. *Sherman: A Soldier's Passion for Order.* New York: Free Press, 1993.

Matter, William D. *If it Takes All Summer: The Battle of Spotsylvania.* Chapel Hill: University of North Carolina Press, 1988.

McDonough, James Lee. *Shiloh: In Hell Before Night.* Knoxville: University of Tennessee Press, 1977.

———. *Stones River: Bloody Winter in Tennessee.* Knoxville: University of Tennessee Press, 1980.

———. *War in Kentucky: From Shiloh to Perryville.* Knoxville: University of Tennessee Press, 1994.

McDowell, Robert Emmett. *City of Conflict: Louisville in the Civil War, 1861–1865.* Louisville: Civil War Round Table, 1962.

McKinney, Francis F. *Education in Violence: The Life of George H. Thomas and the History of the Army of the Cumberland.* Detroit: Wayne State University Press, 1961.

Myers, Raymond E. *The Zollie Tree.* Louisville: Filson Club Press, 1964.

Noe, Kenneth W. *Perryville: Perryville: This Grand Havoc of Battle.* Lexington: University Press of Kentucky, 2001.

Piatt, Donn. *General George H. Thomas: A Critical Biography.* Cincinnati: Robert Clarke, 1893.

Poage, George R. *Henry Clay and the Whig Party.* Chapel Hill: University of North Carolina Press, 1936.

Prokopowicz, Gerald J. *All for the Regiment: The Army of the Ohio, 1861–1862.* Chapel Hill: University of North Carolina Press, 2001.

Ramage, James A. *Rebel Raider: The Life of John Hunt Morgan.* Lexington: University Press of Kentucky, 1986.

Reid, Richard J. *The Army that Buell Built.* Fordsville KY: Sandefur Offset Printing, 1994.

———. *Stones River Ran Red.* Fordsville KY: Sandefur Offset Printing, 1983.

Reid, Whitelaw. *Ohio in the War: Her Statesmen, Her Generals, and Soldiers.* 2 volumes. Cincinnati: Moore, Wilstach, & Baldwin, 1868.

Reinhart, Joseph R. *A History of the 6th Kentucky Volunteer Infantry U.S.: The Boys who Feared No Noise.* Louisville: Beargrass Press, 2000.

Remini, Robert V. *Henry Clay: Statesman for the Union.* New York: W. W. Norton, 1991.

Rhea, Gordon C. *Cold Harbor: Grant and Lee May 26–June 3, 1864.* Baton Rouge: Louisiana State University Press, 2002.

———. *The Battles for Spotsylvania Court House and the Road to Yellow Tavern, May 7–12, 1864.* Baton Rouge: Louisiana State University Pres, 1997.

———. *To the North Anna River: Grant and Lee, May 13–25, 1864.* Baton Rouge: Louisiana State University Press, 2000.

Roland, Charles D. *Albert Sidney Johnston: Soldier of Three Republics.* Austin: University of Texas Press, 1964.

Rothert, Otto A. *A History of Muhlenberg County.* Louisville: John B. Morton, 1913.

Speed, Thomas. *The Union Cause in Kentucky 1860–1865.* New York: G. P. Putnam Sons, 1907.

———. *The Union Regiments of Kentucky.* Louisville: Courier-Journal, 1897.

Sproull, Matt. *Guide to the Battle of Chickamauga.* Lawrence: University of Kansas Press, 1993.

Stickles, Ardent M. *Simon Bolivar Buckner: Borderland Knight.* Chapel Hill: University of North Carolina Press, 1940.

Stone, Richard G. *A Brittle Sword: The Kentucky Militia, 1776–1912.* Lexington: University Press of Kentucky, 1977.

Tapp, Hambleton, and James C. Klotter. *Kentucky's Decades of Discord: 1865–1900.* Frankfort: Kentucky Historical Society, 1977.

Toman, Walter. *Family Constellation: Its Effects on Personality and Social Behavior.* New York: Springer Publishing, 1993.

Tucker, Glenn. *Chickamauga: Bloody Battle in the West.* 1961. Reprint, New York: Smithmark, 1994.

Van Horne, Thomas B. *The Army of the Cumberland.* 1875. Reprint, New York: Konecky & Konecky, 1996.

———. *The Life of Major General George H. Thomas.* New York: Charles Scribner's Sons, 1882.

Webb, Ross A. *Kentucky in the Reconstruction Era.* Lexington: University Press of Kentucky, 1979.

Welsh, Jack D. *Medical Histories of Union Generals.* Kent: Kent State University Press, 1997.

Woodworth, Stephen E. *Jefferson Davis and His Generals: The Failures of Confederate Command in the West.* Lawrence: University of Kansas Press, 1990.

Works Progress Administration. *Military History of Kentucky.* Frankfort: State Journal, 1939.

Articles

Griese, Arthur A. "A Louisville Tragedy–1862." *Filson Club Historical Quarterly* 26 (April 1952): 133–54.

Jenkins, Kirk C. "A Shooting at the Galt House: The Death of General William Nelson." *Civil War History* 43 (June 1997): 101–18.

McMurtrey, Gerald. "Zollicoffer-Battle of Mill Springs." Filson *Club Historical Quarterly* 29 (October 1955): 303–19.

Miscellaneous

Chumney, J. R. "Don Carlos Buell: Gentleman General." Ph.D. dissertation. Rice University, 1964.

Http://sunsite.unc.edu/pub/academic/histo...litary/civil_war_usa/D_H_Maury/DHM.06txt.

Oxx, Francis B. "The Kentucky Crittendens: The History of a Family Including Genealogy of Descendants in Both Male and Female Lives, Biographical Sketches of its Members, and Their Descent from other Colonial Lives." No place, 1940.
Volz, Harry August III. "Party, State, and Nation: Kentucky and the Coming of the American Civil War." Ph.D. dissertation. University of Virginia, 1982.

Index